WORDPLAY

How Words Captivate
Illuminate,
Intimidate,
Inform, and
Imbue Us With Intelligence.

GLENN BASSETT

Copyright © 2013 by Glenn A. Bassett

ISBN#: 1492985384

1. Psycholinguistics
2. Modeling Reality with Words
3. Social Psychology
4. How Culture shapes language
5. How Words Shape Behavior
6. Non-Sense Language

Book design and photography by
Artful Image - Paula Severino
www.artful-image.com

Table of Contents

IN THE BEGINNING:
WORDS AND THE LANGUAGE IMPERATIVE

An inner city teenager hisses a common insult as he approaches another on the street. A switchblade knife is whipped from an ankle holster and slashed at the offending speaker. An hour later after handguns have been sought out, the transaction is resumed. In a matter of moments, one lies dead on the pavement, the other limps down the street with a leg wound. A spoken phrase has ended in a lethal shootout!

An English teacher at a highly rated suburban high school berates a student for poor English on a report. The teacher challenges the student with, "You'll never get your choice of colleges with this kind of performance". An hour after school is out, parents call to ask why their daughter is not home yet. Search of the facility discovers her body in a restroom stall, both wrists slashed with a razor. Verbal criticism has become a death sentence.

The office supervisor completes this year's rounds of performance reviews with her employees. One is criticized for poor attitude and work habits, cautioned to improve and told there will be no annual raise. He picks up a chair and throws it across the room. Communication intended to improve behavior elicits inexcusable rage that results in the offending employee being fired.

In each of these circumstances, a particular culture provides the context in which language is spoken and behavior is evoked. Inner city streets offer little support for fragile self-esteem. Guns are part of the prevailing drug economy and easily obtained. Fear and anger are never far beneath the surface.

Insult invokes retaliation. In upscale suburban communities the expectations of parents and teachers are high. Students compete against high standards. Failure is not an option. Criticism evokes despair. In an ordinary work setting, the use of conventional "motivational" communication with a worker brings a storm of rage. Ever present job stress overwhelms better judgment and self-control.

Words at their core may be no more than conventional representations of sensed and perceived reality. Yet they can produce storms of vigorous, destructive or angry reaction. What gives them such power? Surely, the reality of life itself should have greater influence on behavior than images evoked by words alone. How can they be so loaded with emotion? How does so much feeling intensity become attached to words?

Those human emotions that are wired into the nervous system, fear, surprise, disgust, anger, sadness, joy and love, come already loaded onto their word descriptors. These words are directly attached to feeling experiences aroused in the brain and body. They are natural emotional feelings that are not necessarily mediated by the senses. The experiences themselves are resident in the nervous system and in the mind. Those feelings get associated with words that represent external things, events and ideas through the common mechanisms of Pavlovian conditioning and social suggestion. In association with the things, events and ideas they represent, words absorb the emotional passion of one or more wired-in emotions. Some words become so saturated with emotion that they have little or no coded, referential, rational meaning left in them. Many simple four letter word utterances of anger and disparagement offer only raw emotion as the message.

The importance of language as a primary means of social connection gives words much of their emotional power. Personal status, access to food, clothing, housing, and mating all require language competence. A complex economy of skill specialization where few grow their own food, build their own shelter or spin fabric for their personal clothing requires each person to find a place in the social system. Negotiation of personal need within the cultural envelope demands language use. Language itself becomes a survival, or at a minimum, a coping tool. Without language, life is hard, very hard. Words loaded with emotion become cultural messages that describe and forewarn of life's opportunities and threats.

The sense of real concreteness that saturates words is equally amazing. Even before they become associated with sentiments, words are more than mere labels for things, events and ideas. They are permeated with meaning so rich that they become those things, events and ideas. Branded deep in the inner recesses of the brain, they are our world, our environment, ourselves. Language is a remarkable capability that sneaks up on and takes over the mind. Language is not so much learned as it is absorbed. A child listens, imitates and, somehow, finds meaning in the words spoken by parents, siblings, relatives, neighbors, and others in the common speech culture. Once speech is mastered, there is no memory of former speechlessness, no awareness of having learned. Once acquired, the words that play on our lips are as familiar and unnoticed as the air we breathe. We cannot imagine living and acting without them.

Without words, could we know anything at all? The answer depends on what is meant by "knowing". Experience at some level no doubt exists in the absence of word knowledge but is better described as recognition of the familiar than as knowledge. Knowledge arises out of the use of words to parse, label, remember and recall experience. A living human being is recognized by use of words that demonstrate mental reflection going beyond immediate sensory experience. Everything else is instinct or response to stimulus that needs no words to drive behavior. Knowledge is inherent in a realm that transcends immediate sensation. It is coded into the mind with words.

Translated from speech into the symbols of the phonetic alphabet, written words are doubly distanced from the things, events and ideas they represent. They are no less drenched with meaning. The words you are reading at this moment are not mere ink stains on paper or electrically activated pixels on a video screen. They are language! As you read these words and sentences you immediately share some part of the meaning that I am trying to invest in them. We are two minds in separate skins distanced by time and geography, yet in communication. Taking notice of the written and recorded language we use to communicate with one another puts us in a different dimension of experience. It is near to being a mystical event.

Language use in a community of shared culture proceeds simply enough without necessarily demanding awareness of the words themselves. There is no strangeness to jar consciousness when everyone is on the same page of word usage. Families or communities in isolation communicate simply and naturally, unaware of the words they use. Strangers to the community speak words that lack familiar inflection, meaning and context. Strangers are those who require our full attention if we are to grasp the meaning of their speech. We can never be fully sure what they mean or if they can be trusted. It would be best to avoid them if we can.

Avoidance has become difficult, maybe impossible in this big, crowded, global world. A multicultural society with multiple variations of dialect and language confronts us with strangers at every turn. Simple habits of common speech are challenged. When strange languages and cultures penetrate formerly isolated and insulated communities they challenge shared community. They are stressful, distressing, offensive, and at times painful to deal with. The response is likely to be angry rejection of the stranger and everything he/she stands for. A global, multicultural world full of strangers generates wide spread stress and anger.

As the world has become smaller, more closely interconnected, economically unified and saturated with communication links, that anger becomes more dangerous. It builds to the bursting point and erupts in heated rhetoric that can boil over into retaliatory response on an international scale. Social hot spots where cultures are in serious friction erupt everywhere. The wonderful power of language to create community has been put to the service of its destruction. If that potential is to be tamed, we must examine our words to discover how they form our minds and shape behaviors. That is the object of the chapters that follow.

Part 1 explains how language becomes a cultural overlay upon the animal skills and instincts nature has equipped humankind with. Culture is a long succession of human generations across which language has been invented, refined and passed on through the media of that culture into which one is born. Language is the gift of our ancestors that lifts us above the animal state. The neuroplastic mind shapes itself to an environment of words and ideas. Much is automatic acquisition in the infant mind. Once it is acquired, the habit of assuming language as a natural capability blinds us to the symbolic arbitrariness of words and the conventional meaning we invest in them. We speak with blithe unawareness of our language heritage.

This part explores the ways that language is shaped by social and environmental forces. Language used as a mental model for thinking about and navigating the social and natural world is examined. The remarkable transformation of sensory referenced words into abstractions, essences and ideas is explored. The special power of literacy and the written word to form the mind and transmit language heritage is described. The workings of the neuroplastic associative mind are explored.

The working premise in these early chapters is that the accumulated power of language over generations has shaped human development to a level where it can be argued that *words are our minds and our personal identities.*

Part two explores some of the many weird and wonderful things that human minds are capable of perceiving, understanding and creating through the medium of language. Evidence is adduced for the probability that dual streams of independent consciousness can exist side by side in the human brain. The implications of hemispheric language dominance for the structure of the mind are evaluated. The way words shape and reflect individuals as unique personalities, and the sometimes hard-to-believe power of social authority and suggestibility are explored. The visceral quality of every day word use is examined, and the way that realities are invented is illustrated by lessons from past and recent history. Frighteningly dramatic events, bitter public confrontations, creative forensic recreations, traffic accidents and game styled simulations are used to show how events that overwhelm are inventively interpreted in detail through use of familiar words. The capacity of words to take on emotional intensity is examined and ways of moderating heated emotional rhetoric are examined. The manner in which the infant mind acquires language is tentatively explored.

Part three is about words that do the heavy lifting to advance practical affairs. Lessons are drawn from propaganda campaigns, advertising practices and politics. The great economic debates that drive public policy and divide public opinion on issues of justice are examined. The ubiquity of word play in the immediate social space that surrounds everyone and drives human affairs is revealed.

Part four focuses on how numbers, scientific method and philosophy bring richness to language that both clarify and complicate meaning. The mazes of language created by abstractions in the form of ideas and essences are explored for their capacity to confuse and mislead with their *non-sense.* The power of numbers to influence behavior, despite their otherworldly unreality as pure ideas, is examined. The treacherous complexity inherent in statistics and index calculations is discovered. The powers and limitations of science that lay behind the high prestige of most scientific pronouncements is brought to light, and the ways in which science advances or falters are examined. The contribution of those ultimate spinmeisters, the philosophers, is sketched in outline form from antiquity to the present to illustrate the broad evolutionary path of language.

Part five looks at words as doors to mystical, maybe even spiritual understanding. At this exceedingly abstracted level of language we may perhaps recognize that much of who and what we are comes about because we are a culturally shaped, language-using people. As language is employed to explore the recesses and back channels of the mind, there is opportunity to discover the large extent to which we, as socialized human beings, are the product of our words and the mental map they supply us for navigating our phenomenal world.

This will be an examination of that remarkable, indispensable legacy of language that so greatly enriches life. It is a look at how words permit humans to be more than just homo erectus, homo habilis or even homo sapiens. With the command of language that man has achieved he may indeed have become something closer to a lesser god in his command over nature. Words are his scepter.

PART ONE:

The Construction of Awareness;

Swimming in a Sea of Words

1. How To Build A Mental Model Of Reality With Words

Language is the distinguishing mark of human beings. Of all the tools of civilization invented by man, language is the most powerful and distinctly human. The most primitive culture known to anthropologists has an extended vocabulary that describes the tribe's physical and social environment. Within every culture, basic sensory experience is recognized and articulated with words. Even the higher apes appear to be capable of using words to communicate with humans.

Chimpanzees, genetically closest to man, communicate among themselves in their natural environment and with their human handlers in labs. Troops of chimps in the wild have been observed to signal one another using simple gestures. There is convincing evidence that chimps understand their social world, can mentally model the effect of their behavior on others, and can understand the intentions of other chimps[1].

Chimps clearly do not have the capacity for complex speech but have been taught to communicate in a rudimentary way by researchers who use American Sign Language (ASL) and other devices. Five lab chimps handled by Roger and Deborah Fouts were trained to communicate with their handlers as well as among themselves using sign language. When trained, they could respond to spoken English, translate the words heard into sign language and train their young to use sign language without further involvement of their handlers[2]. The chimp with longest experience signing ASL was reported to use more than 200 signs. If chimps had the physical ability to vocalize – to form speech sounds – they might have a language of their own.

Dogs and cats are often observed by their owners to communicate and even to comprehend words. A pet will nuzzle its owner for attention and "speak" for food. Dogs may grasp without training the meaning of spoken words like "walk", "leash", "food", "car" or "go". They can be taught to respond to both words or hand gestures. The primate brain is capable of recognizing sounds, events, even symbols, and invest them with meaning. Primates can be remarkably clever at managing their environment. But they cannot reflect on their experience and organize their thoughts to better understand or communicate their experience. Humans can.

The unique power of language among humans arises in the creation of social meaning that is passed from generation to generation. History, real and mythological, comes into being in early human societies. Language is a social device that permits sharing of experience and social understanding across time and distance. It permits a "troop" of human beings to create a social culture that is expandable and transmittable to subsequent generations. Absent the social context of a human "troop" the isolated human being is perhaps little different from a chimp in the wild.

The closest thing to that kind of primitive state is the feral child. Cases of these children have been reported for at least two thousand years, first appearing in Greek mythology. Feral children raised in the wild are said to act and sound like their animal companions. The implication of accumulated reports of feral child speech is that lack of exposure to human speech in the earliest years of life will permanently impair the ability to learn language. Cases continue to be reported and there are new reports yearly. The majority of recent cases result from extreme confinement or isolation. The usual result of childhood with little or no human contact, whether feral or isolated, is the absence of learned language. Efforts to teach language are always very difficult or more likely fruitless. It is clear from this abundance of natural evidence that speech heard in very early childhood determines the extent of one's mastery of words.[3]

In the absence of language, human beings are hardly recognizable as human. Children born completely blind and without hearing are pitiful creatures, unable to relate to the physical world and virtually impossible to socialize. The crudest training using the remaining sensory pathway of touch may be possible, but social communication, much less language, is impossible. The legend of Helen Keller does not at all contradict this description. Helen was born fully hearing and sighted and lost these faculties through illness at two years of age. When training in language skill was commenced four years later, she "bloomed" with language capability in a relatively brief time. Preparation for language and speech is accomplished in the first two years of life and use of words typically starts around the age of two. Helen Keller, sighted and hearing until age two, then made blind and deaf, was socially and neurologically "put on hold" until a committed teacher awakened her to the language foundation earlier formed. Helen's new social beginning at age six is a natural demonstration of the importance of language and social exposure in the very early years as preparation for speech. The pathetic state of those born without sight or hearing demonstrates that, without cultural exposure, the mind normally cannot develop beyond the most primitive animal state.[4]

Thousands of years of culture encoded into language are essential to civilizing and humanizing each newborn. It is the tradition of language culture passed on generation to generation that cultivates and enlightens humankind. Learning the language of one's culture comes naturally to children. Unless neurologically impaired or not exposed to speech, the child will acquire the basics of his/her native language by the age of three or four. Babies born into one language culture and adopted into another will learn their adopted language. The capacity to communicate with words exists at birth. Children acquire and use words they hear the way everyone in their surrounding culture uses them.

Words are codes for things, activities, relationships, feelings and ideas. Language is a complex symbol system that encodes experience, allowing it to be set more firmly into memory and, since invention of the phonetic alphabet, as written record. Through written records, linguists chart the course of word usage and development across centuries. Those records show how the working vocabulary of words has continuously expanded the verbal tradition of the culture. Spoken or written stories spread language and enrich common culture passing language from generation to generation. In the present age use of language in communication is so intimately a part of daily living that it is easily taken to be innate. It is a near impossibility to think of daily social life without spoken and written words.

An understanding of how language can be used to manipulate or inform requires close examination of the basic human behaviors, starting with a description of the physical, psychological and social processes involved. Language is a complex symbol structure that encodes experience, allowing it to be set more firmly into memory and as written record too. Language learning is not mere mimicry, though. Cognitive neurologists describe how the brain organizes perceptual experience. Vision is not a meaningless jumble of shapes, textures or forms. Complex visual patterns, actions, affective sensations and sounds are observed and identified as distinct from of their background. Once objects are discriminated out of their chaotic context, words can then be associated with them.

Particularly dramatic evidence of the mind's capacity for pattern construction comes when it is lost through brain injury or disease. Perception is no longer organized. With visual agnosia the brain damaged individual can see but cannot discriminate shapes, even very simple ones. Evidence of the brain's loss of this perceptual organization is offered when the faces of familiar people can no longer be recognized. Agnosia may also occur with the auditory, olfactory and tactile senses as well. Normal individuals can discriminate specific patterns of sound, smell or texture. Individuals with particular kinds of brain damage cannot. Perceptual patterns that were originally perceived as distinctly separate things have become jumbles. Complex perception of visual, auditory or even tactile patterns of sensation allows human language to be invented and acquired.[5]

The normal developing child's brain thus is full of perceived things, actions, and sensations that are naturally discriminated out of their backgrounds and associated with words. In the company of language competent adults, a set of spoken sounds is offered the growing child which is used to tag those elements of perception. This is the way words with object references are learned. Children go beyond referential coding to intuitively grasp complex language structure and meaning merely by listening to adult speech. Abstract ideas are perceived and understood. Connectives to describe relationships between words, articles to give focus or emphasis, categories to describe types, all are intuitively grasped in ways that cannot be fully explained or comprehended. Even the rules of grammar are intuitively understood and correctly used by the normal, growing child.[6]

How this mastery of complexity comes about is something of a mystery. Words as descriptors of specific sensible things, dog, apple, door, or activities, run, eat, sit, are easily associated, even by animals. Humans go well beyond using these directly referential words. It is nonetheless remarkable that a normal child grasps the meaning of words that have no objective referential anchor. Abstractions that reference functions and relationships are easily understood by most children. The human brain seems designed to acquire and use language. That language acquisition is innate to brain structure seems an inescapable conclusion.

Words are clearly the stuff of thinking. Experimental evidence demonstrates that even very young children are capable of constructing and modifying prior experience with words alone. At about the age of two, most children can identify a formerly seen and handled object that has changed when told that a change in its condition occurred while it was out of sight. A toy used in play is identified by name from among other toys, some identical to it. Later, while away from the play room, the child is told that the named toy had accidentally become doused with water. Returned to the room, most children accurately and quickly identify the named toy based on its wetness. The explanation must be that a spoken description of the change alone has activated and revised the child's mental image of the toy. Mere words alter the image of an existing sensory experience and guide appropriate behavior on returning to find the original object. *Words have become the experience of the object.*[7]

There is evidence that words are necessary to retrieval of memory for situations and events. Children age two to four were exposed to a simple, unique event such as a magic trick. A day or so after, their verbal description of the event was recorded with close attention to the words used to describe it. A year later, the same children are asked to recall the earlier experience. It is observed that the words used to describe it are limited to those that were earlier available in the child's vocabulary. There has been no updating of the description to incorporate words learned in the succeeding year. It is concluded that memories for events at an earlier stage of language skill are not revised or expanded with the acquisition of new words. The words originally available for description limit later memory recall.

It would not be too much a stretch to say that words are the memory. The near universal experience of very limited memory for early childhood experiences suggests that, without words, there may be no descriptive memory of those early experiences. Those words that were available when the experience was encountered are the memory. Without words to describe the mind print it is just a picture, reproducible perhaps, but beyond clear verbal description.[8]

Language is learned intact in all its structural complexity. Children quickly go beyond recognizing and learning words for things, events, and feelings. They acquire words like *family, neighborhood, school, friends,* or *work* that describe social situations and conventions. They learn words like *toys, food, flowers, animals,* or *buildings* that are classes of particular things. They know the words for *beauty, soul, truth* even though they are words that are outside direct sensation. Such words are classified as ideas and essences. They lack direct sensory reference and must be defined by other words. They are every bit as intuitively and naturally understood as are the words mama, daddy and bottle.[9] Intuitively grasped, the words that represent abstract ideas become as real as *dog* or *toy.*

By the time language is firmly set in the speech of children, the words are no longer mere codes that stand for sensed things and events. Words *are* things and events themselves. They have become fully bound up with the perceptual and emotional experience of those things and events. Danger and desire, sweetness and anger are all now part and parcel of the language set, indistinguishable from the objective experiences described. The essences of community and family, health and illness, good and bad are as real as dog or toy.

In social, political and intellectual terms, ideas and essences are the linguistic currency of idealists, ideologists and philosophers. They are the tools through which personal experience and language itself become subject to rational examination and conscious reflection. They are the stuff of grand abstract speculation.

Almost two and a half millennia ago, the reality of ideas was enshrined in philosophical discourse by the Greek philosopher Plato. Plato's view was that raw sensory experience was too unstable to be trustworthy. He took the notion of essence to its outer extremity. Reality to Plato was the idea. A bed might be a blanket in the corner of the room, a raised platform, or a cushioned mattress. To Plato, perceptions as realities were mere fleeting illusions. The reality of a bed was the idea of a place where sleeping could occur. A chair was not necessarily a four legged stool or even a block of wood. It was a sitting place. Plato sought to define the essences of common experience. Of central importance to his idealistic philosophy is the notion that sensory experience of reality is a shadow world. Sensory perceptions in his schema were likened to shadows on the wall of a cave. Ideas invest those shadows with more or less useful meaning that forms one's interpretation of and clarifies the shadows. This was an improvement in language. Ancient Athenian Greeks lived in a shadow world of myth and superstition. They had no empirical grasp of natural science. Plato and his mentor Socrates invented language that set the foundation of Aristotelian natural science. It was a useful advance in clarity of word usage. By challenging the childish confusion of that era it made human thought subject to reflection and clarification.[10]

Plato's scheme of reality rested on the notion of dualism, the splitting of the physical from spiritual universes. It was an appealing abstraction that recognized a difference between the experienced and the imagined. Dualism lends to the view that the physical world is changeable and untrustworthy, full of material things that will pass away. By contrast, the world of ideas, the realm of the human soul, endures forever. Platonic philosophy holds that ideas are real, materiality is a dream world. Plato's theory of a dual universe spread throughout the Mediterranean world and was incorporated into the religious schemas that were emerging out of pagan customs. The essential, abstracted idea was enshrined in written form and expanded to become religious ideals that endured across millennia.

In that same age, writing became the mark of higher consciousness. Ideas committed to writing were special reality. Written language and literacy were on the rise in the early Western and Mediterranean world. The written record became an extension of the raw mental experience. Ideas about ideas could be set in print to be reflected upon, permitting the presumed reality of an ideated world to be seriously entertained by literate men.

Writing clarifies experience and thought. Thought put into writing makes one's ideas tangibly and enduringly available for others to evaluate and build upon. With the rise and elaboration of human culture, written copy became fundamental to maintenance of social policy and structure. Writing permitted governing policy to be enacted and enforced at great distances and across time bringing unity to the Mediterranean world. Communication was feasible from incomprehensibly far distances, even beyond the grave. The ability to transform such written communications into speech was high power itself, akin to magic. Life's boundaries of knowledge and experience were expanded out to the limits of the literate world.

Language is an intimate tool that permits one to describe and remember life's experiences. The intuitive embedding of language into one's sense of self and the association of words with emotions makes language the record of each individual's course of growth and development as a person. Once language has been acquired, it becomes an expression of selfness and a personal tool for dealing with one's social and material worlds. Modeled in words those worlds become difficult to distinguish from the words that describe them. Words become one's world, one's reality. To question them is to question the truth of experience.

Words clearly are the greater part of human reality. In the absence of words to identify and isolate objects, events, feelings and relationships in the experienced world, those experiences pass in a fuzzy rush. Words bring focus to experience. They permit experience to be processed in elements that can be remembered and retrieved afterward. In the absence of words powerful enough to describe a strange sensory experience, there may be little choice but to accept another's verbal description of the happening as truth.

Words map the experienced world. To a very great extent, what is seen, heard or sensed in any fashion depends on whether or not it is marked by a particular word. Raw sensory grasp of experience is crude and unreliable. Until mapped onto one's world-view in language, it is largely unintelligible and unmanageable. Experience not articulated in words allows only reflexive, instinctive or habitual responsive action. A mental reality map in words permits analysis of and adaptation to unique events. One navigates the day-to-day challenges of life intuitively with the mental map of words.[10] The accuracy of individual maps of the world is a function of the rigor with which its word elements are tested. Using the medium of language, the personal map is refined through comparison with experience of others. General agreement achieved through these comparisons and reliance on the word of culturally accepted authority is called *common sense.* Critical testing of observation and experience is called *scientific method.* A mature, reasonably accurate mental map of the greater world emerges through a blending of science and common sense.

What each person knows as reality is a function of the word map he or she has assembled through the course of life's experience. If new words and ideas of others fit the map, they are true. If the map works to solve personal problems, it is accurate. The complexity of language allows for ongoing elaboration or revision of almost any map, whatever the age of its possessor. Most become fixed at some stage of life. Assembling the mental map is an adaptive process that can stop in early childhood or continue for a lifetime.[11]

The accumulated lore and knowledge of the language culture is a remarkable human asset. Language may in fact be only a set of auditory or visual symbols that encode the things, events, feelings and ideas encountered in one's life space. Words as sounds, as visually encoded sounds, or as pictures, become so firmly embedded in the human brain that they become that which they represent. They become too real to be recognized as *just* symbols. Words invest us with the power to manage our lives. Personhood is established by the language we use. One person's experience is shared through the speech or writing that describes it. The world is managed and manipulated because it is mapped by language. Words describe known reality. The ultimate question may be, who is in control, the words or the human being?

2. Linguistics And Culturally Unique Meaning

Linguistics is the study of language, principally spoken language. Linguistics as a field of study, though, is not any one thing. It is the formal description of language structure, the way words are classified (nouns, verbs, articles, conjunctions, etc.) and how words are strung together grammatically to form phrases and sentences. It is analysis and study of the way word sounds are formed by the vocal chords, tongue and lips as well as how sounds are captured by the inner ear of the listener. It is the cross-comparison of different languages to examine similarities and differences in syntax structure, word use and meaning. It is the study of how native language is learned by infants and how languages not native are later acquired. It is the study of how language use is reflected in brain function imaging and human behavior.

This list does not necessarily exhaust the list of issues that come under the umbrella of linguistics. Formal linguistics contributes to rigorous scientific analysis of language. Sound production can be analyzed with principles of natural physics. Language structure, so laboriously taught in standard high school English courses, was given mathematical rigor by Noam Chomsky. For this service, Chomsky is widely accepted as the father of modern linguistics. Translating the traditional elements and rules of language structure into rigorous mathematical terms with his 1957 book, *Syntactic Structures,* Chomsky established the foundation of modern day computer languages. His *context free grammar* deals with nouns, verbs, articles, conjunctions, etc. as components of a grammatical system and treats language as pure structure, manipulating words as if they have no referential (sensory based) meaning.

As pure structure, Chomsky's context free grammar operates at what he calls surface structure. Referential meaning of words operates at deep structure. Logical processes can be employed on these independent, parallel levels of language structure to construct simple coherent phrases and sentences. Translation on one level alone is computationally manageable, but two become so complex that it is impractical to attempt. Surface structure is one thing, referential meaning quite another. Chomsky's syntactic structure makes an important contribution to advancing the study of language structure as well as to construction of artificial computer language. Ultimately, though, his approach demonstrates the limitations of mathematics in performing complex linguistic tricks that the human mind does instantly and naturally. Mathematics requires exact definitions of the relevant variables to model a hugely complex process like language. Hundreds or even thousands of variables may be involved. Whether a computer model can ever match the human mind as a language making machine is an open question. The mind's capacity to create a comprehensive mental world map full of adaptive meaning is an incredible and perhaps unmatchable feat.

Each culture invents its own language. On the face of the earth, there are between 5,000 and 10,000 living languages embedded in their respective cultures.[1] How these languages compare and whether there are any universal characteristics that typify language structure is the subject of comparative linguistics. Within the discipline of comparative linguistics there is a well-known proposition called the Sapir/Whorf hypothesis. The general thrust of this notion is that in a survey of world languages the underlying language structures are different and that these differences represent distinct cultural realities arising out of differing environmental forces and social history. Language is a culturally shared reality map constructed over a span of successive human generations. The shape of the resulting reality map produced will vary with social history and experience of the culture. Each will be in some ways unique. A conclusion this explication offers is that, if humans map reality using words that take meaning from culture, different language cultures will produce different reality maps. Indeed, there is evidence that this is the case.[2]

The intellectual intersection at which the study of language culture begins is that of cultural and linguistic anthropology. The language, customs and history of a culture are part of a common fabric. Full understanding of the culture first requires a grasp of its language. Edward Sapir, a twentieth century anthropologist and linguist, obtained his doctoral degree in Anthropology from Columbia University and went west to study the languages of North American Indians. He was chief of Anthropology at the Canadian National Museum in Ottawa for a time and later founded the Department of Anthropology at Yale University. Sapir's insights into the influence of language on thinking are captured in a paper he presented to a joint 1928 meeting of the Linguistic Society of America and the American Anthropological Association in New York City. He observed that:

"Language is a guide to social reality. Though language is not ordinarily thought to be of essential interest to social science, it powerfully conditions thinking about social problems and processes. Human beings do not live in the objective world alone, nor alone in the world of social activity as ordinarily understood, but are very much at the mercy of the particular language which has become the medium of expression for their society."[3]

In that pronouncement, Sapir articulated the role of culture in shaping language and invited others to examine it.

Benjamin Lee Whorf, a Connecticut Yankee, was a chemical engineer graduate of MIT who began his career as a fire prevention engineer. As a student at Yale University he studied anthropological linguistics under Edward Sapir. Though Whorf continued to make his career in the insurance industry his life's interest became the study of linguistics focused on the study of American Indian, Aztec and Mayan languages. Over the course of about two decades he published and presented a number of scholarly papers in the field of anthropological linguistics. His was a mind shaped to linguistics that enabled him to catch the nuances of North American Indian languages.

His work continues to be read and to generate ethnographic and linguistic research.

Of special interest to scholars of the time was Whorf's study and analysis of the Hopi Indian tongue. He linked up with an English speaking Hopi Indian living in New York City with whom he attempted to master the intuitive depths of the Hopi language. Whorf would learn word meanings from his Indian mentor, then practice forming sentences with them. As he practiced and was tutored in their correct Hopi usage, he discovered the intuitive subtleties of the language that described it linguistically. His analysis of the Hopi language was of sufficiently high quality to merit invitation to present papers before the Linguistic Society of America.

Whorf concluded that the structure of Hopi language differs from English in several significant ways. Hopi does not use past, present and future tenses for its verbs. Rather, it has a factual tense that includes everything that has happened and is happening, a future tense of that which is or may yet be, and a generalized verb form that is indeterminate as to time. The notions of time and space familiar to Newtonian physics are absent. Time and space are metaphysical in quality. The Hopi reality map is not the reality of conventional English usage. It takes on qualities of the mystical or occult. In Hopi, there are things of the real world, and things of the heart. The heart offers things unseen that are felt, not experienced, things that are magically awesome. Whorf's description of Hopi linguistic reality is titled *An American Indian Model of the Universe,* published in the International Journal of American Linguistics in 1950.[4]

Whorf's method for analyzing Hopi is representative of the field of linguistics. Unless one is bilingual from an early age, language must be learned from native speakers who are willing to coach the learner. The test of language use is communicating within the linguistic rules of the culture. Language does not spring from a ready-made manual. It is constructed over time within a living culture, passed on generation to generation by the same kind of personal example and coaching. Comparative linguists must tune in to the speech of natives and attempt to communicate with it. Grasping a language's meaning, word by word, phrase-by-phrase is required to understand its structure. One does not understand until one has learned to speak the language naturally and intuitively like a small child.

Anna Wierzbicka, an extensively published linguistic anthropologist, was born Polish, which defines her native language. She is English fluent, and a professor of pragmatics, semantics and cross-cultural linguistics at the Australian National University. Her particular specialty is comparative language.[5] She is best known in her academic community for development of natural semantic meta-language NSM, that permits exact comparison of word meaning across languages. NSM allows the meaning components of words to be broken down into their simplest terms using a set of *semantic primes.* Semantic primes are those concepts in language that are not definable in words. They can only be defined by directly referencing the objective experience they represent. In principle, they should be found in every language. They have so far been recognized in Polish, Mandarin, Malay, Lao, Spanish, Korean, Mbula, Cree (Algonquin Indian), Yankunytkatjara (Australian Aborigine) languages, and, of course, English.[6]

Anna Wierzbicka employs NSM to describe with precision the intuitively analyzed meaning content of important language concepts. Her European background equips her with intuitive working knowledge of Russian and other European languages. Employing English as the comparison language, she has examined differences in linguistic cultures through their keywords by looking at differences in how major concepts that describe personal relationships, history and politics are expressed in Russian and Polish languages. Following is a summary of some of the conclusions published in her 1997 book, *Understanding*

Cultures through their Key Words. The key comparative words of English that were examined are *friendship* and *freedom.* Dr. Wierzbicka finds that these fundamentally rich and meaningful English words have only approximate counterparts in Russian and Polish. She examines and describes in precise detail the influence of national cultural history on how these languages describe friends and freedom.

English uses the word *friend* broadly to reference all qualities of social relationships. Polish people uses three terms, Russian uses five to discriminate degrees of relationship. Cultural differences parallel differences in language convention, and difference in usage mirrors the culture in which the meaning of a word has been forged.

Qualities of friendship are expressed in English with adjectives like *close, casual, long-time,* or *old.* Friends are made easily and pass from states of casual to close through a series of shared experiences, all described as friendship. It is normal to make new friends quickly. In a mobile, mass Western society, relationships can be brief and transient, reflecting the lack of a fixed community that would offer opportunity to develop depth in relationships. Friends are made quickly and in large numbers. This reflects modern cultural expectations. Dr. Wierzbicka notes that in the simpler cultural era of Shakespearian time the English word *friend* was reserved for truly special relationships that required a long span of time for development. Across about four centuries, a change has occurred among English speakers as to what a friend is. It is a change that can be attributed to cultural adjustment and language evolution.

Polish language has three distinct words for relationships, one for equal relationships within group or class membership, another for a close, sometimes intimate friendship, yet another for people who are little more than acquaintances. Each class of relationship is distinct. Polish people appear to need more clarity concerning their relationships than do Americans. The

Polish word and concept of *solidarity,* the name given to the Polish union movement, arises out of a pervasive cultural sense of group equality. This is different from a personal relationship.

Russian friendship is complex and intense. One kind of friendship is extraordinarily close. It is mutual in respect and support, requiring full trust and willingness to come to the aid of a friend in urgent situations. This kind of relationship takes on a quality of the moral absolute that requires coming-to-aid to be a virtual absolute in severe crisis. It is a relation that may be closer than is ordinarily experienced between family members. Russians commonly seek out this quality of relationship. The political and social isolation that is characteristic of Russian culture appears to support the need for attaining this kind of emotionally fervent friendship. The level of commitment demanded would seem extreme to most English speakers.

Russians have another word for a relation based on common interest and perspective. This term is a near parallel of "close friend" in English. It is an intermediary category between the maximum and the minimum levels of relationship. Yet another, different word describes strong sentimental attachment to community, family, language and heritage.

Two distinct meanings attach to a Russian word that has traditionally been used to describe relations with co-workers or collaborators. Under Soviet Communism, this term was co-opted to mean political *comrade,* a term loaded with ideological fervor. Depending on the context, it can mean just co-worker or it can suggest the ideological intensity of political comradeship. With the collapse of Communism, the ideological sense of this kind of relationship has faded reflecting the change in culture and the passing of its use to create a sense of common political commitment under communism. In these linguistic differences, established and illustrated at length by Wierzbicka's explications, clear cultural differences in the meaning of friendship become apparent.

Similar differences extend to other words. At the level of social relationships, issues of history and politics are examined by Professor Wierzbicka for their cultural connotations. She extends the argument for cultural specificity across languages by examining the significance of differential meanings of the word *freedom.*

Freedom in Western history is associated with the right to pursue opportunity and self-interest toward whatever end purpose an individual may choose. There are no historical restraints that hold one back from revising and reinventing social convention and individual style. Freedom in the West is a celebration of opportunity. Historically, this reflects the explosion of geographic space and natural resources opened by the discovery of the Americas. Those venturesome enough to seize opportunity in the New World earned the right to shed old ways and old constraints. All that is required is that one be sufficiently bold to risk stepping into the unknown. It is freedom to be whatever you can be and want to be.

For Russians, there are two words for freedom. One reflects release from social constraint that permits one to act with impunity, even irresponsibly. It is the difference between strictly enforced social or legalistic restraints and no restraints at all. It is Vodka freedom that fully releases inhibitions. Historically, the rigid oppression of rulers and landlords restricted Russians' behavior arbitrarily and brutally. Freedom from this kind of oppression means to shed external restrictions in almost childish ways.

Another distinct Russian word speaks to freedom of movement. Serfdom bound Russian laborers to their landlord under law. Escape was possible but very dangerous. If a serf were caught, there was certain, severe punishment. If escape were successful, it meant life among predatory enemies at the boundaries of the country. This word for freedom is equivalent to release from prison with the right to go where one wants to go and take what risks one must.

The Polish word for freedom is bound up with national identity. It is almost entirely connected with the ideal of national independence. Positioned in the middle of Europe, Poland has been a middle ground of territorial militarism for more than two centuries over which Polish culture has known foreign subjection almost continually. For Polish people, freedom is no superficial thing. It is a moral and national concept of greatest importance. Even on a personal level freedom is invested with moral tone. Professor Wierzbicka observes that freedom for the Polish individual "translates as the struggle for freedom, or freedom of conscience". It cannot be translated to mean freedom from restraint or mere absence of inconvenience. Such meanings are outside the moral bounds of Polish freedom. Freedom is an ideal, not an ideology of individual independence as it is in America.

Working at a University in the sub-Asian Australian continent, Wierzbicka has encountered other significant language cultures that offer opportunity for cross-cultural linguistic comparison. Access to one of the world's most primitive languages, Australian Aborigine, presented an unusual laboratory for comparative linguistic analysis. The exceptional intrusion of English into Japanese culture after World War II has invited comparison of the forces that so dramatically differentiate Japanese and English languages. She contrasts the English concept of freedom with that of Aborigines and Japanese and finds the anticipated cultural differences.

Wierzbicka observes that primitive cultures like the Australian Aborigines have not been subject to the political and cultural clashes of Western society and thus have no words that correspond even remotely with the notion of freedom. They have never known the need for such a concept. This finding suggests that anything not occurring in the environment and experience of a culture does not get represented in its words and is missing from the mind maps of its people.

Japanese language borrows its term for freedom from Chinese and gives it no major cultural importance, even applying a sense of the negative to it. The ideal of freedom as it is known in the West is culturally alien to the Japanese. At the core of Japanese culture are key concepts that emphasize the cultural importance of embracing dependence, non-assertiveness, and obligation to others. Freedom is neither idealized nor widely sought.

This is historically tied to Japan's rice economy. In pre-history a single family could not produce enough rice to feed itself, but a community working together could produce a surplus. Community was essential to a sufficiency of food and to survival. Thus, Japanese culture has enshrined community values in its language and culture. Freedom used in a positive Western sense among some, particularly the young Japanese, has begun to grow in post World War II times, though it is clearly a foreign import.

English is the closest thing to a universal language. It is the most widely spoken, especially so as a second language, and the richest in varieties and subtleties of meaning. As an immigrant who mastered English as a foreign language, Dr. Wierzbicka practices comparative linguistics with special sensitivity to words that have meaning only in English. Certain English words, she maintains, are more than just words. They are cultural scripts that become central and distinctive ways of thinking. Two words that she finds unique in their English meanings are *reasonable* and fair.

The roots of modern usage of the word *reasonable* can be traced in part to English philosophy of the Enlightenment period, especially that of John Locke. To be reasonable, in the most general sense, is to be open to alternative and probabilistic ways of knowing something. This meaning is loosely connected to the notion of applying reason to differences in thinking or viewpoint. Reasonableness is not dogmatic, nor is it excessive certainty or rigidity of thought.

The use of the word reasonable in English also has nuances well beyond this centrality of use. A reasonable salary is one that permits some degree of financial comfort in economic matters. That comfort need not be excellent, nor unacceptable. It is within a range that one can accept. Much the same can be said of a reasonable price, reasonable conditions of work, or reasonably good performance of a musician or actor. If one is reasonably satisfied, it is suggested that conditions are within limitations of personal expectation and desire. If it is reasonable to think or say something, that thought or speech is supportable in argument and also within socially proper or acceptable boundaries.

The hugely important legal phrase "beyond reasonable doubt" has its own meaning. Reasonable doubt plays a central role in criminal prosecution within the English language legal system with its emphasis on the probability of one's knowledge. It is closely linked to English social and political philosophy. It describes a personal judgment that is not exact or certain but is so nearly exact or certain as to clearly suppress doubt. It is a description of how one thinks and reaches conclusions rather than one of how truth or falsity is determined.

In the evaluation of police use of weapons and methods of restraint, there is concern for whether force used is reasonable or excessive. In judging this quality of reasonableness, law officers are held to high standards of imminent threat and handling excessiveness of suspect resistance. In assessing whether someone with responsibility for property or personal safety has exercised reasonable care in guarding them, due vigilance and adequate defensive measures are the suggested measures.

Reasonableness in English language cultures accepts uncertainty and probability as central facts of experience. For the reasonable person, knowledge can never be total or final. One must judiciously consider all of the facts and possibilities and weigh the judgment reached. Indeed it is not a certain conclusion that is reached; it is, rather, always a reasonable judgment. These are usages and meanings that have no parallel words in other languages. They are distinctively English.

The root meaning of the English word *fair* is pleasant, beautiful or light of skin complexion.[7] The use of fair or unfair as a description of sports play, punishment for misbehavior or social prejudice is unique to the English language. Wierzbicka observes that the terms *fair* and *unfair* as used by English speakers "have no equivalents in other European languages (let alone non-European ones) and are thoroughly untranslatable." The cultural script (deep meaning) that underlies fairness and unfairness assumes equality of social standing among those involved that is regulated not by law or even established rules. The rules emerge by consensus among equals and are accepted as a matter of common interest. There is no exact right or wrong, good or bad. The rules are generated out of the activity and interaction of those involved, to be judged by the participants in the game for their "reasonableness". That which is judged as justifiable and mutually beneficial by any reasonable person is *fair. Fairness* is the liberal, free, unconstrained person's idea of socially equitable judgment and action. Life may not be fair, but social transactions in a society of equals should always be.

Anna Wierzbicka and Benjamin Whorf make persuasive arguments for language as a repository of cultural experience. The manner in which that experience is processed and appropriate action is chosen determines and limits the structure of one's native language. From birth, its words and sentences are absorbed as intuitive natural descriptions of reality. Forming words and sentences becomes the mental process through which human and natural potentialities are discovered and evaluated.

Language is invented and refined through the practice of philosophy, law, science and even through simple game-like social interaction. The social needs and circumstances of cultures are expressed in the meaning of its words. Western English-American culture is plural and rich with subcultures that have their own languages and word meanings. This can be seen in the central role words play in contemporary Western political rhetoric as well as in the rules of play for organized sports like baseball. In political matters especially, a word can have very different meanings and emotional associations. Differences, where they can be identified, may be of significance in explaining differences in reality maps. In particular, even within the same language culture, an individual's theory of how and why the world works shifts with variation in word meaning from subculture to subculture. In intra-cultural matters, people often talk at one another without communicating. They talk past one another using the same or similar words that do not mean the same thing. Twenty-first century English language political rhetoric is full of this kind of discrepancy.

There are those in the US who favor armed intervention around the world believing that it is necessary for maintenance of international order. Others reject the use of armed force as inherently immoral and counterproductive to world peace. Careful attention to the arguments put forward by each position will reveal major differences in the meaning of core words and of reality maps in use.

Militarily enforced world order starts with the premise that conflict among cultures is inevitable and national security requires maximum military response to every threat. Social order demands that enemies fear massive retaliation. From this view, national security after the September 11, 2001 attacks on America had to be restored by inflicting such severe pain on its enemies that they would never again attempt such an attack. Restoration of security after such an event is the traditional duty of young men who must courageously do battle with the enemy as soldiers. Pride in one's nation is expressed through willingness of the young to risk death defending its freedom and security.

The individual variation on the massive retaliation reality map is the belief that freedom is preserved through possession of weapons that strike fear into those who would limit or take it. A reputation for meanness and brutality is thought to make one invulnerable. At the core of this reality map is the presumption that individual self-respect requires one to respond violently in the face of *any* humiliation. It is the attitude that underlies bar fights, gun rights advocacy and inner city gang shoot-outs.

Rejection of armed force argues from the premise that brutal retribution is never more than a temporary solution. Retaliation only humiliates and must eventually result in counter-retaliation. It arises from the emotional need for revenge. Revenge is driven by pride that is humiliated. War is pride against pride. Sending young men and women into armed battle to restore pride is foolish and fruitless. Security comes not following mutual exhaustion from warring but from acceptance and enforcement of rule of law. Without respect for others, there will not be respect for the law. Humility and mutual respect are basic to personal security. Excessive pride is evidence that one lacks confidence and self-respect. Issues of respect cannot be settled by war.

The most important differences in these reality maps are in the words *fear* and *pride.* There is also a difference in the meaning of *freedom. Fear* for the military enforcer is a mix of threat, anger and humiliation. The experience of fear is a gut-level, adrenaline rush that justifies and requires maximum response. Anything less will result in humiliation at best, threat to survival at worst. *Pride* is knowledge of superior strength and resources. It is the conviction that one's retaliatory capacity is unbeatable, winning is inevitable. Freedom in this view is a sense of security built on superior strength and firepower. *Freedom* is the capacity and the right to act without restraint in maintaining that security. This is the meanest kid on the block reality map of freedom and security.

From the anti-military perspective, *fear* is a barrier to rational analysis and response. Fear is surrender to retaliatory instinct that justifies resort to violence. The experience of fear is a signal to search out understanding and resolution of the problem. For anti-militarists, *pride* is a dangerous, delusional emotion that makes enemies of the simply disagreeable. *Pride* overestimates the intentions of the enemy as well as judgment of the ease with which he can be subdued. *Freedom* is the right to act prudently and responsibly without undue restraint. This is the rational problem solving reality map of how to pursue national and personal security.

The same words used with different meanings for each of these respective world views enables communication but not understanding between strategic positions. Meaning arises out of different reality maps that have different chains of causation from the point of initial conflict to end resolution. They guide action down different paths. The languages of each subculture talk past the other using the same words infused with different meaning.

Added to this contemporary clash of cultures is the view of a large block of fundamentalist religionists who are disgusted and alienated by what they see as a breakdown of morality in the modern world. Fear of sweeping change that may swamp traditional values produces righteous anger toward the whole sinful world. Freedom is license, liberal rationality denies faith, traditional moral values have been abandoned, sin rules. There is no way to take pride in any of this awful evil. They turn to the apocalyptic biblical view of a final war that ends with the second coming of the Messiah, especially if the total war is waged in the Holy Land. War is acceptable if it brings about the kingdom of God with expectation of ultimate peace on earth. Let the Lord smite his enemies. Let war be waged. This reality map is wholly distinctive to itself. It is the apocalyptic theory of *fear* and *freedom*.[8]

These sub-cultural scenarios are illustrations of how the meaning of words shape action. They become actionable scripts that determine what the problem is and how it must be handled. Words thus used are not so much what is thought as they are a way of thinking. Words determine what we know or "have in mind", and what we see, or "give attention to". Words permit a grasp of what is happening, how to react and how to participate in every domain.

Understanding the structure of almost any social event is difficult or impossible without well defined words to describe it. One must speak the language to know what is happening. There is, for instance, great inherent complexity in the game of baseball. One must command the right words to follow and understand the game. To the naïve observer, baseball is a game of hitting and throwing a smallish ball, about the size of your fist. A player with a slender stick attempts to hit the ball. If the ball is hit successfully, straight away and not off to the side somewhere, the player runs to the right down a line toward another player. Players on the field try to get the ball and throw it toward another player on the field who is beyond the runner. If the thrown ball is not caught by that player, there is a lot of excitement and the runner keeps running. If it is caught on the fly or ahead of the runner's advance, he walks back to his bench.

This is a naïve, uninformed though basically accurate description of baseball as a game. One need use only common sense words to describe what is visible. In homes throughout America there are undoubtedly many wives who would agree that this is what they see in the play of baseball on television. They have no knowledge of what is a hit or a walk, a strike or a ball, an error or an out. True fans go deep into the details of the game on every play. They attempt to penetrate the strategic thinking of the players and the decisions of a team's manager.

To understand baseball, you must know that every action during play has a name, and is recorded as a number statistic under that name. Every term is explicitly defined so that there is little confusion in the statistical record. Where there is room for confusion, a judge is appointed to decide what statistical category the play belongs to. When the ball is thrown – pitched - and caught at home plate without being hit, the umpire calls a strike or ball. To be judged a strike, the ball must pass through an imaginary zone over home plate. Otherwise it is a ball. A hit off to the side (outside the "base lines") is a foul and is a strike, but cannot be the third strike. Three strikes ends the attempt at bat, four balls is a free walk to first base. Tapping the ball to the ground in front of home plate is a bunt. A hit ball that falls to the ground before being caught is fair and in play. A ball that might have been caught or trapped but wasn't may be judged an error. The base line from home plate to first base is one side of a ninety foot square infield. Home runs must be hit over the outfield fence or wall. And so on.

It does not stop with definition of the elements of the game. Batters have their "at bats" calculated to three decimal places to measure the percentage of hits in a game, a series, a season, or a career. Pitchers have the number of balls and strikes counted for a game, a season or a career. Statistics for hits, walks, home runs etc. are calculated for individual pairs of pitchers and batters. Managers change pitchers and other players as they see opportunity or need. Everything goes on the record. Real fans memorize the statistics and talk the game with knowledgeable enthusiasm.[9]

It is the words that define and describe it that make any game rational, intelligible and meaningful. Without the words and a grasp of their meaning, it is all throw the ball, hit the ball, run. While the game may be interesting, even fun, to watch, it remains nothing more than vigorous activity as long as there are no words to define it. That would describe the experience of the most rabid baseball fan watching a British game of cricket.

To the uninformed American that game culture makes no sense until the overlay of its own special words is mastered.

In just about any specialized activity confusion prevails in the absence of words that describe its processes. The practice of law requires accurate knowledge of legal words and the processes of courts. The practice of medicine requires that names of diseases, medicines and medical procedures be exactly understood. Mathematics requires an understanding of fractions, integers, algebraic equations and calculus integration. Words are fundamental to each reality map. Meaning is more than words. It goes beyond words into the realm of language structure. Language structure shapes thought into chains of causation and identifies cultural and environmental priorities. Every language culture has unique words and meanings that reflect cultural history. Meaning and history determine how peoples from different language cultures think and understand their phenomenal world.

Comparative linguistics requires special talent. One must be or train to be intuitively multilingual. Languages must be compared intuitively for the meaning of words, phrases and sentences. The comparison experienced must then be clearly and accurately expressed in words, perhaps even separately in the words of each of the languages compared. That may not always be fully possible, since some languages are more complex and extensive than others. English is the reference language of modern cultural linguistics because it encompasses more varieties and qualities of meaning than any other living language. It is the master map against which others are compared. No one should assume that it is a complete or final map. Language is continually being expanded and reinvented. A culture never stops adapting its mental map. Words keep being invented.

3. Culture And The Language Imperative

The culture one is immersed within prescribes the way individual behavior will be shaped and conformed. Language is foremost in determining the shape and quality of culture. The shared reality of any community is represented in its language and is the reality model passed on to every new generation. Subtle and not so subtle instructions for thought, belief and action are carried in language. Of all forms of behavior learned from one's culture, language is the first and most central. Even the special accent characterizing a culture's speech is a mark of cultural identity. Shared language is the ticket of admission to intimate social exchange.

Culture conveys the mores of a people. Acceptable and unacceptable action, proper or improper speech, holy or wicked ideas are all prescribed by culture. Departure from cultural convention is rebellion. Those qualities that describe a social group's culture are its truths. If those qualities do not wear well with an individual, he/she may opt for status as an isolate, an excommunicant. In an earlier age, to be cut off from one's community was a virtual death sentence. It still takes strong character to endure lack of a social anchor.

The power of a community of culture lies in its ability to enhance survival, quality of life and longevity. A common language allows for clearly communicated signals of danger and opportunity. Cooperation increases success in competition for survival. Hunting parties are more likely to bring home a kill. When it is a large kill, sharing in the community serves the communal good. A community has a better chance of warding off attacks from animals or other tribes. Communities can withstand death or injury to one or a few members without breakdown of order. There is clear safety in numbers all around.[1]

A shared language lets accumulated communal knowledge be passed on. Dangerous people, animals, or foods are clearly classified and labeled. The alarm can be sounded of impending danger. Socially dangerous or disruptive behaviors can be verbally blocked. Lacking built-in reflexive or instinctive responses, human beings must assess a situation, then try and err or, alternatively, fall back on cultural wisdom. Humans are flexible in their choices of behavior, the most adaptive of all the primates. They learn from every circumstance. Within a community, that learning is shared. It need not be repeated through every generation. Language is the storehouse of a culture's experience and knowledge. Culture teaches customary behavior that maximizes health and survival. An instructive contrast showing how this comes about can be drawn from comparisons of Japanese rice culture, American West cowboy and gold rush culture, and middle Eastern Bedouin culture.

The influence of rice culture on unique Japanese word concepts goes much deeper than the significance of a single word. Beyond the muted value of freedom in Japanese language, the entirety of Japanese culture is shaped by rice farming. It would not be unreasonable to claim that the uniqueness of Japanese character was itself formed in its rice paddies.

Constrained by limited land space the Japanese early learned to manage their resources in an eco-friendly way. Rice, well suited to the soil and climate, is both labor and water intensive. Preparation of water for rice ponds must be accomplished within a narrow time frame and rice must be planted in all ponds on the same day. There are no great rivers in Japan. Effective use of water means that such water flow as available must be carefully managed. A series of ponds that exploit the natural flow of rivers offers most efficient use of that water. Japanese farm families live together in tight village clusters around the water and rice fields. To maximize rice production, action must be collaborative and free of friction. Competition for status or resources among farmers would risk rupturing the cultural fabric of the community and hazard starvation.

Dependency on cultivation of rice as the staple crop shaped the most basic social customs of the Japanese. Only a small part of the Japanese population is today engaged in rice production. The social culture of more than one hundred million people nevertheless emphasizes, above all else, that harmony and accommodation are required for its production. The overarching emphasis in Japanese social arrangements is group consciousness and harmony in relationships. That requirement directly flows from the demands of rice agriculture.[2]

Harmony and accommodation is expressed by a single, one syllable word in Japanese; *wa.* In the strictest sense, wa is not translatable. Wa is not just getting along with others. It is complete immersion of oneself in the group to the extent of full submission to group purposes. Wa means anti-individualism as well. One must not stand out. A Japanese saying has it that *the nail that stands up will be pounded down.* Individualism is spoken of only as a negative, undesirable quality.

Social conflict in Japanese culture is strongly discouraged. Japan has far fewer lawyers than does the US or Europe. Litigation is rare. Open conflict over contracts or business arrangements is unusual. Japanese culture captures the values that suppress conflict in two significant words, *on,* and *giri. On* is said to constitute the foundation of Japanese morality. Again, the word is monosyllabic and essentially untranslatable to any English (or other language's) terms. In part it means the receipt of a benefit that carries heavy obligation. There is simultaneous gratitude and resentment in the receiver, who must bear the obligation with grace and goodness. *Giri* carries a complex meaning that partly overlaps *on.* There is a parallel implication of debt and obligation with an extension of meaning into the realms of duty, honor or justice.[3]

Wa, on and *giri* impose on Japanese culture some requirements that, in English, could be described as huge *social trips.* It demands an all-pervasive social harmony where gifts and favors are taken as burdens of obligation that impose a duty to acknowledge and repay. One must not stand out, one must not complain, one must accept. It need be no surprise that group suicide among the young is common in Japan. Extreme submission of selfness to the greater good exacts a heavy personal toll.[4]

This is a culture that overwhelmingly values the interest of the community above that of the individual. Japanese go to extraordinary lengths to avoid social conflict. The vast part of decision making is collaborative, even to the point that it is often impossible to hold any single person responsible for the result. From a Western perspective, this would be impossibly oppressive and irresponsible as well. It is not all bad, though. One of the strengths of this culture is the remarkable degree of conscientiousness displayed by the Japanese in their jobs. Japanese manufacturing processes call for full participation of workers at all levels in the solution of design and production problems. Unlike Western practice where a trained engineering expert solves such problems, the Japanese work group finds a consensus solution. This group includes production workers, supervisors, and specialist engineers, all working within the constraints of *wa, on* and *giri* to achieve the best solution.[5] The extremity of commitment willingly offered to solution of a common problem is well illustrated by the willingness of Japanese workers to repair at terrible personal risk those nuclear reactors damaged by the March 2011 earthquake.

Group decision making that takes into account the inputs of *every* member imposes a heavy burden of internal communication on its members. A group of only ten people offers 45 possible pairs of individuals who potentially may need to communicate with one another to produce group consensus. There are 120 different trios, over two hundred unique quartets, and so on, that could need or want to communicate. Consensus can become dauntingly complex.

Japanese meet these intimidating demands by expanding their opportunities to communicate. Rather than go home at quitting time, it is customary for co-workers to cluster in after-hours saki houses for the purpose of building strong group unity through communication. They meet with their work group to communicate about work and other issues. Informality and alcohol loosen tongues. The skills, knowledge bases and personal uniquenesses of group members are identified through informal communication. Strong foundations for group decision making are cultivated.

Top-down management decisions are rare in Japan. While the elders of Japanese society enjoy the highest mark of respect from the young, they seldom if ever use their position to make unilateral decisions that impact those subordinate to them. They participate in the consensus building but do not dominate it. Good feelings are too important to risk with arbitrary executive decisions.

Japanese culture is well characterized as extraordinary togetherness. Continually adapting to scarcity minimizes opportunity for and concern with gathering wealth. The Japanese are a remarkably leveled people. Ninety percent of Japanese are said to describe themselves as middle class. Top executives of Japanese companies do not award themselves the lavish salaries typical of Western Corporations. Job advancement is a blended function of seniority and merit. Though Japan may have lost World War II to the technological superiority of the US, it achieved domination of the US Auto market by virtue of superior industrial organization based on full, consensus based communication and work problem solving. For its severely limited geographic size, Japan has built one of the most vigorous and prosperous economies in the world. Its culture must get the credit for much if not most of that success. Few Westerners would be comfortable living with Japanese cultural demands.

The cowboy/gold rush culture of the old American West, celebrated in endless movies and novels, illustrates how the rupturing of stable East Coast colonial culture was brought about by the sudden availability of boundless western land. The lure of wealth, gold, and rich agricultural territory pulled the boldly ambitious into the emptiness of a new country. Language played a limited role in this new, Western culture. It was a culture of wit and grit. Hard experience, ad hoc communities and guns met social need and resolved arguments. The culture that emerged shaped a society that valued rugged independence and self-sufficiency. Only as much community was tolerated as might be needed for cooperation in crisis. Illiteracy was widespread, and the "good book" was more a decorative icon than a source of social guidance. A wealth of natural resources offered plenty of room for error and bad judgment on the part of these hard working pioneers and frontiersmen. Western culture was wide open and roaring. In some places, it still is. Each man learned for himself what it took to survive. Life spans were short and exciting.

Rifles and guns were essential in hunting game for food and for protection from danger. The initial rush into the West and its gold fields was an individual adventure. Over a twenty-five year time span wagon trains carried families over the Oregon trail to the Pacific coast to claim rich farm lands of northern Oregon and central California. With the arrival of transcontinental railroads, great tracts of open land permitted family farms to flourish throughout the mid and far west. In contrast with Japanese rice agriculture with their tight clusters of family homes, western farmers lived in isolation, often miles removed from any other family. Social events required travel and were treated as recreation, whether the occasion was a barn dance or a religious revival meeting. Formality prevailed for such occasions, and best appearances were emphasized. Disagreement may have occurred with neighbors or in social settings, settled with conflict that may have ended in gunfire where things got out of control. A tradition of cool headed, watchful independence came out of these cultural experiences. Emphasis on qualities of self-reliance and personal initiative are firmly imbedded in the language of US western culture. The special ideological quality of absolute freedom, a characteristic of America, is at its core.

Americans have seldom worked together comfortably in groups. Industrial America was and is mechanized to the maximum. Heavy capital investment drives the economic system. Workers are cogs in a machine. Tightly specialized jobs requiring little or no training that can be consistently and reliably performed by minimally trained workers were long the norm. The US is a nation of independence minded individuals working alone within a formal, largely machine like structure -- if they work within any structure at all. Relations are constrained by simple rules enforced to avoid the potential for conflict. Poor or marginal performers are fired. While it may be shocking to see it happen, basic grievances still may be settled with guns, even in cities and offices.

Americans find it very difficult to make decisions as a group. Differences are either emphasized or suppressed. There is strong tendency to establish a pecking order of social priority through competition and friction. Open disagreement occurs with those at or below one's level until the order is set. A superior's positions and decisions are publicly agreed to, then faulted in private.

In the absence of full communication and consensus, groups in America tend toward quick, superficial agreement. Preservation of good relationships and feelings will be maintained through discouragement or squelching of differences. If the leader signals a preferred solution, the group rapidly comes together behind it. Alternative courses of action are ignored or dismissed. There is little patience for consensus building. Identifiable risk is ignored or played down. Agreement that is reached quickly often results in a solution that is shallow. Americans are independent decision makers who temporarily suppress their independence in groups. Bad group decisions are a frequent result.[6]

The language of Western American culture tends to be terse and abrupt, characterized by single words and brief phrases, loaded with meaning and spoken with confidence. Those who speak fluently and sensibly in consonance with common cultural values become its cultural standard bearers. Preachers, selected for their special linguistic fluency, enjoy high status and exert wide influence. Speaking skill sets leaders apart, making it a mark of personal status. The Westerner says only what needs to be said. He leaves the talking to others. The words that characterize his culture are heavy with reverential meaning like independence, self-reliance, privacy, liberty, freedom.

The sudden clash of Islam with the West has made improved understanding of Arab cultures a cultural imperative of the twenty-first century. Before the discovery of oil in the early twentieth century, the Islamic middle east was dominantly a Bedouin culture. Viewed through the prism of Western culture, Arabia was a mysteriously exotic land of camels and veiled princesses. In truth, most Arabs eked out a bare existence from a harsh desert land. It was, indeed, not so much exotic as it was simply backward. Government was tribal, nations existed in name only. The Arabian peninsula is especially characterized by great scarcity of resources (other than oil). The most critical lack is water. The exceptionally arid climate of the peninsula makes it one of the harshest regions in the world for maintenance of life. Much of the desert region that runs down its spine is uninhabitable. There is little water available for support of agriculture or livestock. Only those eastern areas adjacent to the Gulf of Persia offer any life support at all.

The culture of the Arabian middle east is as harsh as the land. Tribes compete with one another for water and arable ground. Death is always near. If the climate does not kill, neighbors quite possibly will. Tribal culture is anything but placidly cooperative. The Arab way is expressed simply as " Me against my brother, me and my brother against my cousin, me, my brother and my cousin against the world." Depending on how close to thirst and starvation an individual or tribe is, readiness to cooperate increases. The law that regulates this irregular social fabric is, literally, *The Word.* The Quran and religious fatwa determine what is good and just. There are no secular courts to assure consistent interpretation of the law. Young men memorize the Quran as their guide to social living. When uncertain, one either looks within or to a respected Quranic scholar to find the answer. Knowing and interpreting law is open to anyone with sufficient Quranic prestige. Higher education in Arabic nations is dominated by Quranic scholarship. Interpretation of The Word shifts with social and environmental circumstance. Ultimately, survival in this brutal desert is a function of who is best fitted to its harshness. The Quran provides the basic moral and legal rules that guide adaptation of social and personal behavior.

It is instructive that Arabs revere *The Word* as almost no other culture does. Challenge to The Word or to their Prophet is mortal challenge. Life is full of desperate dilemmas that mere humans are not genetically programmed to meet. The Word is the place to look for answers when they are needed. As a result, much cultural time and energy is focused on understanding and interpretation of The Word. Readiness to use raw power to enforce a particular interpretation is always close to the surface.

The culture of Arabia is shaped by a cruel environment and a special linguistic heritage. Given the uncertainties of life, the desperation of striving and the limitations on personal fulfillment that the pre-oil Arab world offered, the pillars of Islam served as an important constraint on volatile impulses and energies. Mass prayer five times daily creates community and leavens the bleakness of daily life. The Word is significant social glue in this hostile and fragmented society.[7]

Language is the accumulated experience of a culture that is passed on in words. Once in use, it is much more. Language establishes cultural and personal identity. It provides a sense of connection and community that offsets the trials of life. Without that connection we are lost in a wild, unfathomable universe. Language and culture are tools for organizing and meeting the challenges of that universe.

4. Intellect And The Written Word

The history of western culture tells the story of how mental models have evolved and emerged. Western society left the intellectually stale middle ages when Christopher Columbus tested a fresh model of the physical world as a globe. Success in discovery of the new world destabilized Europe, setting the stage for global navigation, mass communication, religious fragmentation, nation building, and buildup of wealth made possible by the industrial revolution and expanding science. Literacy was indispensable to that progress and the printing press was absolutely requisite to the spread of literacy. Indeed, the printing press is almost certainly the most important invention of the second millennium, easily comparable to the invention of the internet. The explosion of intellectual innovation that created this new era could not have occurred without it.

Records of human activity and culture are a recent human invention. Crudely drawn prehistoric pictographs are known. The record of a hunt from at least thirteen thousand years ago is portrayed in the figures of running animals on a cave wall in Lascaux, France.[1] In addition to such pictographs, tools and artifacts are the record of human presence until language appears. With invention of a phonetic code for the spoken word sometime around 1,000 BCE, the written record emerged and expanded in the millennium leading up to the Christian era. By the first century of that era, the written word was in relatively wide spread use throughout the Roman Empire. Roman and Greek literature were well developed. The far-flung Mediterranean legions of the Roman Empire were coordinated by written orders from Rome. Greek history and philosophy flourished. The early Christian Church was organized and ministered to through the writings of St. Paul and other early church fathers. Written language created communities at a distance and stabilized their stories so they could be communicated across time and distance. A story on paper ready to be read and orally recreated was a miracle of informational transmission across human generations. The written record with its special power became the foundation of social order even though, for most of the next two thousand years, literacy was limited to the educated elite.

Until the fifteenth century, literacy was a virtual monopoly of priests and clergy. Through the middle ages, for all practical purposes, the written word was owned by the Church and largely inaccessible to the common man. Books were for the educated, literate elite. What the common man knew of ancient literature was read aloud to him. The low incidence of literacy and the rarity of written copy gave religion domination over community and culture. With the invention of the printing press, secular science could advance independently of religion and theology. Scholars could communicate with one another through written tracts using common vernacular language.

Printing on paper was not necessarily new, but without movable type it was tortuous and inefficient. Prior to 1450 nearly all written communication was hand inscribed. An army of scribes was needed to reproduce one copy of any traditional manuscript. The total product of a single copyist monk's life might be as much as two complete Bibles. Small, impractical advances in mechanical printing had occurred. A flat, hand etched wooden surface could be hand inked for impression against a sheet of paper using a crude press. Because wood deteriorated with successive applications of ink the potential for advancing the written word on etched wood platens was limited.

The printing press was invented when Joseph Gutenberg brought together a set of critical elements in an act of creative genius. The limited letter set of the phonetic alphabet made it practical to assemble individual cast metal letters, letter by letter, line by line, to form words, sentences and pages for printing. Gutenberg's inventiveness went further. He was a silversmith with enough knowledge of metallurgy to know that letters cast of lead alone would quickly oxidize. He alloyed lead with tin and antimony to produce a stable metal print face that could be assembled, printed, broken down and reused again. The quality of the finished print was enhanced by a special mold that formed metal dies for rapid, reliable production of high quality typeface. The press was adapted from agricultural use for pressing fruit into wine and cider. To make the printed page more durable Gutenberg substituted oil for water as the base of ink. His assembled trays of type were inked and the paper was pressed to transfer the image. Books could be produced in hours rather than in years. The ground was set for an explosion of literacy.

Prior to introduction of the printing press with movable and reusable type, a university library with no more than 100 volumes of books was the norm. Within a half century after its introduction in 1450, nearly all the ancient literature of Greece and Rome had been published and the Holy Bible had been printed in most vernacular languages of Europe. The accumulated wisdom of western culture was available to any literate citizen. Scholars, starved for access to written secular classics, now had them for personal reference. Martin Luther could print and distribute his ninety-five theses to found the Protestant reformation. Printing was a truly revolutionizing invention.[2]

Literacy spread quickly after invention of the printing press. Accelerated spread of literacy came as the industrial revolution provided the cheap paper and leisure time for the luxury of reading. Nonetheless, large pockets of illiteracy continued to exist during the ensuing five centuries. As recently as 1970, one-third of the population of the world was illiterate. Literacy is not always encouraged by government. It can challenge existing authority, religious or civil. With reading comes knowledge. Knowledge confers power and independence. It is disruptive of social order. Ideas born of the printed page are potentially dangerous to prevailing authority. In the era of American slavery, teaching blacks to read was actively discouraged, subject at times to criminal prosecution. Literacy would "ruin" a good field hand or house maid. In Brazil as recently as 1960 it was illegal to teach peasants to read. Literacy has long been the test of personal and political status in many parts of the world. Political power was often preserved through maintenance of forced illiteracy. The social and economic significance of the written word helped invest the written word with still greater power and prestige.

The written word is closely associated with religious belief. The most accessible printed book since invention of the printing press has been the Bible and the only book in many Christian homes prior to the twentieth century was the Holy Bible. In the nineteenth and early twentieth century traveling bible salesmen blanketed the United States placing a bible in every home that could afford it.[3] It was the book from which many learned to read. Family history and genealogy were inscribed in its pages. It was held and read aloud during solemn moments. Magic and awe were on every page. It was and continues to be a holy icon in its own right.

Written copy of every kind has special authority. It can only be guessed how much greater authority there is in writing for those who cannot read. Hearing the word read by literate authority must be an awesome experience. When illiteracy is one's social reality, the written word is invested with wonder. To the illiterate, writing is magical, reading is awesome, perhaps terrifying. Inability to read is disconnection from the wider world of knowledge and awareness. Illiteracy is an immense social and economic liability.

Prior to the nineteenth century, most word maps were religious in quality. The Word is the currency of religion and religion is the divine mental map. It uses big abstractions to cover large gaps of uncertainty. Scientists attempt to fill some of those gaps with empirically derived truth. Religion supplies the revealed truth of authority, science seeks discovered truth of disciplined experience. This describes the ground of conflict between religion and science in the present day world. Both religion and science depend on formal, written language to communicate their big, special, idea and word-based truths.

The written word is concrete and stable; the spoken word is ephemeral. Writing exerts its own authority. Literacy changes the rules. Writing extends the availability of the word so that individuals can independently interpret and question its meaning. The doors are opened to competition among differing interpretations of the written word. Religion fragments into sects, each with its own interpretation of holy writ.

As if to mock the division between religion and science, science fiction offers rich play on reality creation. Ordinary physical reality is invested with magical qualities in much current day adventure fiction. There are no limits on the imagination in these constructed realities. Nor is there any requirement that they be accepted as reality. One may accept, pretend to accept, or merely be amused by possibilities science fiction represents. It is the possibilities that are celebrated. Today's science fiction can become tomorrow's reality. Flying carpets and magical communication across distance was the science fiction of former times. Flying around the world, listening to radio and watching TV are commonplace today. There is no way to know how much science fiction is yet to be realized. Much is still poorly understood about the physical universe. What seems like wild imagination today could reflect potential for future discovery and new reality.

Language, words and ideas are the vehicles that have carried humankind forward into startling new realities, inventively created by a brain that seems to insist on knowing how the universe works. The remarkable capability of the mind to invent explanations is revealed in split-brain experiments of Roger Sperry and Michael Gazziniga detailed in the following chapter. Their research demonstrates that the mind of man easily becomes an alternative reality maker. That reality could not exist without language. The construction of a comprehensive model of human experience requires a community of minds working together across time and distance using written language. Mere speech dissipates in the wind. Written ideas can be examined critically to be improved and tested against the experiences and ideas of others.

The written word sits patiently until it is discovered and read. It sits on the page for all to read or hear read. Unaided memory is no longer a possible source of confusion or error. The written word is communication that any literate person can access and challenge. It advances social stability through the written record of agreement. Contracts reduce important agreements to writing so that the intentions of all involved can be later determined. In major legal cases, testimony in a court of law is instantly transformed into writing or otherwise recorded electronically for later written transcription. Once recorded, it is the record of the law.

Speech and writing involve wholly different skills and processes. Writing takes speech to an entirely different mental level. The phonetic alphabet visually encodes the sounds of language. This is actually code at a secondary level. It is representative of and superimposed on speech sounds. Reading introduces added mental steps into the comprehension of language. It begins with extensive retraining of the visual cortex of the brain. New neural pathways must be formed that ultimately connect through the visual cortex to the language centers of the brain. The phonetic written code is first converted into sound images to be comprehended. Learning readers often read aloud, literally listening to the words they articulate. Gradually, words bypass the sound association stage. Most people learn to decode the meaning of the word "stop" by instantly translating when seen on a red hexagon. Fluency slowly comes. Reading sentences fluently is a high level skill. It demands a large investment of time and effort. Civilized societies support readers, primitive ones don't. Books are a product of social advance, wealth and leisure. In terms of human history, published secular books for a mass market are very recent. A mass market of readers who seek out the stimulation of ideas in the written word is a product of the industrial revolution and modern education. Literacy and progress are Siamese twins.

Writing changes the way the writer thinks. Evaluating one's own written words uses the written word as an extension of memory to give perspective and allow comparison. The written words of a writer that have been put on paper are reprocessed through the eyes and visual cortex where they can be evaluated by both hemispheres of the brain. This is a powerful way to check one's mental word map for clarity and meaning. Editing one's own writing puts discipline into thinking and expression. It allows very complicated arguments to be constructed in words and later examined for comprehensiveness, accuracy and consistency. It is in the special discipline of reading one's own words that thinking is improved. With practice, thinking in written words diverges at length from thinking in spoken words. Flow and consistency are introduced that have the power to convince.

The originator of published written words is called *an author*. *Authors* wield the *authority* of written words. Generating original stories or ideas carries a special quality of authority. If a new story contradicts the authority of an existing one, its (the new story's) authority (author) must be challenged or even destroyed if the old reality is to be saved. Written ideas can become issues of life and death. Economic ideas of nineteenth century philosophers produced war and revolution in Europe and spawned the Soviet Union. Encounter at the boundaries of major world religious communities can be deadly. The written word is dangerous. Writers are revolutionaries. The pen (or the keyboard) is their weapon. Their brains are shaped to wield the weapon of language. Journalists and authors process the words of their minds differently from ordinary folk. They read, criticize and evaluate their product as they write, especially so when making an argument for a critical audience. As they do so, they cultivate and refine their mental word maps.

In the construction of meaning, speaking and writing differ in major ways. Non-writers, as well as those who read with difficulty, can find it unnatural and tedious to generate analytical arguments. Their words will lack clarity and consistency when used in debate or argument. Intuitively understood meaning is rarely exact. It is a common observation that many words have multiple, different meanings. Intuitive speech allows alternative meanings to be substituted freely in use. Meaning can be conveniently or accidentally revised from one utterance to another almost in the style of a pun. Until disciplined with practice, intuitive speech is always sloppy and lacking in discipline. Intuitive speakers give their words color with body language. They stutter and repeat and correct as they go, revising and clarifying when their audience becomes confused by poorly chosen words. Writing requires that the unevaluated, intuitively produced language of speech be transcended. Writing demands discipline in language use. Writers have only the words themselves and must use them thoughtfully to create meaning for unseen, unknown readers.

The mental map of intuitive speech allows for inconsistencies and contradictions. Much of it is a kind of shorthand that compresses thoughts around core ideas. Spoken thoughts are poorly remembered for anything other than their salient, key words. Writing one's thoughts on paper and later reading them separates the acts of production and evaluation. This allows inconsistencies and contradictions to be discovered. Good writers become good speakers by practicing the formation of coherent sentences. Words are no longer loosely cobbled together as with intuitive speech. For use in thinking, speaking and writing, the mental map is expanded to include usable phrases and sentences that have been tested in writing. The meaning that individual words possess and convey is enhanced and extended by how they are placed in the context of other words. The language culture of speakers is thus quite different from that of non-writers. One is intuitive and personal, the other critical and rational. The associated mental maps are also different. In that difference there is potential for critical minds to clash with intuitive minds.

Intuitive speech deals in words that address immediacy. Spoken language is fluid, full of ambiguities and easily modified from one situation and time to another. That makes it useful to salesmen and politicians. Political rhetoric, indeed, is a language of speech and slogans. Speeches are modified to fit the audience, sometimes on the spot, and slogans are revised as necessary. The unreliability of political promises is renowned. The ephemeral quality of intuitive speech allows easy later amendment. Political communication put into written form is appropriately called *spin*. Political "platforms" and press releases are carefully crafted for maximum ambiguity. In the pre-film and television world of intuitive speech, that was good enough. In the modern age, patterns of sound are immediately recorded electronically for later replay and evaluation. Modern aggressive journalism by those trained as writers is supported by a ready electronic record of every public political speech. This has changed the political environment in the late twentieth century. Spoken words of politicians are videotaped and stored for easy retrieval so that contradictions can be put side by side on the nightly news. Lack of clarity and consistency is made obvious. Politically, exact records of intuitively generated words are quite inconvenient. Politicians have had to become experts at spinning messages that maximize easy slogans, avoid clarity and evade the hard issues.

The politician who cannot give up the convenience of intuitively spoken ambiguous words is easily skewered on his or her inconsistencies and revisions captured on videotape. Spokespersons and supporters of the politician may sincerely cry foul. "You don't understand what he (she) is saying." In the shifting contexts of intuitive language, that claim may have merit. In the standard language of politics, intuited understanding of the words may be good enough. In the broader realm of rational and reasonable word meaning comparisons are nonetheless used to demonstrate fuzzy, inconsistent thinking. The power of literacy skill has invaded intuitive life of politics.

The brain of a writer needs to be rewired for two handed word making. Writing as a modern profession is mostly *keyboard* mediated. The words flow through the fingers that depress keys on a standard QUERTY keyboard. Old-fashioned typewriters took the code directly to paper with ink impressed by a hammered typeface. Keyboards such as the one on which these words were written enter code for the alphabet directly into electronic format, store them in computer memory and display them on a screen before being transferred to paper. For most writers, the keyboard is the indispensable interface with the recorded record. On a keyboard, words can be transformed into written copy with great efficiency and speed as the written word flows out of the fingers onto the printed page. Rewriting and editing for clarity instantly revises existing copy in electronically mediated computer memory. New and alternative word realities are created efficiently and rapidly, rammed into computer memory by hands and fingers on a keyboard. The once trickle of published words has become a torrent.

Keyboard entry adds new mental dimensions to the complex of literacy skill. Rapid keyboard entry is a two brain, two handed activity. Distribution of alphabetic letters across the keyboard requires bilateral coordination of the hemispheres. Normal frequency of vowel usage in words is about equally divided between left and right hand of the QUERTY keyboard. Written words are expressed by the motor functions of both hemispheres of the human brain. Writing with a keyboard is a whole brain activity. Typing at anywhere from thirty to a hundred and fifty words a minute is not consciously mediated. The brain that has been retrained to express itself on a keyboard is different. Thinking is changed.

Analysis and clarity in communication require skill beyond natural, intuitive speech. The written word stands on its own ready for interpretation, acceptance or challenge. A community of critical thinkers can lend their individual specializations to refinement or revision of the reality offered by the written – and electronically recorded -- word. Experience can be shared and the intensive testing that is required to identify disciplined versus intuitive thinking can occur. In examining complex or confused issues, experience can be parceled out among a community of thinkers using the written word. The power of a community of minds can be brought to bear on testing uncertain reality when the issues are put into writing. Science advances and culture is enriched.

Writing expands the capacity of an unaided memory by adding storage capacity. Ultimately, no one can hold in mind at once all the elements of a vast and complex reality scheme. Remembering and clarifying the meaning of words requires some reliable means of fixing them for later recall and examination. Writing down one's thoughts permits large funds of reality ideation to be fixed as a memory-independent record. Once captured in writing, these ideas in memory can be compared and evaluated by their author. The recorded ideas of other minds can be added to the mix. Writing clarifies and expands ideas. Written words push reality creation beyond the limits of an individual mind. The written word is potentially an eternal memory.

Language is a miracle of human invention. Words as tools for labeling the elements of human experience have special power. The written word is a higher creation yet. It may be fitting to hold the written word in all its forms as Divine.

5. How The Neuroplastic Associative Brain Acquires Language

The radical behaviorist John B. Watson once famously asserted that if someone would

> "Give me a dozen healthy infants, well-formed, and my own specified world to bring them up in, I'll guarantee to take any one at random and train him to become any type of specialist I might select – doctor, lawyer, artist, merchant-chief and, yes, even beggar-man and thief, regardless of his talents, penchants, tendencies, abilities, vocations, and race of his ancestors."[1]

It was a bold, and in many ways, outlandish claim, though one that could not easily be dismissed. The dominant psychological phenomena of the time, Pavlovian behavioral conditioning, persuasively alluded to the potential for such human malleability. Behavior could, to some extent at least, be shaped with purposefully designed behavioral reinforcement schedules. Behaviorists like Watson thought they could stretch the notion to account for any kind of human conduct. They asserted there were no mind or mental processes in the brain. It was all just stimulus ->response. The brain could not help but respond to its environment.

The appeal of Watson's brand of behaviorist psychology held sway in the popular and professional imagination for an extended interval of time, until the superficiality of its audacious overstatement had to be recognized. Cavalier rejection of human mental phenomena ignored the obvious. Human experience is just more complicated than a reinforcement schedule. Humans argue with themselves about what to say or do. Much of their behavior is articulate linguistic noise produced by lungs and vocal cords that is acquired, not trained. Language sets humanity apart from other species in powerfully important ways. The emergence of a capability like language could not occur just from a reinforcement schedule. A rich cultural context that offers the infant opportunity to practice its production and use is essential. The long history over which language has been invented and elaborated has accumulated a comprehensive kit of tools that a child need only accept and use. Each newborn child is offered a kit of culturally communicated linguistic and physical tools that invite mastery. It is not necessary for each generation to conceive and physically construct a hammer, a lever or pulley. One must only recognize their utility. Nor is it necessary to perpetually reinvent articulated sounds as the names of important events or things. One can use the catalog of spoken words already available in and employed by the child's culture. Culture is a mold that shapes the mind and the quality of human life.

That humans are shaped by their cultural setting is beyond question. Watson recognized the cultural imperative in stipulating the need for "my own specified world to bring them up in. . .". Culture is so central and critical to formation of personality and tool use that it becomes one of those things that "goes without saying". It is so all-pervasive that it disappears into the background. Taken to its ultimate end, it can be declared that the newborn human is a blank slate waiting to be shaped by those experiences imprinted by its environment and that the human condition is limited first and most by the shape of human culture. Change its shape and you design a different kind of person. From some angles of view the human organism again does indeed look to be infinitely malleable. It was that vision which Watson seized on.

The limitation of Watson's behaviorist methodology lay in its absolute focus on rewards and punishment offered by a contrived reinforcement schedule. Culture itself is a marvelously complex, natural and uncontrived reinforcement mechanism. It is Godlike in its design and power to influence. No one person can orchestrate it. The closest mere humans may come to shaping culture is through the calculated design of their social institutions. Much of that design will still be determined by natural events as well as by competition among contending institutions and the influence of long standing tradition. Total redesign of utopian communities and states has a way of being either unstable or of turning inhumanly bizarre.

The nearest thing to total redesign is removal of cultural influence through isolating the child from its influence. When this happens it becomes obvious that exposure to language culture is crucial for its learning. Acute isolation or abandonment denies the child opportunity for cultural development. Isolation will certainly block language acquisition if imposed from birth into the critical early formative years. With no exposure to language of the parent's culture, the child cannot use or comprehend speech and will not adapt socially. Those rare instances in which a child has been "adopted" by animals describe emergence of social behavior that is to a remarkable degree like that of the adoptive animal parent. The assumed characteristics of a civil culture are entirely missing. In their place are only the qualities and characteristics of the child's adopted culture. If the child survives at all, it is as a beast- like creature. Even if merely isolated from human interaction for a brief time after birth, a child will be seriously impoverished of language skill. If isolation persists into late childhood, there may never be any real grasp of language. When ultimately exposed to language the isolated, untutored child is bewildered. At best only a limited few words will ever be grasped.[2]

The extreme limitation on language acquisition found in severely sequestered children mimics that encountered in attempts to communicate symbolically with chimpanzees and other higher apes. Within closely constrained limits apes can be trained to express their needs with hand signs and lexigrams. Training methods employed are, indeed, largely if not wholly dependent on Pavlovian behavioral reinforcement. As attested to by their trainer/handlers, language trained apes nonetheless do communicate with humans in meaningful but limited ways. One chimp, earlier equipped with a version of American sign language, extricated itself from the purgatory of an experimental medical laboratory by furiously signing for help. At their limited worst, language impoverished humans can do as much.[3]

The difference between apes and humans is the facility with which humans as infants absorb speech from their cultural environment. Those instances where language does not "naturally" emerge are troublesome oddities. The human brain seems designed to use language. The debate in the linguistics community is over whether capacity for language is genetically built into the brain or is somehow acquired. The argument for inborn genetic language structure has long stalled in dead end speculation. The more likely case is one that favors the extraordinary plasticity of the brain as an adaptive cognitive organism. The normal human brain adaptively constructs itself to absorb language and syntactic structure.

The Plastic Brain[4]

The extent of neuroplasticity in the human brain is astonishing. The plastic human brain exhibits remarkable capacity to adapt to almost any circumstance, however extreme. Following many kinds of brain injury that impair motor or perceptual capability, lost skills can be retrained. The younger the age of injury, the fuller the recovery afterward. If there are enough pieces of the former capability remaining, they can be stitched back together or reconstructed in another part of the adult brain. In response to circumstance, the brain uses its remarkable associative capability to repair itself. Supported by the brain's associative processes, learning as a process of skill and knowledge mastery can continue throughout life.

It is at and near the inception of life the human brain's neuroplasticity is most remarkable. The extent of adaptation by the infant brain seems almost without limit. Sea Gypsies, a nomadic people of Southeast Asia, are born to the sea. Their children learn to swim and dive before they can walk. To accommodate the problems of light refraction in water, their brain adapts neurologically to produce clarity while swimming and diving. Adaptation is natural to every growing child. Exposed very early to musical instrumentation and notation, children can become accomplished composers and performers before they enter puberty. Challenged to adapt to its environment, the infant brain seizes the opportunity. Language is among the foremost of the challenges it meets successfully. Autistics are the major exception. The autistic brain appears to be structured to acquire language best through mechanical processes such as behavioral reinforcement schedules.

The ubiquity of language as an element of developed social culture assures that most children will naturally acquire their native language, though the quality of language immersion offered will inevitably vary from one social circumstance to another. Normal children exposed to a rich intellectual environment achieve an earlier and richer command of language. The quality and intensity of word usage encountered in the environment largely determines level of language skill attained. Those less immersed in a rich linguistic culture develop speech more slowly and less intensively. Because the normal brain shapes adaptively to its environment, the quality of language environment encountered by each infant is critical to development. Language skill acquired becomes the foundation of personhood. In the context of nutrition and caring offered by a rich culture, the more or less socially competent human being emerges. Language use is critical to present day civil society. In that society we are recognized as a person by the words we use. Without words, we remain beasts.

How The Infant Brain Works

How mastery of language comes about is a subject of long-standing research and controversy.[5] Best up-to-the-moment evidence suggests that specific cognitive capabilities of the normal infant brain are critical. The child must recognize and respond to objects as being independent of their background context and distinguish sequences of change that occur among them. It must recognize that objects persist in time and space. Individual pieces of experience must be seen as unitary wholes, separate from other pieces and from the background. People, things and activities must be independently noticed. Articulated sounds must be discriminated from background noise. These are fundamental perceptual skills that are the foundation of language acquisition. They are the things and events that words will attach themselves to.

Infant psychology research offers a basis for identifying those cognitive skills that are normally required for language acquisition.[6] Psychologists present pre-linguistic infants with simple animated cartoons in an environment otherwise free of distraction. As a movie show unfolds, the potential of particular pre-planned events to capture the infant's attention is observed. From these studies it is established that, at various stages of development, infants can discriminate animate from inanimate figures. They notice changes of state like attachment or detachment and attend to purposeful, goal oriented action. It is concluded that most infant brains have the capacity to differentiate their sensory experience among objects and actions, even textures and qualities. The developing brain parses elements of experience into component parts of sensation offered by the physical environment, thereby allowing association of words that will later designate them.

The Probabilistically Associative Brain

For specific words to become associated with perceived objects and actions, relationships between things, events and sounds that overlap them must be noticed. The brain easily associates events that occur together. Experiences are organized by the intersections where they collide. The brain literally fabricates itself physically to map those correlated experiences into an organized record of sensory experience. In the normal brain the natural process of language acquisition progresses continually throughout life as words are associated and re-associated with experience. Once language is established in childhood, new experiences, new words are integrated into the language matrix of the brain. Old experiences, old words are quickly retrieved and understood because of their long standing association in the brain. On the foundation of neural impressions formed from contact with language culture in early childhood the brain continues to adapt by adjusting connections within the existing associative structure in a probabilistic manner.

As the brain develops and accumulates sensory experience in the language environment, it probabilistically associates a set of distinctive sounds with those objects, actions, textures and qualities as they occur jointly. Words start to represent sensory experience to the developing child. The human brain's capacity to parse and associate experiences that occur together in time enables the child to build a comprehensive verbal, mental map of its experience, taking its code from the language scaffolding supplied. The more organized and sharply focused that environment is, the easier it will be for the child to master the complexities of verbal mapping. A stable culture reproduces these skills in each new generation. The plastic human brain's aptitude for association of concurrent sensory events does it naturally.

All brains are not necessarily of similar structure at birth. Some patterns and kinds of external stimuli may shape brain structure and function in utero. Some differences in structure may be genetically determined. As a result of these differences, departures from normal language development will occur. A common difference is the autistic syndrome. In autism, brain structure does not seem to make the usual probabilistic associations between experience and word. The brain does not generate the critical associations that are the foundation of language use. The autistic brain may form its record of the phenomenal environment as a kind of moving picture that fails to parse sensory experience into its elements. Speech acquisition for the autistic brain is not "natural". Absent requisite cognitive brain structure, a program of intense stimulus/response conditioning may be necessary for anything approaching normal language skill to be achieved by autistics.

Language is Sometimes Invented

Under favorable circumstances, the plastic brain can even invent language. The immense utility of language to coordinate social action provides incentive to discover and make use of language in some form where it is absent. Within the context of culturally structured social interaction, language will spontaneously emerge as the indispensable tool for maintenance of social order. Illustrative of this process is the response to genetic deafness in isolated speaking communities. Signing communities have arisen naturally throughout the world from time to time where some of members are been born deaf due to defective genetics. To integrate its deaf members into the larger community, a system of hand signs are created and used by all, deaf and hearing alike. An organized community of the deaf has been observed to support such invention. Students in a Nicaraguan school for the deaf ignored teachers' attempts to teach lip reading and invented their own unique signing system. In the early stages of invention, signs were mostly crude pantomimes. When passed on to younger deaf children, signs took on an increasing degree of grammatical ordering. Verbs, nouns, adverbs, and adjectives began to appear. Once a set of crude but workable signs were in place, young learners found it natural to match the "words" of signing language to cognitively parsed elements of sensory perception.[7]

The human brain's ability to associate language code with differentiated sensory experience is the absolute requisite of language acquisition and use. Its capacity to wire and rewire while adapting to language makes the normal infant brain a language magnet. Once infant attention is focused on discrete fragments of its sensory environment, it can begin to sort and match them against the prevailing language code. The brain adaptively wires itself to this purpose. It connects code with the experience probabilistically.

Experience and Code Ultimately Fuse

Language thus acquired is much more than code. Memory of the original experience lies behind every word and grammatical device. That experience is resonated when the word is spoken. Linked to remembered experience, language as code disappears from view and associations become so complete that the code becomes indistinguishable from the experience. Each repeat of that experience updates and refines the association. The code itself eventually takes on as much sense of experienced reality as that which originally resided in the experience itself. As experience accumulates, language shapes, refines and accumulates perceptions of raw experiences and summarizes them in cohesive lumps of association, all connected in the language center of the brain. In this organized form, language becomes a quasi-actual reality.

Words and language are out front and obvious, obscuring all the background action. The sensory experience associated with and behind language hides in the shadows of language usage. It is the stuff of the mind and is beyond view of the mind's eye. The associative process itself is so pervasively ubiquitous that it cannot be hidden. Words just naturally pull other words behind them as they tumble from the mouth. The most obvious demonstration of contrived association occurs with simple word association. Instances abound. In response to the word *man* the associated response may be something like *woman,* or *strong.* Association with woman-ness is based on sensory discrimination of gender. Pairing masculinity with strength reveals association with the male role. In further association, *woman* may be paired with *mother* or *sister* evoking a sense of feminine roles. The idea of strength may associate with *muscle,* or *sweat,* revealing underlying connection with work effort. *North* evokes *south* understood with mental images of a map or compass. *Good* calls up *bad.* Word associations are inherently superficial but logical. Word association comes easily to the brain. Word games that demonstrate associative skill play out nightly on television. Responding to a word or phrase cue, the brain quickly makes a memory match in the language center and activates an appropriate response. These exercises demonstrate the pervasiveness of associative processes among words themselves.

Though ordinarily obscured, the underlying sensory foundation of language is observable and accessible through invocation of the associative processes that bind them. Ideas can be deconstructed into their associated component experiences. The association of a word with its experienced image is revealed in the instruction to "think of" something, such as "think of a woman" or "think of work". Awareness will now go below the level of simple verbalization to that of sensory experience. Thinking of a woman will typically bring up mind images of one or more specific women. One's mother, wife or sister, the face of a celebrity or a friend will be triggered by the word *woman.* The most likely image is the recovered experience of a real woman. Thinking of *work* will evoke the image of one's workplace, office, desk or tools. Or, it may call up the picture of a product or other work outcome. Thinking of something *strong* may evoke the image of a sumo wrestler or a highway bridge. Thinking of *water* will summon the image of a river, waterfall, running spigot or pitcher. Thinking of *beauty* generates the vision of an attractive face, a lovely landscape, a morning sunrise. Thinking of a *road* produces the picture of a familiar street or highway. Most nouns and adjectives will evoke a mental association with underlying sensations when attention is called to thinking of them. Many evoked images will be clearly graphic, actual things or events. The brain easily interconnects these sensory memories with their associated words when cued to *think* of them. It is this complex neural network of mental associations between word or phrase and their underlying sensory memories that gives words, mere symbols in themselves, instantly recognizable meaning that requires no translation. A special quality of association occurs when mnemonic memory systems are employed to associate words or numbers with images so that words or numbers are made mechanically recallable.

Many verbs evoke the equivalent of an action sequence or script that goes beyond mere image. "Think of where you might have put them down" in response to "I can't find my keys" may elicit a mental recapitulation of recent movements. It can call up images of those places where missing keys have previously been found. The instruction to "think of what you enjoy most doing" will evoke images of actual moments of pleasure. Some action instructions call up complex scripts. Directing someone to "Go take a walk outside and cool off" is an instruction to leave the current situation and attempt to change one's attitude with activity that can draw off excess feeling tone. It paints the picture of someone figuratively blowing off the steam of anger or frustration. Coaching someone to "go ahead, have a try" at a new skill implies that there is no harm in attempting and failing in the action, but suggests potential for fault in unwillingness to attempt it. Almost any action statement or instruction can be elaborated into a script that brings to mind complex behavioral sequences of activity.

Words are Real

Once acquired, one's native language, associated from infancy with referenced sensory experience, is beyond mere symbolism. It can be said that words are mere symbols of underlying experiences, but that is an almost vacuous assertion. Each word is a centralized summary of those experiences that have come to be associated with it through the course of real experience. It is the summarizing of sensory imagery by organizing associated memories that makes language so powerful. A single word evokes multiple experiences, compressed into a core of meaning by their principal similarities, yet nuanced by their varied dissimilarity at the fringes. These nuances are neatly cataloged in a thesaurus and explicated by a dictionary. *Beauty* is dictionary defined as "the quality or *aggregate of qualities* in a person or thing that gives pleasure to the senses or pleasurably exalts the mind or spirit." In thesaurus terms *beauty* may include synonymous qualities of attractiveness, loveliness, or exquisiteness. Attraction pulls one toward something, loveliness inspires warmth for the object, exquisiteness evokes awe of workmanship. The word *beauty* packages all these qualities into a single signal word evoking a sense of the totality. To appreciate the power of how this comes about, one can imagine the plastic brain reaching out to connect all these experiences together at a central place in the cortex where the simple, two syllable word *beauty* is located. As the word is spoken or read, all those qualities are instantly drawn to it. Words become the experiences they represent. They centralize, organize and summarize our memory of sensory experience into a rich fabric of meaning.

The Language Center as The Brain's Executive

To become useful for social communication the lexicon of language must also be associated with the motor centers for speech. The language center usually centralizes meaningfulness and communicative expression of that meaning in a single master record that becomes the center of language execution. This accounts for the peculiar status of the brain's language center. It is almost always located in only one of the twin cortical hemispheres, most often the left. The right hemisphere has been shown to comprehend spoken and written language though it usually cannot produce it. When the right hemisphere is surgically disconnected from the left it will respond appropriately when commanded to point or choose. But it does not speak. The language center is the center of a complex associative process connected by neurons to memories stored in all parts of the brain. As such it is the executive department of the mind for purposes deciding what to say. Anything less than lateral centralization would literally divide the mind and could impede speech production.

The Language Center is also Abstraction Headquarters

The plastic brain creates associations between words and words, words and experiences and experiences with other experiences. When a word is heard or chosen for speech, the brain activates the associations that underlay that word with other words and with experiences. The relative richness of those associations establishes the generality of the word's use. As general appropriateness of use rises, clarity of centralized meaning is reduced. Eventually, a substantial degree of abstraction develops. The word can then become so broadly general in meaning that it is largely or wholly detached from sensory experience. It emerges as an abstracted *idea*. One set of words has such great potential for broad, non-specific use that they are immediate candidates for full abstraction. These are the cardinal numerals. They lend to theoretical abstraction at the highest level.

Adaptation is the Brain's Forte and Purpose

It is remarkable how fully the human neuroplastic brain can form itself to its environment. Indeed, it is tempting to speculate that the infant brain has potential to adapt itself to any environment. When the child is transplanted out of one language culture into another it does exactly that. The Chinese infant adopted early into English language culture will fluently acquire English speech. The Western language scaffolding will mold the mind to its local tongue, not to that of the original mother land. The abandoned child will take on the character of the environmental scaffolding that exists. The more elaborately developed and refined that scaffold, the more elaborate will be the child's development. In a developed culture, each new life adopts the scaffolding package prepared for it by previous generations. Culture largely if not wholly determines who and what we become.

Behaviorist John B. Watson was really not so far off the mark with his outrageous claims for possession of godlike power to shape human character. He was mostly guilty of excessively overextending the potential for effectiveness of behavioral reinforcement technology. The human neuroplastic brain is remarkable in its capacity to organize its environment into networks of sensory association without reinforcement. In the presence of cultural and social structure that includes a mature language system the brain forms itself to map the prevailing environment in word concepts as a matter of adaptation. During its growth through infancy its neural tentacles literally leap into action to create an analytical record of its environment. Words and phrases are associated with sensory experience by an experience hungry brain. With time and use those words come to define and explain that environment, allowing it to be modified and redesigned. The cultural scaffolding, early absolute in its influence on the developing brain, is itself made plastic by the emerging mind.

The full scope of linguistic structure emerges over time with further growth of child and brain. Most of that structure can probably be credited to the complexities of association capable in the plastic brain. Significant differences in the syntactic composition of different languages are readily accommodated by the developing brain. Beyond words alone, phrases, sentences and, ultimately, high level abstractions all take on associated meaning that is instantly comprehended. It may even go beyond the raw data of sensory experience to construct the vision of a hidden reality of structures that underlie nature. The brain is a natural scientist, observing, questioning, analyzing, associating probabilistically, creating new awareness. It is a marvel of adaptive plasticity.

PART TWO:

The Mind's Structure -

Revealed in Word Play

6. Psychology And Language; Is The Speaking Brain Your Mind?

Sensory grasp of reality is a seductive thing. Sense of sound, sight, feel are rich, engaging experiences. Absence or diminishment of one sense can enhance the richness of an alternative sensory pathway. The sensory apparatus of the mind seems tuned to maximize the quantity and quality of sensory input taken from the environment. It is all so rich, so riveting, so real, sometimes surreal. Illuminating the inner reality of experience is the object of a variety of scientific disciplines. Psychology, Social Psychology, Cognitive Psychology, and the emerging brain sciences all put forward explanations. The twentieth century explosion of world population in league with rapid advances in these sciences has added new insights into the workings of the mind. Much remains to be discovered.

Among psychologists of the late nineteenth century there was no consensus as to whether they were philosophers in the classical sense or practitioners of a new and separate science more closely related to biology. In the decade of the 1890s, a Russian physician and psychologist, Ivan Pavlov, observed that dogs could be trained to salivate at the sound of a bell if, on earlier occasions, the bell had sounded when food was offered. He had discovered classical associative conditioning, a phenomenon so closely identified with him that it is called Pavlovian conditioning. His widely reported experimental observations firmly set psychology on it own course, one more closely associated with experimental physiology.[1]

John B. Watson, an early American psychologist, is generally credited with establishing the behaviorist movement in psychology with the 1913 publication of his article, "Psychology as the Behaviorist Views It". Watson passionately seized upon Pavlov's demonstration of classical conditioning and made associative learning the foundation of all psychological phenomena. He firmly believed that, with the proper behavioral conditioning, he could shape virtually any human ability or character, boasting that he could "take a (child) at random and train him to become a ... doctor, lawyer, merchant chief, beggar man or thief."

Behaviorism builds on the associations that Pavlov demonstrated possible between unconditioned stimulus, conditioning stimulus and behavioral response. Although mental processes to Watson were too subjective to be the stuff of experimental description he nonetheless stopped just short of ruling out all mental phenomena. The twentieth century Harvard psychologist, B.F. Skinner went the remaining distance in founding Radical Behaviorism.[2] Skinner dismissed all things of the mind as metaphysics, unsuitable for scientific study. He single-mindedly pursued the experimental analysis of behavior, inventing the operant conditioning chamber and other devices for experimental measurement of behavioral reinforcement schedules.

Skinner was something of a utopian who believed that, as described in his book *Walden II,* social order, happiness and morality are all achievable through application of a scientifically created behavioral reinforcement schedule. Like Watson, he was convinced that any behavior could be changed for better or worse with conditioning. Because modifying language use with classical conditioning was the most difficult of all conditioning tasks, Skinner addressed that task with the publication of a book length program of action titled *Verbal Behavior.* In it he argued that word play can be fully explained in terms of conditioned associations.

Words, speech and reading were clearly the most difficult elements for Skinner to reduce to operant conditioning and reinforcement schedules. To overcome the problems of making verbal behavior researchable in the framework of radical behaviorism, he created a new behavioral philosophy of language. He argued that verbal behavior is the product of the immediate environment operating on all past history of verbal behavior. In addition to his standard four-term contingency and reinforcement model of behavior he invented a set of six new theoretical word concepts called "elementary verbal operants". His explanation of how verbal behavior is produced through associative conditioning and without intervening mental activities is an example of nearly pure inductive philosophy. For one so totally committed to rigorous experimentation as the foundation of science, Skinner spun out his argument with little more empirical foundation than the fact of Pavlovian conditioning. It is a grand theory that is still in search of demonstration. In applying his conditioning schedules to words Skinner may have overreached his science and discredited behaviorism. There nonetheless remains a viable argument that much of polite conversation may be little more than an ongoing sequence of behaviorally conditioned word responses.

Skinner's theory of conditioned language went too far for structural linguist Noam Chomsky. Chomsky argued original language learning by infants could not possibly be produced by any form of operant conditioning. Infant language learning arises out of social interaction accompanied by trial and error word usage. Chomsky argued further that the ability of adult humans to create unique language structures and even make up new word constructs demolishes the entire framework of verbal behaviorist theory. Unique language structure and meaning could not possibly result from conditioning alone. The inventiveness of Skinner's own verbal theorizing about verbal behavior stands as supporting evidence on that point.[3]

Nonetheless, through the middle years of the twentieth century Skinner's radical behaviorism was the dominant premise of psychology as the foundation of product advertising practices. In the end, the overwhelmingly real subjective experience that one is a thinking person plus evidence that the mind can function quite independently of sensory input led many to reject Skinner's orthodoxy. Operant conditioning was too shallow a foundation for the study of all human behavior.

Pavlovian conditioning is a powerful and robust phenomena, but it does not explain all, perhaps not even most, human behavior and experience.

Much more is now known about the working structure of the human brain. Powerful instruments are available that can locate and measure the extent of brain activity intervening between stimulus and behavior. Advances in psycho-neurology have come with the invention of MRI, magnetic resonance imaging, and PET, positron-emission tomography, instruments that allow brain activity to be captured as pictures showing where oxygen is taken up by the firing of neurons. The location of brain response to sensory input is thus approximately established by observing oxygen surges that feed working neurons. This enables research to describe not just brain functions but also to specify neurological connections within the brain that identify the physical locus of behavior.[4]

Since mid-twentieth century, the field that now carries the label *cognitive neurology* has expanded rapidly. Research by psychologists Roger Sperry[5], and Michael Gazzaniga[6] focused on the functions of the cerebral hemispheres, the loci of conscious awareness and sensory data processing in the brain, using so-called *split-brain* patients. Sperry's work was sufficiently innovative and important to gain him a Nobel Prize. Still carried forward and amplified, his work offers an important window on how human consciousness emerges.

The core of the very extensive body of Sperry's and Gazzaniga's cognitive neurological research examines what happens when communication between hemispheres of the brain is physically severed. Their research piggy-backed on other neurological work that sought to find a remedy for the destructive effects of grand mal epilepsy. Severe epileptic seizures could be substantially controlled, it was found, when the corpus collosum, a limited bridge of neurons that connects the bases of the cerebral hemispheres, was surgically cut.

Formerly the treatment of choice for grand mal epilepsy was frontal lobotomy, a drastic procedure that destroys the frontal section of a cerebral hemisphere and can leave the patient semi-vegetative. By contrast, Commissurotomy, the surgical procedure that merely separates the hemispheres, appears to have little or no effect on speech, intelligence, personality or behavior. The patient talks and acts normally, as if no brain surgery had occurred. The result begs the question as to just what the function and utility of two hemispheres may be. For Sperry and Gazzaniga commissurotomy opened a door to discovery that the separate hemispheres may work as independent units. On passing through that door they found remarkable things.[7]

A series of critical research procedures were designed to test the hemispheric brain functions of commissurotomy patients. The lateralized structure of the nervous system was exploited to allow independent communication with each half of the brain. The human body is duplicated left and right in various ways. Curiously, many of the sensory nerve paths serving the left half of the body connect to the right side of the brain, while the same arrangement connects nervous input from the right side of the body to the left side of the brain. Vision is very specific in this regard. The retina of each eye is vertically split down the middle into neurons on the right side of each eye feeding the left brain, while those from the left connect into the right brain. To communicate selectively with the hemispheres researchers used a visual projection system that flashed an image to only one side of each retina while the eyes were front focused.

Sense of touch is also lateralized in crossover fashion by the hemispheres of the brain left to right, right to left. Independent tactile input from the hands could be obtained by hiding the hands behind a screen. Lateralization of sensory input allowed discrete visual and tactile communication with one side of the brain or the other as desired. What the commissurotomy patient *saw and felt* could be restricted to the side of the brain where a message was directed.

One other important neurological factor comes into play with this experiment. Language capability, reading, writing and speaking, is usually and largely, if not wholly, a function of the left hemisphere of the brain. It has been recognized since the nineteenth century that damage to the left hemisphere can render a person mute. If the damage is experienced in youth, it may be substantially overcome through neurological adaptation and development. In older people, loss of language capability as a result of left-brain injury may be permanent. Similar injury to the right side of the brain rarely impairs language ability at all. For practical purposes, the left brain talks, the right does not.

Thus, it is expected that an image flashed onto the right side of the retinas (and to the left hemisphere) can be identified by speaking its name, while one sent to the left retinas feeding the right hemisphere will go unrecognized, or at the least, unverbalized. If some object, a comb, for instance, is visually presented to the left hemisphere of a commissurotomy patient, the response of the talking brain will normally be, "I saw a comb". The same image flashed independently to the mute right brain by way of the left half of retinas, will appear to have been missed. When an array of objects that includes a comb is set out before the patient, the left hand can point it out when asked what was seen.

In one version of Gazziniga's experiments, the image of a chicken claw was flashed to the left brain and the image of a snow scene sent to the right brain. The subject of the experiment was asked to point with both hands at a set of pictures that included a chicken and a shovel. The left hand pointed to the shovel as the right pointed to the chicken. "Why did you pick the shovel? asked the experimenter. "Because a shovel is useful for cleaning out a chicken house" responded the speaking brain of the subject. Ignorant of the real reason for choice of the shovel, the left brain "made up" an explanation. Given lack of real knowledge and awareness, words that seem to fit the situation were chosen by the talking brain to create a plausible reality that fitted the case. This experiment seemed to show that two separate and distinct streams of experience were operating in the same head, though only one of them (normally) expresses itself through speech.

For the great majority, about nineteen out of twenty people, the left brain is the language dominant hemisphere and does the talking. The right brain has at least some speech capacity in about five percent of people, and is the sole language center in about one percent. The distribution of speech locus and the fact of normal left hemisphere speech specialization are well established. Surgery to the left hemisphere of the brain will likely impair or destroy speech ability. Prior to brain surgery that might disrupt speech, left or right lateralization of speech function must be determined for normal, corpus callosum-intact patients. This is done with the Wada test. Sodium amytal is introduced into the carotid artery that serves one side of the brain, momentarily anesthetizing that hemisphere. The test is then repeated on the opposite side of the brain. Speech capability is determined by observing the side that falls mute. Results of the Wada test confirm that left hemispheric specialization for speech is near universal. Data accumulated with use of this test allows estimation of the frequency of language lateralization in the hemispheres. About nineteen times out of twenty, it is the left hemisphere.[8]

In most individuals, speech is fully lateralized in the left hemisphere. Though it is rare, partial or full speech function is sometimes located in the right brain. Speech may be both spoken and understood or it may be understood, but not spoken by the right brain. As a usual thing the right brain has no language capability and appears unable to either comprehend or respond to spoken commands. The expected state is one of behavioral torpor. The right brain seems merely along for the ride. When speech is lost through damage in the left hemisphere, there is question as to what quality of conscious experience remains. It is communicating in speech through words and sentences that establishes the fact of a conscious, thinking person. It is reasonable to ask whether the mute right brain is conscious and thoughtful, or is not.

Indeed, what does the mute right brain contribute? Is it capable of thoughtful action, or is it limited to automatic, reflexive responses? Socially appropriate use of language is standard evidence of autonomy and awareness. We may ask what happens to those faculties when the left brain shuts down and the right brain has no apparent capability to speak or write words? Gazziniga and Sperry continued to exploit the division of vision and touch sensation to communicate separately and exclusively with the mute right brain. They cleverly devised tests that would address these questions.[9]

To evaluate ability to recognize and reason with words, they arrayed in open view before a subject ten small objects that included *things* like a cup, knife, pen, orange, etc. When the written word for one of these objects was flashed to the left visual field, (the right hemisphere) the left hand would point to the correct object. Reversing the process, a set of cards on which the words for those objects were written was arrayed in view, and a picture of one was flashed to the left visual field. The mute right brain responded by pointing with the left hand to the correct written word, exhibiting the ability to comprehend the written word. Word and object were consistently associated by the non-speaking right brain.

The test for aural speech comprehension was somewhat more difficult because input cannot be limited to one ear or the other. Subjects were instructed to press a button with the left hand when a word spoken matched the correct one from a series flashed to the left visual field (still the right hemisphere). The test was extended and elaborated by using a short descriptive sentence of an object, such as "used to tell time", and by flashing a series of words to the left visual field that included the word "clock". The task was consistently performed with success. The right brain also had no difficulty retrieving the correct object by feel from behind a screen when the word was spoken.

Subjects showed that they could reason out the identity of a common object by feel. An object was placed in the left hand behind a panel and examined. The subject was subsequently asked to raise the left hand to identify that object when the names of a set of objects was read aloud in random sequence. Object and spoken name were consistently matched. Language capacity in the mute hemisphere was next tested by requiring the subject to respond to words that described object texture or shape. Comprehension and understanding was apparent for complex words, those other than simple referential names. The mute right brain could sometimes even correctly spell simple words with four inch block cardboard letters manipulating them with the left hand out of sight behind a panel. This could be done while the experimenters carried on an independent conversation with the talking right brain as the left hand carried out its spelling task, demonstrating ability to focus intention and reason with ideas in the presence of distraction. Through these tests, the mute right brain offered evidence of capacity for conceptual thinking, understanding and independent awareness. Gazziniga and Sperry concluded that there is "considerable comprehension of language present" in the mute right brain despite the lack of spoken language.

The phenomenon of divided consciousness that is demonstrated when the brain hemispheres are surgically separated has since spawned a variety of fad theories claiming various sorts of functional specialization in the normal, intact human brain. The right brain, for instance, is sometimes credited with greater capability for spatial visualization. Graphic and artistic skill is thought to be a right brain function and the right brain is said to think in pictures rather than in words. There is no credible evidence of such specialization. The best evidence supports the notion that hemispheres are, indeed, normally though not always, specialized for speech and that each possesses the ability to take over missing functions lost by the opposite hemisphere. Both hemispheres are fully engaged in processing sensory inputs. Sight, smell, touch, taste, hearing as well as the various motor functions of the body are all coordinated through the respective hemispheres into which nerves feed. Muscular coordination also is coordinated by the brain hemispheres. Hemispheric specialization is largely limited to language functioning. Injury to the speaking brain is commonly overcome by the adapting brain.

The hemispheres can and do work in similar ways.

In those normal individuals whose corpus callosum is intact the mute right brain remains an enigma. It may support the left brain in some speech functions, or may seem to be totally uninvolved. Given its lack of speech, it cannot explain itself. It does, though, appear capable of initiating independent action of various kinds. That action may at times be in conflict with the action initiated by the left brain. In Dr. Strangelove style, one arm may extend to strike as the other moves to restrain it. There is no doubt that the mute right brain is capable of entertaining an independent stream of consciousness. Sensory and motor functions are certainly present in both sides of the brain. The question is one of how separate and independent that experience can be.

There are limitations to the Sperry-Gazziniga studies. Split-brain studies must be carried out with a very special population -- persons suffering from grand mal epilepsy and subjected to the major brain surgery. There could be differences in the brain structure or mental function among these individuals that lead to epilepsy. The dominant normalcy of language location in the left hemisphere means that commissurotomy will usually produce a verbally expressive left brain and a mute right brain after the hemispheres are separated. Independent response from each hemisphere strongly suggests the existence of an independent stream of consciousness in each. The mute right brain can understand some language and is capable of intellectual activity. The extent to which that independence occurs in the intact, human brain remains unknown. A variety of human behaviors are supportive of potential for independent initiation of action by the hemispheres of an intact brain. Multiple personality phenomena, dissociation of experience in hypnotism, and sociopathic behavior all point in this direction. Split consciousness is an idea worth pursuing for its potential to explain some of the observed inconsistencies and abnormalities in reality maps that may be maintained within multiple minds.

Communication between left and right hemispheres in the normal, surgically intact brain may be extensive in some people, or it may be limited in others. The brain is remarkably plastic. The corpus callosum can develop differentially in different individuals. It can differ among individuals in the number of connecting neurons that cross the bridge. Fewer neurons in the corpus callosum, providing limited cross connections, may produce considerable independence of thought functioning in normal humans. Small strokes in the corpus callosum could disrupt communication. Some individuals may be capable of tuning down or turning off inter-hemisphere communication, either permanently or temporarily. In normal functioning humans, the two hemispheres of the brain may coordinate in great harmony. In some, as in commissurotomy patients, they may hardly communicate at all. Dr. Jekyll and Mr. Hyde personalities might result from presence of a toggle switch type of function across the corpus callosum.

One common experience reported by many normal people is that of a living, invisible being hovering near, even communicating with them on a continuing basis. Reports of angels, religious figures, relatives and others who speak to provide emotional support and comfort are commonplace. It is not a great leap from the evidence of split brain research to the possibility that an independent stream of consciousness in the mute brain can be sensed and related to. Confusion and erratic, unsocial or immoral behavior may arise out of mixed impulses flowing from the independent hemispheric experience flow. It would be entirely reasonable to interpret sudden reconciliation of previously warring motives and purposes as some kind of a magical or spiritual event. Hemispheric independence in normal humans could account for many otherwise extraordinary human behaviors.

The notion of humans weighed down by multiple inhibitions pervades clinical and Freudian Psychology. Inhibition of response has been demonstrated in a vast number of experiments on verbal training. The commonplace observation that people can say one thing and do another illustrates the capacity for dual motivation. The widely recognized character trait of integrity includes in its dictionary definition the descriptive terms "unbroken, wholeness, uprightness, honesty, sincerity." Human behavior that lacks these qualities is easily noticed. Simple dishonesty or insincerity can readily inflict pain on others. Brokenness of character can be dramatic and tragic. That brokenness might result from hemispheric disconnection or competition.

Hemispheric independence need not be so dramatic. There may only be minimal competition between left and right brain for initiation of action. Two words may come to one's mouth at once because they are generated in two places. Inconsistency of word or behavior might be ordinary forgetting (inhibition?) or just poor recall that permits revision of past events to fit present need. With attention and effort the hemispheres can probably be taught to work together toward a common goal. Independence does not necessarily seem to be a liability, and it certainly is a possibility.

The experience of monitoring oneself as one speaks and acts is, indeed, much like becoming of two minds. Experiments with surgically divided cerebral hemispheres suggest that hemispheric independence might be a quite plausible description of the neurological mechanism underlying self-control. Other behaviors and skills suggest close integration of the hemispheres. Whether the hemispheres are opposed or are working in tandem may determine the level of mental skill displayed in highly intense mental activities. Reporters and police interrogators must use all their mental resources to achieve their purposes. Training one's self to be an effective information gatherer with live, real-time interviews can be revealing. One must observe and remember what one has said and done while attending to the specific words and body language of the interviewee as everything is simultaneously integrated and evaluated. Complex events are observed, processed and comprehended in detail.

Some kinds of performance are so demanding that engaging more than one hemisphere would seem to be absolutely necessary. Musicians in performance can confront high complexity of mental and physical activity. The master or mistress of a great pipe organ, for instance, must simultaneously read three staffs of music, monitor two to five keyboards and a thirty-two note pedal board, listen to the quality of the musical output and make decisions as to additions or deletions of tonal stops while manipulating ten digits and two feet to reproduce the written musical notes as musical sound. These and other parallel activities such as acrobatic flying or open slope skiing can require extraordinary management of sensory physical and mental inputs to achieve the desired result.

An untrained, unintegrated mind would certainly have trouble with any of such tasks. It would inevitably produce errors and lapses in the management of complex environmental circumstances. The accomplished organist, skier or acrobatic flyer can not only manage them, they can identify problems that occur in the performance and describe them in words after the event. Training to these levels requires language and a comprehensive language map of the activity. Description and improvement of performance depends on knowing the words that describe elements of performance. The organist "knows" that the wrong tonal stop is a clarinet, not a trumpet, the wrong chord a diminished not a major seventh. The skier "knows" that the angle of approach to the turn was either ten degrees off or exactly right. The acrobatic flyer "knows" that stall speed is approaching. These same experiences to the average eating, sleeping, working, procreating human being are entirely evanescent and transitory. The training, instrumentation and social support required for their mastery is demanding and lengthy. The appropriate words must be learned to observe, record and recall these fleeting experiences with reliability and accuracy. Awareness of complex realities like these requires a complex, trained, integrated, *word filled mind.*

The propensity of the brain to unaccountably produce seemingly non-consciously directed experience suggests a hidden source of experience. An injury to a specific temporal area of the brain for instance, has been observed to produce noticeably unusual behavior. "Temporal lobe syndrome" as it is called, sets off an intense commitment to religious belief, the need to constantly write down everything that comes to mind accompanied by bizarre sexual behavior.[10] It is the sort of acting out that would, at one time, have been attributed to possession by a demon or spirit. Driven by forces that could not possibly have been grasped as natural, the brains of both the possessed and observers of psychic possession could be expected to offer an endless variety of fanciful explanations. Acceptable attributions of cause would usually be those already sanctioned by the culture and supported by those in authority. Under some circumstances, such behavior might be interpreted as indication of divine inspiration, spawning a new religious movement. Under others, it would be evidence of evil possession that would result in torture and execution. Spiritual and demonic experience might be a specialty of the right hemisphere. It is, after all, usually just sitting there, listening. One might expect it to respond in some way.

Brain injury can produce a variety of automatic behaviors, but injury is not always necessary. The brain can be chemically stimulated to elicit unusual and unexpected experiences and actions. The growth and development of every human nervous system can vary in small and potentially significant ways. A slight difference in brain growth that occurs from normal intra-uterus positioning during infancy is thought by some to be sufficient to produce right-handedness with left-brain language dominance. Minor injury or advantage in sync with growth will shape that growth. Thus, there is potential for every human being to be very much like every other human being, though unique. The force of cultural tradition and language structure confers considerable commonality to every individual mind-map, though each will still be special.

Human mental functioning and experience are highly variable in quality, probably much more so than is assumed. The way individual brains work is by no means uniform. The fact of speech and word use is the strongest evidence of both similarity and difference in mental life. It is through words we know the mind to any extent at all. The physical structure of the brain that allows communication through language reveals how similar and different people can be. Experiments with split brain subjects demonstrate that words are the surface of subjective, social reality. The relationship of the brain to language acquisition and use can partially be observed in these experiments, though the exact workings remain largely speculative. Words are the keys that must unlock the secrets that remain.

7. How The Brain Restores Order When Chaos Prevails

Psychology professors sometimes employ a simple trick on their students to demonstrate the limitations of accuracy when observing unexpected events. In the midst of a class lecture, a confederate will charge into the classroom, shout something, maybe nonsense or in a foreign language, produce a loud noise and exit. Students are then asked to write down their personal eyewitness account of what occurred. Written accounts are gathered. Descriptions may include description of an outright attack on someone, usually the professor, with weapons described as seen in the hand of the intruder or of bystanders. Descriptions are subsequently summarized, read aloud to the class, and the event reenacted with help of the confederate. After reenactment, the confederate remains and explains in detail what actually occurred.

The human brain looks for order and consistency. Ancient man seeking sleep under the stars looked up and saw amazing order. Lions, bulls, fish and other vivid images formed themselves out of the twinkling stars. Order came out of chaos. The more fertile of working imaginations put their observations into words and communicated them to others. Marvelously, the simple suggestion of heavenly order resulted in matching observation. The skies were full of mystical creatures. We might speculate that less imaginative individuals on being told of these things in the sky pretended to see them just to avoid appearing odd. Social conformity can come about in many and various ways. Personal interests, motives, needs and feelings are continually filtering experience. Perception is subject to multiple sources of distortion. Order is easily created where it does not exist. Where words are found that seem to fit the situation, the appearance of order emerges even more quickly. As split brain research has shown, the mind readily makes up an explanation for otherwise unaccountable events. It brings order where there is little or none. That order is often pure conjury.

A genuinely bizarre instance of false reality created by overzealous word play occurred in the case of the "Norfolk Four", arising out of the 1997 rape and murder of a young Navy wife, Michelle Moore-Bosko.[1] Several hours after discovery of her body, police began questioning Danial Williams, a Naval seaman neighbor living in an adjacent apartment. After more than eight yours of interrogation, Williams offered up a taped confession of the crime. When it was found that DNA found on Moore-Bosko did not match that of Danial Williams, police concluded that he must have had an accomplice. They turned to the nearest possibility, William's seaman roommate, Joe Dick. Following extended interrogation, Dick too offered a recorded confession. When Dick's DNA failed to match that found on the victim, police concluded that there must be others involved. Upon interrogation, Dick implicated another seaman, Eric Wilson. After extended interrogation, Wilson confessed. When his DNA was tested, it too failed to match the rapist's DNA from the crime scene. Police concluded others must have been involved and returned to the ever cooperative Joe Dick. This time Dick implicated seaman Derek Tice. Returned from Florida where he had since been transferred, Tice, after extended interrogation, gave up a confession and identified three other men as accomplices. Dick and Williams offered a guilty plea and were not tried in court. Wilson and Tice were convicted by juries on the basis of their taped confessions. The other three individuals identified were indicted but, because evidence was insufficient, not tried. With the conclusion of trials, police and prosecutors were confident all seven were guilty.

Eighteen months after the murder, a woman named Karen Stover received a letter from Virginia Prison inmate Omar Abdul Ballard in the course of correspondence with him. In it he threatened to murder her if she did not send him money and "nasty pictures". To underscore the reality of his threat, Ballard admitted in writing to killing Michelle Moore-Bosko. Karen turned the letter over to authorities.

Ballard had been known to the Boscos, and was likely trusted by Michelle. Sometime before the murder, Michelle and Bill Bosco had given Ballard sanctuary as he fled a mob of neighborhood men angered by Ballard's beating of a woman with a baseball bat. Two weeks after Michelle's murder, Ballard was arrested for the rape and beating of a teenaged girl at a location a mile from the Bosco's apartment. At that time police already had William's confession to the Bosco murder and did not connect the two incidents. When the new information on Ballard's involvement was checked out, his DNA matched that from the Bosco crime scene. Confronted by police, Ballard confessed, saying he acted alone. A year later he recanted his confession and implicated the Norfolk four, ostensibly "to avoid the death penalty".

Confessions offered by the Norfolk four contained numerous discrepancies and were difficult to reconcile with the crime scene. Other than the murder victim's body on the floor in the bedroom, there was no sign of struggle. Before discovering his wife's body, Bill Bosco had entered the quiet and undisturbed apartment on return from ship duty, assumed his wife was out, showered, and shaved before finding the grisly scene. If eight people had been in and out of the apartment participating in rape and murder, the uncluttered condition of the apartment would be hard to account for. Then there was the fact of no DNA match to any of the seven seamen imprisoned or indicted in the crime. Only the taped confessions spoke to their guilt.

The cases of the Norfolk four were reopened by the Innocence Project in the Cardozo School of Law at Yeshiva University. Argument was offered by Project counsel that confessions were false. Clemency was requested of the governor. To make clemency less of a political issue in Virginia, Richard Cullen, US Attorney and former Virginia Attorney General announced his belief that, on the basis of scientific evidence and crime scene evidence inconsistent with police and prosecution theory of the crime, he was personally convinced of their innocence. Police, prosecutors, judges and family members of the victim continued to insist that the right men are in prison and their implication in the crime by Ballard had settled the matter. How could four men falsely confess to such a horrible crime, they asked. Ultimately the substantial weight of evidence prevailed. The Norfolk Four were pardoned by Governor Tim Kaine and released after eleven hard years in prison.

The evidence that such confessions frequently occur is convincing. Under the intense pressure of an experienced police interrogator, suspects, guilty or otherwise, do break down. Members of a jury confronted by the survivors of a horrible crime do feel compassion and an urge for justice. The accused's voice on tape calmly admitting and describing the crime is impelling. Those words sound as real as words can be. The police "solve" the crime and go on to other issues. Their own words to prosecutors and courts must be defended as real when the matter is reopened five months, a year, a year and a half later. Before the court of law, justice is blind, permitted only to weigh the evidence. Much of that evidence is words; the words of police, the words of witnesses, the words of the accused, the words of prosecutors and defense attorneys. Those words create the arguments out of which convictions are drawn.

False confessions, false memory and erroneous eyewitness identification all testify to the unreliability of human memory and observation. Unless one is specifically trained to perceive at a level of great detail, crude impressions that are easily prompted with suggestion are the likely result. Accuracy comes with disciplined observation. Antique dealers identify types of wood, note specifics of construction detail, see signs of wear and other details in historic furniture. Trained portrait artists focus on shape of face, nose, chin, ears and other distinct features of appearance. Geologists see specific crystalline structure in rock formations and identify the age of fossils in them. Skilled accident and fire investigators spot the exact point of impact of cars on the road, or the incendiary flash point of a fire in a structure. They are trained observers who can describe the small details of these events where others are left with only a vague impression. They command the words necessary to describe their observations. To the expert eye, order exists in seeming chaos. To the untrained mind, false order will more likely be found in it. Eyewitness testimony used to convict perpetrators of crime is particularly vulnerable to such error.

Faced with the reality of a violent crime, few can stand by as dispassionate observers of the event. Though some details of the happening may be seared into memory, most will become a jumble waiting to be sorted out. Accuracy of individual eyewitness testimony will vary from witness to witness just as in the psychology class demonstration. It will become false testimony to occurrence of an event that lies outside the person's working mental map of reality. Much of that testimony will be spurious because the mind lacked words to construct it at the moment of happening. In recalling the event, though, witnesses can exhibit high confidence in its accuracy and will fill in the blanks with imagination.

Yeshiva University's Innocence Project uses DNA evidence to refute faulty eyewitness testimony and overzealous police work. To date it claims credit for reversal of 200 false convictions. Typical is the case of Jerry Miller. The victim in the case was accosted in her parking garage at night in 1982. She was beaten, robbed and raped before being forced into the trunk of her own car. On attempting to leave the garage, attendants recognized the car and stopped it. As the rapist fled on foot, the attendants heard the victim in the trunk and released her. In a police line-up, Miller was identified as the fleeing attacker by the two parking garage attendants and the victim. Even though identification of the victim was tentative, the sum total of eyewitness testimony and evidence was sufficient for conviction. Though there was no rape kit, semen on the victim's clothing was kept as evidence. Twenty-four years later, DNA testing of that semen exonerated Miller.

In 1983, Scott Fappiano was convicted of the rape of a police officer's wife in New York City. The rapist entered the house while husband and wife were asleep, tied up the husband and attacked the wife. At trial, the wife identified Fappiano in a line-up, though the husband did not. Despite a mismatch in blood type from the crime scene, Fappiano was tried twice, almost acquitted the first time, and ultimately jailed for a term of 20 to 50 years. Preserved blood evidence exonerated Fappiano twenty-three years later when DNA testing became available.[2]

The role of mistaken eyewitness testimony is recognized as the principal factor in more than 75% of the wrongful convictions overturned by the Innocence Project. Depending on the circumstances of a police line-up or the nature of witness interrogation by police, wrong identifications made become fixed in memory. Even after a lengthy lapse of time following the crime, eyewitnesses can hold complete confidence in their wrong memory of the event, confidently offering a story that sways a jury. The emergence of DNA as extraordinarily accurate evidence in criminal prosecution has reopened the issue of police line-up and questioning methods. Some of those convicted wrongly were on death row. Because only those cases where DNA evidence was preserved offer possibility of reversal, estimates are that exonerations achieved by the Innocence Project represent only the tip of the wrongful conviction iceberg.

Doubt as to the accuracy of much eyewitness testimony has long been put forward. Early twentieth century psychologists Alfred Binet (think intelligence test) and Hugo Munsterberg (think Harvard) published studies arguing that methods of interrogation used by police officers had significant influence on witnesses' recall of the event. Prosecutors and police of that time were not happy to hear criticism of their methods. They summarily dismissed the competence of psychologists as critics of law enforcement techniques. Continuing psychological research had little effect. Prevailing approaches to interrogating eyewitness testimony went unchanged until the late twentieth century. The improbable accuracy of much eyewitness testimony then began to be successfully challenged by good psychological research methodology and recommendations for its improvement entertained.

Experience from the Innocence Project supports the conclusion that eyewitness accounts may be the least reliable kind of evidence. Reliability can be improved if better police methods are used. Research identifies some of the factors that can be used to predict witness unreliability. Cross-race identification and situations involving disguise heavily contribute to inaccuracy. Lengthy exposure to the perpetrator during the course of the crime is associated with greater accuracy. Undue pressure on an eyewitness by police interviewers can create distortion of memory or generate false memory. These influences should probably be obvious when testimony is offered, especially if a defense attorney questions deeply enough. Otherwise, a jury may have little choice but to believe what it hears. Eyewitness testimony is impelling, especially when confidently offered.[3]

The conclusion that should be taken from science based recommendations for evaluation of eyewitness testimony is that there have been and likely still may be many rush-to-judgment convictions based on bad eyewitness testimony. Detectives, prosecutors and judges facing political pressure for a conviction accept it to get the job done. This makes it easy for those found wrongfully convicted to argue they were arbitrarily and unfairly deprived of freedom and reputation by a flawed process of justice that could and should have been recognized as such. Large lawsuit judgments against the State can follow. A further cost may be that well-meaning but overzealous prosecutors and police officers can be charged with misconduct, ending otherwise meritorious careers. False confessions can incur serious social costs.

In crisis, there may be great pressure to explain in words what has happened. Individuals under pressure can be overwhelmed by the stress of the situation. The capacity of their mental maps of sensory reality is exceeded. Few people are willing to believe or admit to this possibility. It is disturbing and frightening to acknowledge that the edge of one's reality map has been breached and that confusion prevails. Order must be maintained in one's phenomenal world, even if at the cost of fictionalizing a part of it, even if error and disorder are inevitable. Demonstrations of erroneous observations are offered regularly on sports television. Close plays on the football field are called by experienced officials, then overturned on review of televised replays. Bad calls on the baseball field are dissected on replay, and the offending officials are angrily accused of incompetence. But a game can move too fast for totally accurate sensory judgment even from trained specialists. It is difficult to admit that "I really can't say what happened". Overly confident accounts of intense, fast moving events should always be distrusted. Even expert accounts may be flawed.

Fictionalized experience is not limited to eyewitness accounts. The phenomenon of false memory gained wide public exposure in the decade of the 1990s. Psychotherapists faced with patients whose anxieties seemed untreatable looked for evidence of repressed childhood sexual abuse by family members as source of the problem. Deep therapy that sometimes included hypnosis appeared to uncover old incidents of family incest or abuse that could account for patients' emotional distress. These supposed events were explored and elaborated upon through therapy sessions. The patient was then encouraged to confront the offending family member with their "memories".[4]

Much like overzealous crime investigators, therapists were too quick to guide recall and plant memory seeds. Overly cooperative patients constructed scenarios of the presumed early abuse and acted on them as if they were an accurate retelling of an actual happening. Confrontation between family members was often explosive, rupturing long term loving relationships.

Accused abusers did not accept this situation passively. They sought legal council and explored the methods used to "uncover" these supposedly repressed memories. Stories of the abuse were examined for factual basis and found flawed in many ways. No one else in the family recalled anything that would support the recovered memory. Second opinion therapy uncovered misleading tactics of the first therapist that would, in and of themselves, account for false memory. Lawsuits followed.

People who are under emotional stress who lack an adequate mental map of the social world cannot defend themselves or cope competently. They are eager to try any suggestion that might offer release from the pressure. Made-up reality that has any plausibility at all is created and accepted.

It is remarkable just what simple suggestion under stressful conditions can do. Some false confessions of crimes are wholly unsolicited, voluntary and still obviously false. Because of the variety of motives that can produce them, voluntary false confessions are dealt with as a special concern of psychological research. Susceptibility to suggestion of all kinds is one of the more common causes. Some bogus confessors may even believe they are guilty. Other false confessions are coerced with threat and emotional pressure. A suspect may confess just to get the interrogator to let him alone and then recant the confession once the interrogation is past. A significant proportion of coerced confessions break down the subject's sense of reality to the point where they come to believe they must be guilty. The art of suggestion applied to interrogation can be practiced too aggressively. Trickery, not truth, prevails.

This is not just speculation. Suggestibility has been closely studied by psychologists and the processes involved can be convincingly demonstrated.

One such study was conducted by the Psychology Department of Williams College in Massachusetts. Students were recruited as participants in what was represented as a reaction time experiment. The task was to instantly depress the individual computer key as its letter or symbol was announced. Key entry subjects were specifically warned *not* to touch one very specific computer key when responding to experimental cues because the computer could "crash" and data would be lost. The time pressure of work varied, with some subjects allowed slightly more than one cue each second, others receiving cues at the rate of about forty cues a minute. About a minute into the task, the computer screen went blank by prearranged plan. An agitated experimenter accused the subject of having hit the forbidden key. He/she was asked to sign a confession admitting to the mistake and was sent into an adjacent "waiting" room where a confederate, supposedly also a subject, asked what had happened. The subject's answer served to determine if he/she accepted fault for the error. Subjects were then returned to the laboratory and required to reconstruct how they pressed the wrong key so others could be helped to avoid the same error. The object of this final procedure was to learn if the subject would voluntarily make up imaginary details related to the supposed error.

Of 75 subjects, 52 signed the confession when asked to do so, 21 accepted full responsibility when telling the confederate what had happened, and seven invented a story of what had happened when pressed to explain the mistake by the experimenter. Working under greater time pressure made a large difference in acceptance of responsibility. Only one-third of those working at a slow pace signed a confession, whereas all of those working at a fast pace did so. As best it could be determined, two-thirds of the fast paced subjects came to believe they were truly at fault for the screen failure. The pressure of circumstances contributes significantly to suggestibility.[5]

These were not social dropouts hustling on the street. The average SAT score for this student population was 1300. Subjects from this socially upscale community were of well above average intelligence. The experimental scenario they were subjected to reveals how methods routinely employed in police interrogation can persuade innocent persons to accept personal guilt for a supposed wrong action. Compared to crime suspects in custody, isolated, faced with real police officers, these were self-assured, relaxed people. The worst they had to face was a bawling out from an upset research professor.

These conditions are familiar, though. The centrality of emotional pressure in convincing subjects they are really guilty is of great importance to false confessions. Facing an unfamiliar situation under pressure can stress anyone's reality map to its limits. One cannot easily perform under pressure and grasp the discrete elements of that performance with accuracy. Order will be imposed. It will be created, made up, or confabulated. Attention to and awareness of the details involved in many performance routines can be achieved with training. Accurate or close to accurate observation becomes possible when words that identify the details are acquired. Trained observation can be demonstrated and attested to. In the absence of training and competence in the circumstances, it must always be assumed that one who is confused or upset by the unfamiliar cannot fully know what he/she has seen, heard or done. Despite confusion, they may nevertheless detail in words the event.

Many people pass through their immediate environment as if in a slight fog, unaware of events that should deserve attention. Depending on the mental set of the individual, only those more dramatic situations will make an impression. People attend to details when they possess the words that encode enfolding events. For those without words that fit, sensory experience will be compared to the words of an existing mental map and judged on a best fit basis. They will make the best sense they can of the situation with the words they have. That which does not fit an existing map may be creatively filled in. Where critical words are missing from the mental map accurate observation and recall will not be possible and details of the experience will be either missing or seriously distorted. A violent, unexpected event such as assault or rape can only be recreated in detail with words. Enough opportunity to observe *and being in possession of relevant words to describe it* will determine the accuracy of eyewitness or victim testimony. The better, more complete existing mental map will produce the most accurate recall. Dealing effectively with events that come at you fast requires continual expansion and updating of the word map.

Individuals vary greatly in their openness to revision of the mental map they use to comprehend events. Some resist strongly. Defense of the existing map requires that the experience be revised according to the existing map to preserve a stable world view. Personal revision of the resister's mental map occurs rarely and wrenchingly. The mental model of the world chooses abstract words to label those events that go beyond the usual. Efficiency requires that the word poor language map include large abstractions that soak up big blocks of experience without discriminating nuances. A few essential, ideational terms like *justice, truth, freedom* or *integrity* will take on huge significance because they work well at filling in big blanks. Communication with others who share similar big abstractions proceeds with minimal disagreement because it is difficult to identify differences in their meaning. With the big abstractions, major differences in world map coexist without conflict because they are not recognized and confronted. Social order is preserved at the price of superficial understanding.

Yet, not every mental map is necessarily rigid. Some individuals are sensitive to small differences in sensory experience and open to change. Their mental map is frequently expanded and upgraded. Errors are made and corrected. Details are closely attended to and new words are found to label specific sensory reference points. Confusion is tolerated and novelty is accommodated by learning. Their mental map is complicated and unstable, but highly adaptable. It easily permits revision and change. The process of sorting out disorder is continual and may be pursued with enthusiasm. Language use is disciplined to master the great variety of special terms necessary to describe this level of complexity. Any abstractions that remain unchallenged are isolated to realms of experience that have yet to be examined closely. Those realms are reopened for revision when they fail to produce needed clarity.

A chicken and egg dilemma prevails with the question of how to explain such large differences in mental models in use. Does something that might be termed intelligence increase the scope and complexity of the mental map? Does tolerance for messy, intense social exchange permit experience to be more fully tested, allowing regular revision of the mental map? Does limited intelligence allow large ill-defined abstractions to obscure important details and oversimplify the mental map? Or is it the relative richness of the culture one is exposed to that determines the flexibility of one's mental map. Like most such questions, the answer is likely to represent a rough equality of contribution from all sources. Early exposure to complex and comprehensive language usage may provide a favorable foundation for later expansion and revision. Fear of confrontation and criticism may limit social interaction that could allow comparison of mental maps. Lack of belief in one's ability, or unawareness of opportunity to achieve better, lack of understanding for social relationships may be a central limitation. Language is a social skill that opens doors to another's experience.

A caveat, though, is needed. Whenever social interaction is limited with a partner whose mental map is composed of overly abstracted or impoverished language it may be best not to demand too much clarity in word meaning. Everyone has his/

her own outer limit of tolerance for confusion where sensory overload occurs. Some individuals are fragile. Their limit is easily reached. They may confess falsely to restore agreement and order to their situation or leap to conclusions to fight off confusion. They may cling to flawed eye witness memory out of desperation for closure. Some will withstand great stress before losing their grip on reality and some will quickly break at the edge, some continue to bend and adapt. When the hard won mental map representing one's personal reality crumbles and words fail, bizarre behavior and outcomes will likely be the result.

8. Social Responsiveness; Authority, Conformity and Suggestibility

The central importance of language in human social development cannot be overstated. Language permits organization of the perceptual world and identification of critical resources necessary for survival. It is literally the ultimate human tool. It should be no surprise that words can take on a reality that is equivalent to or exceeding that of perceptual reality. Without the aid of words, the lessons of threat and benefit, good and evil, can only be learned from direct, hard experience. Words warn; experience can cripple or kill.

From an early time, humans learn to accept what they are told (in words) as true. Unless, of course, the words are *lies*. Lies are the lessons taught with anger and fear. Truths are the lessons taught with love and acceptance. Discriminating truth from lies depends on what those who are accepted and trusted say are truth and lies. Early reality is social reality formed by dependencies and learned through example. Words are the wellspring of both. It is reality shared through the medium of common language. Minds are formed with words alone. Children as young as two can use words to update and revise experience. Young minds can recognize changes that have occurred but yet unseen using words alone. Word dependence forms early. Eventually words become the substance of reality.[1]

Words may become a crutch. Those who find shared reality too comfortable to abandon will maintain dependence on some form of accepted social authority to solve dilemmas of word ambiguity or social conflict. In circumstances of great hardship or threat, reliance on accepted, trusted authority can be near total. In isolated, closed communities women and children are punished for failing to heed the head man's words. Survival dependencies are total and must be maintained. A stable, relatively safe environment is required before independence of judgment can emerge. Personal independence of judgment is attained when words as descriptors of perceived phenomena come to be critically questioned. A community characterized by a variety of independent authorities that differ, even on small issues, is enough to open the door to critical judgment. Many communities never achieve that level of independent thinking. Letting authority lead is comfortable. Only a few rise above it.

A common strategy for dealing with confusion is indeed, to follow orders from someone in authority. This generally means spoken or shouted orders. Soldiers are trained to respond instantly and automatically to orders. Anything less would mean chaos in the heat of fighting. Training for military or paramilitary operations emphasizes response to the command. In emergencies where there is no preexisting social structure, the individual most confident or claiming the most relevant experience may exercise control through commands issued. The term *command* is used with good reason; in circumstances of high stress and great confusion, effective, orderly response requires unquestioning response. The commander should be the best trained or most experienced in dealing with the chaos of combat operations. His/her judgment will be basis of action for all members of the group.

In a more subtle way, social prestige can play a similar role. Those who lack experienced or trained response to a novel condition will follow the lead of another who seems to know what to do. Willingness to follow the suggestions of others, even total strangers, simplifies decision making when confusion prevails. One need not struggle excessively to gain a personal grasp of uncertain reality. Someone else will supply the judgment. Social influence is the basis of what most people call leadership. This is less a matter of skill at leading than it is willingness of followers to be influenced. It is the general prevalence of human suggestibility that makes social influence work.[2]

An appreciation of the power of suggestion can be drawn from examination of what it takes to *resist* suggestion. To reject suggestion, one must firmly have in mind a need to resist. That need may arise from something as basic as readiness to reject any suggestion from the emanating source because it is prejudged untrustworthy. The source may be known or thought to be generally unreliable or, in a specific situation, wrong. Alternatively the source may be rejected simply because the actor wants to follow an alternative course of action for personal reasons. In some instances, the actor may be too confused or fearful to act on any suggested course of action. Inaction appears to be the safe course. In each of these circumstances the suggestion must be specifically and intentionally blocked by the actor.

Acceptance of suggestion is easier and will likely occur whenever action seems necessary and the actor has no idea of what to do. There may also be acquiescence when other courses are known and available but are overridden by willingness to be cooperative. Acquiescence can be no more than basic social participation. Wanting to be accepted, liked, involved, all may be sufficient to bring about acceptance of another's suggestion. The phenomena of behavior under the suggestion of a hypnotist is the very close equivalent of playing a role suggested by the hypnotist. Cognitive dissociation in a sleep-like state may enhance suggestibility creating an extraordinary willingness to cooperate.[3] Thus, as compared to the active behavior required for rejection of suggestion, acceptance can be simple passivity.

Faced with a strange or confusing situation for which there is no useful reality map, suggestion can offer the best available course. Offered with confidence, suggestion may be accepted without question or hesitation. Behavior that is response to another's suggestion can have the effect of simply substituting the other's judgment for one's own. Uncertainty or inexperience can be sufficient basis for accepting a suggested response to any situation. The cognitive switches that reject suggestion input are few, specific and largely rational. Those that accept suggestion more likely allow it to slip through a leaky mental filter, rationally unexamined. Responding to the offered suggestion fosters social exchange and permits the actor to slide thoughtlessly past large gaps in his/her reality map. Accepting another's judgment over one's own saves the painful time and effort of trial and error learning, and leaves another to take responsibility when it doesn't work. Suggestions from others are a great convenience in life. When they are wrapped in what seems like authority, they can be near irresistible. The force of legitimatized authority is demonstrated by research from the immediate post World War II era when peace and stability returned after a time of anger and hate. Social scientist Stanley Milgram's often cited experiments in authority and suggestibility arose out of concern for how something so terrible as Nazism could happen. Milgram's research design illustrates the ease with which authority can evoke cruel actions in quite ordinary people. They are thus a necessary stop on any tour of suggestibility.

Yale Psychologist Stanley Milgram wanted to know why people would obey evil commands from seeming legitimate authority. Ordinary citizens were recruited through newspaper ads and told they were participating in a study of ways to help people improve their memories. On arrival at the laboratory, each recruit was paired with another "recruit" – actually a confederate of the experimenter. One of the two, always the confederate, was assigned as the learner and hooked up to what appeared to be electrical shock apparatus. The actual recruit was designated the teacher. The teacher was to help the learner memorize a series of word sets, and was to administer an electric shock to the learner whenever an error was made. The supposed shock generator consisted of thirty levels on a scale of voltage running from 15 to 450 volts. When the learner made successive errors the "teacher" was instructed to choose the next higher level of shock. Confederates made ample errors, offering regular opportunity for escalation of shock level. In response to the shock "administered", the confederate reacted with cries of pain. There was no actual shock, but the recruit "teacher" had no way of knowing that. The confederate was portrayed as just another person off the street, like the teacher recruit. When the teacher hesitated to throw the lever, the experiment supervisor would simply say to "go on". If an objection to continue was raised, the supervisor would assure the recruit that he accepted full responsibility.

Remarkably, ninety percent of "teachers" when working alone could be induced to press the "shock" levers all the way to 450 volts, this in spite of clear cries of distress from the learner. Only when another confederate, added as a co-teacher, refused to continue further did the recruit refuse to go further with administration of shock.[4]

The demonstration was stunning. So much so that Social Scientists of the time were loathe to accept it as representative of ordinary behavior. Milgram modified his procedure in ways suggested by critics, repeated the study multiple times, and got substantially the same results. It made no difference whether the administrator of "shock" was a college student, a person off the street, highly educated or relatively uneducated. All followed orders. At Stanford University shortly after, Philip Zimbardo demonstrated much the same phenomena in the infamous "Stanford Prisoner Experiments". College students were recruited as paid participants, and arbitrarily divided into groups of guards and prisoners. Almost immediately guards began mistreating prisoners. An experiment intended to last two weeks was cut short when prisoners began to break down under stress. The harshness with which guards readily treated prisoners was difficult to believe.[5]

Response to these findings was so intense that, ultimately, the social science community drew up ethical research codes for the express purpose of preventing future such experimentation from being carried out in the name of Science. It was all just too terrible to deal with. Damn that suggestibility stuff!

Nonetheless, these demonstrations demonstrate that willingness to follow orders and suggestions from authority can be almost without limit. Mere words from any authoritative source can induce almost any kind and extent of behavioral response. Everyday behavior is pervaded by conventional conformity to the extent that independence of thought and action beg to be explained. The influence of suggestibility goes further than authority alone. Peer groups of friends and even strangers can exert influence on individuals through example alone.

In the same post World War II decade as the Milgram experiments, a study was designed to measure just how much the direct evidence of one's senses can be challenged and distorted by the social pressure of strangers in a group setting. Social psychologist Solomon Asch recruited male college students to participate in an experiment described as a test of perceptual accuracy. Parallel vertical lines of differing length were displayed on white posters to groups of 7 to 9 individuals. A standard line was displayed separately on one poster. On a poster next to it, three comparison lines were presented. Two of the three lines were sufficiently different in length to permit easy rejection. The third matched the standard. The task was to pick the line that matched the standard. Differences in length of incorrect comparison lines were large enough so that anyone with normal vision could easily match the standard. Twelve different sets of cards were presented in twelve experimental trials. In each trial, members of the group were verbally polled in sequence as to which line was the correct match to the standard. Answers were recorded.

Unknown to the real research subjects, the group was bogus. The experimenter had formed a panel of confederates who were instructed to pick a line on every trial after the second that *did not* match the standard. Only one member of the group was the actual research subject. A stranger to the others, this person was placed near the end of the group in sequence. The true object of research was to learn if, after hearing others make wrong choices, the actual subject would be swayed to follow the group *against* the evidence of his own senses.

The thirty-one research subjects tested in this manner showed wide variability in their reactions to this extraordinary situation. About one fifth of them chose the correct match on all trials, demonstrating full independence from the group's example from the third trial on. All others chose the group's (wrong) answer at least once, and about 40% matched the group's (wrong) choice three or more times. Two individuals followed the group's example on all trials. Independence of judgment is variable and distributes from strong to weak. The large majority of subjects, though, were at some point swayed by the group's bad judgment.

The process was closely observed by the researcher and his assistant. As comparison trials progressed past the first and second trials and the discrepancy in judgment was experienced, confusion and bewilderment overcame the faces of most subjects. Nervous fidgeting was observed. Some subjects would stand to see the posters more clearly. Obvious agitation of this sort characterized the behavior of only one member of each group, the research subject. Confederates acted as if nothing unusual was happening. At the conclusion of the trials, a "group" discussion of the process took place. The experimenter commented on the disagreement that had occurred, and inquired if one person could be right and the rest of the group wrong. Experimental subjects clearly and unambiguously expressed their confusion over the discrepancy in judgments. The confederates were then dismissed and each subject was interviewed in greater depth to assess his experience in these trials. Finally, the actual purpose of the research was revealed to the confused subject.

The research subject's candid interview comments were fully summarized by the researcher. It was clear from them that the experience of having to choose between trusting one's own sensory experience and disagreeing with the group could be an intensely distressing one. The level of confusion varied widely. Some were upset, some matter of fact. However, all subjects admitted they had faced a personal dilemma when the discrepancy in judgments became apparent. All who chose to make an independent judgment contrary to the rest of the group felt uncomfortable and experienced difficulty doing so. It was emotionally distressful to be the lone deviant in the group. They quickly came to awareness that something was very wrong. The other members of the group (confederates) appeared to confidently make independent judgments that seemed to rule out conspiracy. It seemed to most that there had to be some misunderstanding on their part. As trials progressed and discrepancies continued, subjects began to believe that there was something wrong with the way they were reaching their judgments. Perhaps they were misperceiving as a result of some visual illusion. Self-doubt began to grow. Even the most confident and independent of the subjects were visibly shaken by the experience. They reported afterward feeling isolated and perplexed. The social tension created by the structure of the situation prevented them from reaching the easy, logical solution. They could not see that they had been set-up by the experimenter and his confederates.[6]

The Ashe conformance study represented a seminal research design in its time. Since mid-century when it was first carried out hundreds of nearly identical research studies have been conducted by social psychologists world wide. Researchers in 1996 who undertook to review and compare studies that used the Ashe or a closely similar design identified 133 separate experiments involving 4,627 participants across 17 countries over the near half-century. As would be expected, level of conformance varied but, on average, it matched Ashe's original result. Social pressure consistently produces conformity contrary to sensory evidence in a large proportion of individuals. Under some circumstances, it can produce an entirely false reality.[7]

The habit of agreement may be deeply set early in life. The rebellious are punished, the cooperative are rewarded. While a limited proportion of questions may require critical examination and invite controversy, most social exchanges invite only agreement. Agreement at all levels of language use is necessary for smooth, agreeable communication. Agreement starts with common recognition of the sensory phenomena referenced by words. Even small differences in the meaning of words can create misunderstanding and friction. Shared word meaning is unmistakably the currency of shared community. It should not be such a great surprise then that when agreement must be expressed publicly in words, minor differences in authority status can influence one's judgment of the phenomena perceived. "The boss is always right." In the case of the Ashe study that authority was established by numbers alone. Groupthink prevailed.

Social comparison is of such great importance to assessment of phenomenal reality that obvious disagreement cannot be easily dismissed. These were young men, college students, socially competent and articulate. Being at odds with their peers on a simple task nonetheless shook their sense of reality. How much easier it would be to assault the confidence of a small child or someone in fear for their life if they disagreed. In these terms the confessions of the Norfolk Four make complete sense. It would be expected that only the strongest, most confident, would hold their ground of belief, and then only with difficulty, whenever agreement is demanded by authority.

The power of social persuasion to overcome the personal values of another is illustrated in the phenomenon of the Stockholm Syndrome. This behavior occurs when a captive who is subject to total control by the captors for a length of time begins to identify with the values of the captors. A well known and widely publicized instance of Stockholm Syndrome is the case of Patty Hearst, granddaughter of the publishing magnate William Randolph Hearst. In February of 1974 Ms. Hearst was kidnapped from her apartment in Berkeley, California by a self-styled guerilla group that called themselves the Symbionese Liberation Army. The SLA, as it became known, demanded that the Hearst family distribute food to the needy in California as ransom for Patty Hearst's release. After six million dollars in food had been given away, the SLA reneged on the deal. Then, a mere two and a half months after being kidnapped, Ms. Hearst was photographed holding an assault rifle and shouting commands at frightened customers while SLA members robbed a local bank. Patty had apparently gone revolutionary. Captured with the group in September of that same year she was put on trial for bank robbery, was convicted, and did prison time.[8]

The Stockholm Syndrome takes its name from the robbery of the Kreditbanken of Stockholm Sweden. Hostages in the bank were held for five days before they were freed. In that brief span of time they had identified emotionally with their captors, so much so that captives defended their captors to the authorities after being released. There are even reports of reversal occurring where captors became sympathetic with the plight of their captives. Shared reality can readily become common reality, especially so under conditions of extreme emotional stress.

Manipulation of the social environment to induce political or social attitude acceptance or change is a variation on this process. The label sometimes applied to this kind of reality shift is *brainwashing*. The Chinese army invaded Korea in 1950 in the political vacuum that followed the expulsion of Japan from that nation. US occupation troops still in place in the south of Korea raced north to defend as Chinese troops surged across the

Chinese border. In the chaos that followed, many US prisoners were taken by the Chinese.

US prisoners of war were subjected to extensive psychological measures by their captors. They had to deal with harsh physical conditions and coercive persuasion (repetitive word assaults) designed to socially disrupt group cohesiveness. The approach employed could be translated from Chinese as "brain rinse", a method widely used in China to bring the population into conformity with Communist thinking. A CIA operative working as a news reporter in the Korean theater invented *brainwashing* as the catch term to describe this method.

The mere suggestion of mind manipulation made brainwashing a threat to many. Much mythology grew around the word. Brainwashing was thought to be too insidiously powerful to be resisted. Allen Dulles, CIA director, claimed that it causes the brain to become a phonograph playing a disk put on its spindle by an outside genius. Willingness to accept the power of suggestion was total. The reality was not so dramatic. Close evaluation of the results following the return of POWs after fighting ceased determined that very little if any real ideological conversion had occurred. Some POWs went along with the program to avoid harsh treatment, and a few recorded propaganda confessions were taken by the Chinese. Only a small number of real conversions occurred. Those who succumbed tended to be individuals with rigid, conversion-prone personalities. Seeking final truth, these individuals seize on ideological dogma, sometimes going from one dogma to another. The mythology of brainwashing has nonetheless prevailed and continues to describe what some see as one's (someone else's) brain being taken over and controlled by a manipulative genius. It is a theory of an implanted reality that is largely fanciful. Suggestibility requires a common social setting to work its magic. Minds are not computers that can be programmed at will.[9]

Computers when they first emerged in the 1960s and 1970s were thought by some to be thinking machines. Computer programming was viewed as a method for forming or reforming that thinking. Among some psychotherapists, programming became a metaphor for attitude change and the notion became widely popularized. Shorn of its negative brainwashing associations, implanting a new reality map in humans through attitude restructuring was pursued as therapeutic procedure. For the disturbed, it was theorized, all could be made well by implanting new words into individual reality maps.

Therapeutic reprogramming was a brief lived fad that had some successes with personalities like those effectively brainwashed in Korea. It was marketed as Neuro-linguistic Psychotherapy and, though generally discredited, is still in limited psychotherapeutic use by some practitioners.[10]

The flaw in this methodology is failure to appreciate that rationally dry-cleaned words are not the stuff of thinking and communicating. Culture is the context within which word meaning is established. Reprogramming, to the extent that it is possible, requires a change of cultural context. Traditional cultural programming takes place in the family and then through a series of steps at schools, up to and including colleges and universities. The significance of the cultural context in forming the mental maps of youth is reflected in the present day politicization of public education. Every persuasion of social, religious and political viewpoint seeks to shape the thinking of the young through its own brand of systematic acculturation. Acculturation *is* mental map programming. It is not just a new set of words to describe a familiar sensory reality. It is not mere attitude change. It is language development through cultural immersion at its foundations. Attempting to manipulatively alter an existing world view ignores the differences in word meaning that make up cultural and individual mental maps.

Words are loaded with attitude. Attitudes are more lasting and durable than some would make them out to be.

Attitude change can be brought about in many if approached with patience. Simple persuasion can sometimes change attitude up to and including a shift in politics or ideology. Credible, balanced argument is the most likely path to successful attitude change. It is most likely to succeed with those whose attitudes are only partially formed or somewhat tentative. The persuader who gives credence to more than one side of an issue exhibits balance and fairness that helps persuade. The most powerful lever of change, perhaps, is the reputation and general attractiveness of the information source. The arguments of acknowledged experts who exhibit rationality and avoid emotional excess in their use of words are most likely to influence others.

It is remarkable how powerful words are in shaping and reshaping anyone's behavior and world view. A large part of the populace is always looking for answers to difficult personal, political, ideological, or factual issues. Words that satisfactorily supply reasonable answers will often be accepted when there is confusion. Those who would persuade will take maximum advantage of that readiness to exert their influence.

9. Words And The Inner Experience

Relating realistically with others requires that a simple rule be followed: never presume to have intimate knowledge of another's inner experience. Inner psychological life is wholly personal. Accessing another's personal experience is primarily through words, sometimes in pictures, partially by observing actions. The only experience that can be directly known is one's own. What you know about the experience of others is inferred from what you know about your own. And even your own experience can be very confusing.

Human beings are different. Outward appearance suggests something of the quality of inner experience. Words may partially reflect both description of feeling as well as present mood. The listener/observer takes it all in, compares it to the words that describe his/her own experience and makes guesses about what is going on within the other. Psychologists call this *attribution*.[1] Words and actions that appear to match our own suggest an equivalent experience. Familiar patterns of description and expression are presumed to result from experiences like our own unless there is evidence to the contrary. Some inner experiences are very different. Color vision is not universally experienced. Everyone who is sighted can see black and white but not everyone sees the world in color. Those with color blindness will likely guess that it is something alike to shades of grey. Where non-correspondence of any kind with another's experience exists, the likely solution will be best-fit attribution – aka, a guess based on whatever experience you personally own that seems to fit.

Lacking anything better, attribution helps people relate to one another as if they are like-minded souls. Laughing at the same jokes, completing one another's sentences, enjoying the same entertainments all suggest compatibility. Deep compatibility is a very special relationship, and many go through life never finding a soul partner. Friends are just assumed to be like minded. The office embezzler, the acquaintance who goes berserk with a weapon, the spouse who unexpectedly files for divorce then become demonstration of the extent to which they have never been known at all.

The failure to discover incompatibility in relationships most often arises from an inability to talk personally and openly. Relationships go forward on a superficial level that avoids wandering off the established path of shallow communication. Discussion is limited to things like, How is our mutual friend Joe or Jane? Have you been to the gym lately?, How was your vacation? Personal communications may be compartmentalized by specialties. The lawyer knows our financial worries, the minister or best friend is familiar with family problems, the physician has a record of our symptoms and illnesses. The next door neighbor knows about our pets and gardening interests. No one knows all about us. Even parents never had a clue about most of our childhood experiences and feelings.

The practice of psychiatric or psychological counseling may come closer to full personal disclosure than does any other relationship. Granting another the right to ask penetrating personal questions is extraordinary. Needing to pour it all out to a sympathetic listener does happen in psychological therapy as well as in some other very special personal relationships. Sometimes deep personal information is manipulatively extracted. Skilled police interrogators set up situations that produce self-revelation, sometimes self-incrimination. Very close marriage relations can permit full self-disclosure. Very bad divorces can result from trust that has been betrayed. Opening one's self can be risky. Best friends not infrequently become worst enemies. On discovery of unexpected dissimilarity the emotional polarity of the relationship can sharply reverse.

The safest strategy in relationships is accept what you see and make no presumptions of attribution or gratuitous sympathy. Knowing another's experience is not easy. There are few ways to let another know your inner life short of blurting it all out in a flood of words. That may gain contempt, pity or disgust. Alternatively, an avenue of deep respect and full communication may open. It's a gamble. Unless there is willingness to put it all in words and test the relationship, friends are people you smile at and little more.

Friends can be made and enjoyed because we have words. Words are a large part of what is shared in common. When we use words to describe inner experience, we can never be fully sure that our meaning is the same as another's. There are only limited common, objective points of reference to be shared. Differences become apparent only when behavior gets weird. Out of control or whacky says "uh-oh, I don't relate to that."

Not long ago, strange and incomprehensible behavior in a close community was either *of God or of the Devil*. Religious authority dealt with it accordingly. The inspired were venerated, the feared were tortured or exiled. Nineteenth century secular psychology found other explanations. A new vocabulary of mental life was invented by Sigmund Freud and Carl Jung. Causes in the form of drives and instincts explained strange behavior. Ego, superego, libido were said to be the source of behavior and experience. Freud attributed much behavior to repressed sexual experiences and desires. He is criticized for making too much of sex as the source of inner life, though many people do seem obsessed by it. Indeed, no one can doubt the potency of sexual urges. Freud may in some respects have labored the obvious. His more significant contribution, perhaps, was in the creation of a language for describing the innermost nooks and alcoves of the mind.[2]

The Language Of Temperament

Freud's language has its own vocabulary which is useful because it references behavior that can be related to. Doing so he provided us with words to identify behaviors formerly lost in the shadows of the mental map. He invented the concept of *repression* to describe the seeming inability of patients to recall those events that were too upsetting or painful to face. The evidence of repression is rediscovery of hidden memories through the process of psychotherapy. The patient who rejects the known facts of past events or present obvious realities is in Freudian *denial*. Making up an elaborate explanation for why something has or has not happened is *rationalization*. The patient is *projecting* who avoids admitting the reality of personal illness, injury or fault by insisting it is someone else's problem. The stubborn individual who will not give up on a difficult or impossible task is *anal retentive*. Most present day high school students regularly use this language to describe their own behavior as well as that of parents and fellows.

Much of Freud's mind theory is now taken to be his own *rationalization* of patient behavior. The language of psychoanalysis has nonetheless become the standard in talking about ordinary behavior. Freud's words are mainstream popular psychology. They are often surprisingly useful for categorizing and understanding some behaviors. In their way, they were a breakthrough in lifting the veil on inner human experience.

Karl Jung developed a distinctive parallel descriptive system to categorize and explain psychological types. Fundamental to Jung's scheme were the qualities of *introversion* and *extraversion*. People are either inwardly reserved or socially outgoing. Within each of these groupings Jung identifies four cognitive types; *thinkers* versus *sensualists* and *feelers* versus *intuitionists*. His terms are inherently abstracted and confusing. They seem ill defined and overlapping. Jung's theory of the mind emphasized unconscious needs and desires as causes of action as did Freud's, but differed substantially in terminology. His words are more mystical in quality and have enjoyed less popular acceptance in common usage. His psychological types, though, could be taken as the beginning of human personality theory. As personality descriptors, indeed, they were a useful start.[3]

As used in Jung's approach, personality theory provides words that describe the quality of others' inner experiences. Uncovering personality types proceeds on the presumption that noticeable differences in human temperament are deeply encoded into language. If individuals honestly describe themselves in those words, it may be possible to form a picture of their inner experience.

With this presumption as their base, twentieth century personality psychologists literally scoured language for self-descriptive words that could be used to describe human personality. Starting with the adjectival words identified, thousands of self-descriptive inventories have been invented and tested. To bring order out of this confusion, a community of personality psychology researchers applied statistical analyses to what were judged to be the most meaningful words. In the 1970s their word search boiled down to a limited set of the most likely descriptors of personality. A large number of people were asked to accept or reject these words as personal descriptors. Statistical clusters were identified. Five relatively independent word based factors were chosen to describe and differentiate human temperament types.[4]

These five consensus factors have been given a variety of labels. Most often they are described as *openness to experience, agreeableness, outgoingness, conscientiousness* and *anxiousness.* Alternative labels can be used as a matter of preference or judgment. There remains some disagreement over the best factor labels. Once a cluster of words is identified that seems to isolate one of these temperament typologies it is not always easy to reach accord as to the single word or phrase that describes the whole category. Slight differences in descriptive tone are found in each individual researcher's preference for labeling. Taken as a whole, each factor cluster defines itself as a quality of temperament ranging from more to less. Each thus represents a range or scale on which a person can vary in a quality of temperament. The dimensions themselves can be thought of as polarities of temperament that do not necessarily reflect desirable or undesirable qualities at either polarity anchor point. Descriptions are shaded to be as neutral as possible to allow that polarity to come through. The following descriptions are offered for present purposes:

Openness to Experience encompasses qualities like curiosity, imagination, inventiveness, readiness to explore and encounter new experience. One who is not open to experience would be cautious, conventional, conservative, avoidant of novelty and slow to change.

Agreeableness is cooperative, consenting, sympathetic, uncritical, nice behavior. The opposite end of the range is critical, direct, even confrontational in social relationships, and may shade into qualities of suspicion or stubbornness.

Outgoingness takes in qualities of high energy, social confidence, active involvement in living, as well as enjoyment in working and being with others. The other end of the dimension is self-sufficiency or withdrawal, timidity, and relative noninvolvement in social activities.

Conscientious has the quality of duty, self-discipline, commitment, principledness, and dependability. Its absence is marked by behavior that is free spirited, unpredictable, undependable, erratic, impulsive or undisciplined.

Anxiousness has to do with one's emotional state. One who is anxious is intensely aware of changes in the environment, easily upset, quick to take the defensive or avoid fearful situations, typically on edge or highly alert emotionally. The other end of the scale suggests self-assuredness, emotional stability, even a certain stoicism.

These *big five factors*, so-called, are potentially useful descriptors of common human temperaments and behaviors among all English speaking peoples. The definitions suggested for them here are commonly used though not universally agreed on. Not every experience of openness or anxiousness, etc. is the same and there is some overlap among them. But the way in which these qualities combine together to identify observable variations in human personality do make it easier to understand another's temperament and actions. Care should be taken not to put too much emotional meaning into the words used to describe them. Something positive or negative can be made out of either polarity of each of these dimensions. Every quality of temperament has some useful purpose. After all is said and evaluated, these are only descriptive *words*. It is quite possible that we do not yet have all the words needed to describe the fullest depths of human experience. Full knowledge of inner life still escapes us. As tools for beginning to understand how one person's actions and world view can differ from another's, they can be useful.[5]

Words used to describe personality may differ across languages. The claim has been made that the big five personality factors are applicable in general to all Western language cultures. Because personality structure research had its beginnings in the US based on the study of English words, such a claim could be guilty of overreach unless independently verified on similarly descriptive words from German, Italian, French, Greek, Hungarian, and Russian languages. In fact, research on temperament descriptors from those European languages does offer substantial evidence that the same *big five* factors show up in all of them. There is one interesting discrepancy. A separate, sixth factor, named Honesty-Humility emerges from nearly all of these languages. Europeans appear to place more emphasis on the qualities of honesty, sincerity, and fair mindedness versus, greed, boastfulness or pompousness compared to Americans. Differences on these dimensions may arise out of the greater importance of these qualities to cultures historically based on monarchies and autocracies.[6] The Sapir/Whorf hypothesis suggests that one should expect *some* differences in description of personal qualities across cultures. It nonetheless appears that cross-cultural personality factor research confirms that the Big Five are close to universal in Western culture.

Were it not for descriptive words like these, there would be little to go on except basic body language in plumbing the depths of inner experience. Smiles and scowls would have to do. For the most withdrawn of individuals, there may exist a deep secret life that evades expression even in those terms. If one will not cooperate and talk, we can be fully shut out of that private experience. Words are its primary form of expression.

Inner Voices

For some, inner life is filled with words. The average person has an active inner dialog of words going on during a good part of any day. Some may talk aloud to themselves as part of that dialog. Things to do, people to talk with, places to go, all figure in the ongoing babble. From time to time, almost everyone hears voices in their heads. Some hear voices most of the time. Voices may be identified as those of strangers, friends, family members who offer help, demand action, criticize, comfort, whatever. Reports of personal voice experience are becoming more common as "voice-hearers" form self-help groups to deal with their experience. The evidence of potential for multiple streams of consciousness in a brain lends considerable credibility to claims of such experience.

The long history of psychosis in human beings adds further argument for the verity of these experiences. Among schizophrenics, the statistics for voice hallucinations (the psychiatric terminology) run about 75%. Some of those who cope with persistent voices say that when voice-hearers (their terminology) are distressed by what voices are saying to them and thereupon seek help, they expose themselves to diagnosis as schizophrenic. Indications are that far more people live and cope with their voices than seek psychiatric assistance dealing with them. The cause of voice-hearing can be described variously as illness or mental quirk. Preference for one description or the other may depend on how disturbing the voices become, how pervasive the experience is and how much tolerance the individual has for them.

Curious to test the extent of voice hearing, a Dutch professor of psychiatry, Marius Romme, went on Netherlands television to invite participation of voice hearers in a group of similar minded persons. Four hundred fifty people responded. Questioned as to their distress at hearing voices, one-third said they were able to cope with voice-hearing and lead relatively normal lives. His initiative led to the creation of self-help Hearing Voices Networks (H.V.N.s) in the Netherlands and Britain.[7]

Participants in H.V.N. groups share experiences of hearing and coping with their voices. Some describe the experience as uncontrollable chaos. Others tolerate voice-hearing without great distress. According to one observer of a voice hearing network group, "most members of the group spoke of their voices in the way that comedians speak of mothers-in-law: burdensome and irritating, but an inescapable part of life."

Some humans, perhaps a great many more than might be expected, live with heard voices during a large part of their lives. Voices do not easily go away. The better course for some hearers is to listen to and maybe understand what voices have to say. Some are described as supportive, even witty, others as cruel and abusive. Patients interpret the meaning of voice messages as best they can, often as messages from their unconscious. Voice-hearers, it would seem, do not fully or easily understand their own inner life. One thing voice-hearing does establish is that the brain does communicate with itself using words.

Voice-hearing is often triggered by intensely emotional experiences, such as sexual abuse or bereavement. Physical injury to the brain may bring it on. Once active, the voices may be inescapable and continue for decades. Voice-hearing may result from special structuring of the brain that is either genetically or developmentally generated. Voice hearing brain structure that is normal to most may be exaggerated in voice-hearers. Injury or trauma may trigger brain structure that produces or increases voice-hearing. The mute right brain that seems to exist independently in many people may hijack the language center and start expressing itself. The root causes and mechanics of the phenomena are yet to be examined in any depth. Most heard-voices – hallucinations if you prefer – will still be treated psychiatrically as repressed emotional trauma. In a curiously roundabout way, that may be an appropriate point from which to begin. Those words would *not* be heard if it were not for the presence of language capability already in the brain. Repressed anger and hurt might well be expected to seize language in seeking expression. Words shape lives and drive action. Words permit social coordination of activity that raises society to incredible levels of wealth production. Words are the tools of analysis that drive experiment and exploration of strange phenomena. Words distress and frighten. Words are the media of personal human connection. Personal communion between kindred minds can create comfort, joy and peace. On occasion those minds might be in the same head.

Beyond Sensation

The range of truly extraordinary neurological experience goes far beyond the words of the Big Five personality factors and inner voices. The twentieth century's population explosion in concert with advances in neurological medicine have opened doors to truly strange inner experiences. Visions of angels, friends, animals, etc., do occur within the mind without apparent sensory input. These need not necessarily be religious experiences. They can occur without any religious training whatever. The brain appears to be capable of generating experience independent of sensory input. Knowledge of these experiences is accessible only with words.

The visual brain, for instance, has a talent for filling in the blanks. Each human eye has a blind spot where the nerves that serve the retina exit into the brain. A simple visual test will usually find that spot. Mark two black spots about three inches apart on a piece of white paper. Hold the paper as if the dots are on the horizon. With the right eye closed, fixate the left eye on the rightmost dot at a distance of about twelve inches. Slowly move the paper toward your face. At some critical distance the left-most dot will disappear. You will know it has disappeared because the texture of the paper now appears to be continuous at that point. There is no hole or other indication of blindness because your brain has filled in the blind spot to match the surrounding field of vision. The eye is blind to its blind spot. The brain is its own editor.[8]

A variety of visual tests can be found on the web at www. blindspottest.com that demonstrate the brain's ability to fill in the blanks for those with curiosity to explore them.

People with visual loss resulting from macular degeneration, cataracts or retinal damage can be subject to sudden, unexpected hallucinations in the sightless regions. Though there is clearly no capability for normal sight in the blind field of vision, various images, children, flowers, circus clowns, animals may appear. Movement of the eye will erase the vision. There is no confusion about these being hallucinations. The experience is easily accepted and explained as a product of brain activity. The brain seems to want to create visual images, perhaps especially so when the eyes no longer generate them.

Injury to the visual cortex of the brain caused by stroke, accident or surgery can also produce blind spots in the visual field, called scotoma. The brain will create images in these areas. James Thurber, the celebrated author and cartoonist, suffered injury to his right eye as a child. Progressive deterioration ultimately left him completely blind in that eye. Instead of blankness, his visual field became active with hallucinations.

His blindness was full of images and color. Describing this experience to his doctor, he wrote:

"Years ago you told me about a nun in the middle centuries who confused her retinal disturbances with holy visitation, although she saw only one tenth of the holy symbols I see. Mine have included a blue Hoover, golden sparks, melting purple blobs, a skein of spit, a dancing brown spot, snowflakes, saffron and light blue waves and two eight balls, to say nothing of the corona which used to halo street lamps and is now brilliantly discernible when a shaft of light breaks against a crystal bowl or a bright metal edge."[9]

Thurber's blindness was total in one eye. Damage to the visual field of the brain is often only partial. The visual cortex maps the retina, so that when partial blindness occurs, normal vision is experienced in the undamaged part of the map, but a blind area is experienced corresponding to the injured part of the cortex. Patients with this kind of blindness often experience hallucinations within the blind area. The visual brain is so adept at producing visual images it can create them within itself whenever visual input from the eye is missing.

Without words to describe strange happenings like these, there would be no way to discover the inner mysteries of the brain. The inner reality of pain, pleasure, color, form, and meaning depend on the well monitored experience of a healthy brain to avoid distortion and maintain a confident balance. A reasonably accurate map of physical reality depends on a relatively undistorted inner reality. Correcting and avoiding distortion is achieved by comparing one's inner reality with that of others. At every step, words are indispensable. Inner reality is articulated and understood with words. Words are the building blocks of the reality map. They are the currency of communication and social exchange, the keys to awareness and self-understanding.

10. Words of Passion

Expression of emotion does not necessarily require words, though words may often be accompanied by audible outcries of distress, disgust or joy. Such vocalizations may have been the beginnings of language among primitive man. It is behavior that can be observed among the higher apes in the wild. What can also be seen in near relatives of man are facial expressions of fear, anger, disgust, surprise, sadness, and joy, amplified with appropriate body language. The average dog or cat is quite capable of expressing happiness or fear. Feelings are hard wired into the primate brain.

What is different with humans is the ability to recognize the feeling of emotion and describe it in words. Emotion is a visceral level physical reaction of the body to things and events in one's life space. Emotions are experienced more than they are sensed. The words that describe them have more inherent visceral reality than do other words. The interrelatedness of brain and body in experiencing emotion is clear and unmistakable in experiences of love, fear, anguish, hatred, disgust. These sensations reach into the body and seize it. The uncertainty is in whether emotion happens in muscles and organs at the visceral level and is then experienced in the brain, or begins with a sensory experience in the brain that triggers the visceral response. Whatever! Emotion is clearly more than mere mental contemplation. It is physically experienced.

Those who experience intensely emotional reactions of fright or disgust know the distress that is felt in the gut. That distress is difficult to ignore. The importance of physical reaction to the quality of emotion experienced can be demonstrated in the changed emotional experience of individuals with transected – severed – spinal cords. Experience of bodily emotion must travel to the brain through the spinal cord. In the absence of communication along this pathway, the mental feeling of emotion becomes discernibly muted. The higher the break in the spinal cord, the greater the diminishment of emotional experience. The experience is described as one that lacks the raw visceral component of emotion. Higher mental functions continue to construct a partial experience emotion that is without most of the visceral kick supplied by the body.[1]

With effort and practice some degree of control can be obtained over strong physical reactions to emotional situations. The experience of stage or performance fright is common among aspiring actors and musicians. With time and experience the intensity of reaction can be suppressed and, in some people, extinguished. A central element of a conscious program of control over emotional response is to recognize and describe it in words. Reflection on and analysis of the experience can amount to talking oneself through one's anxieties. If nothing else, the severely reactive individual can recognize the source and quality of emotional reaction and assure others it will pass. Words are an important part of rationally managed emotion.

When Words Are Shorn Of Emotion

The common sense conception of the brain's function depicts it as the place where rational thinking happens. Thinking can be either clear or confused. Dealing with strong emotional experience is thought to require cultivation of rational, reasonable thinking that mutes emotion and preserves clarity. Educated, civilized individuals take a certain pride in thinking clearly and rationally. They use rational arguments and make rational decisions. Emotion is thought to interfere with sound judgment. Rationality is expected to bring about superior decisions, those that are good, fair or reasonable. This is partly due to a distinctively Anglo-English cultural prejudice for *rationality* and *reasonableness* in all things that was championed by the eighteenth century English philosophers Hobbes, Locke, and Hume.

Rationality in its mathematical meaning describes the quotient of two polynomials. The meaning of rationality as clear thinking is a long way from the root meaning of the words ratio and rational as mathematical concepts. As clarity of thinking, rationality is a metaphor that derives from the notion of precise quantitative thinking. That which is mathematically rational can be expressed in simple, integer form. Rationality as thinking is sound, clear consideration of the issues. Mathematics offers precise, final answers. Rational argument is straightforward and unconfused. Bewildered or unclear argument is irrational. An irrational number is one that cannot be expressed as a simple ratio. It can never be completed or resolved. By parallel logic, rational argument can be accepted because it is simple, direct and clear, final.

To think reasonably as opposed to emotionally means to exercise recognizably sound judgment and avoid excess in word or action. It can also mean consistency of thinking, simplification of an argument or avoidance of plain foolishness. It is openness to new ideas and evidence. Reasonableness is sometimes associated with the use of socially positive and acceptable language, or just thoughtful behavior in general. The words *logical, rational* and *reasonable* are interchangeable in describing positive simplicity and directness of words and action. Blatantly emotional use of words is prejudicially taken to be the indicator of irrationality and unreasonableness. Rationality and reasonableness as thinking that has been stripped of feeling content is itself irrational.

Much such expectation for rational clarity and reasonableness in use of words is hopelessly naive. Feeling pervades language and thinking so intensively that its influence cannot be avoided. Precise use of specific words can seem stilted and unusual. Language is full of imagery and metaphor that evoke images. Such language in usual discourse is more common than sterile rationality. Indeed, it is the emotional imagery of words that give them charm and humanity. The emotional loading of words gives them color (to apply a commonplace visual metaphor). Metaphors make reading interesting. Good writing, for instance, is described as *fluid* to describe the smoothness through which meaning and imagery are created. The graduate of a career training program is said to be *equipped* with or to have *mastered* the necessary knowledge to obtain employment. Literally, water or gas is fluid, equipment means physical tools or gear, and mastery is social dominance. They are invoked as feeling laden visual and auditory echoes of their literal meaning to enhance language. Simile makes use of vivid imagery to enliven (!) language. One who refuses to communicate or inform, for instance, is said to be *stonewalling* to portray their stubbornness. Poetic, lyrical speech is fun to hear and easily understood. The emotional loading added to words makes them more than dry symbols. They are invested with enhanced clarity and interest.

The extent to which language is filled with imagery and emotion underscores the importance of emotion for communicating. Advertising and propaganda exploit the richness of language to influence attitude and action through imagery and expressiveness of wording. Language is extended and enriched in doing so, even though that may mean lost precision of meaning. Indeed, exactness of meaning may be largely abandoned leaving emotion alone as the message. Words with feeling content connect. Dry words, sterile of feeling, bore.

In matters of personal security, cold rationality of argument offers little comfort. Attack to one's person must be defended and may demand retribution. The anger that was felt by most Americans at the destruction of New York's World Trade Center on 9/11 had a distinctively retributive quality. The result was a general readiness to support some kind of retaliatory response. The administration's invasion of Iraq was in parallel with that readiness. Even most of the usual anti-war doves in Congress sensed the nation's mood and approved of war. In a climate of public anger options other than military retaliation were never seriously considered. Invasion of Iraq was an emotionally driven decision that was thought to be reasonable for the times.[2] That kind of distorted rationality, though it occurs frequently in moments of anger, is not necessarily inevitable. The decision process that produced war with Iraq can be compared to that which is documented for the Cuban Missile Crisis which, while equally intense in emotion, was rationally controlled.

In October, 1962, Nikita Khrushchev, Chairman of the Russian Communist party, confident that he could take advantage of the inexperience of newly elected President John F. Kennedy, began building intercontinental missile installations 90 miles off the US shore in Cuba. Aerial intelligence revealed the build-up within days of its start. Rather than tip his hand to Khrushchev or inflame US public opinion, a justifiably outraged Jack Kennedy began an intensive evaluation of the build-up and asked the CIA for an estimate of the expected missile readiness. Simultaneously, vulnerability to an offshore missile strike and appropriate positioning of US military forces was evaluated. Military leaders favored an immediate preemptive strike on missile sites in Cuba while they were under construction. The military was held in check by Kennedy's stubbornly reasoned cautiousness. When it was judged prudent to announce the crisis to the US and the world, he began a series of carefully considered communications with Khrushchev. The extent of military readiness for war was calculated to communicate Kennedy's absolute resolve to see the missiles removed.

Generals and admirals, inflamed by Khrushchev's actions, trained for war and, commanding awesome weapons of retaliation, had their fingers on the trigger every step of the way. That required Kennedy and his Secretary of Defense, Robert McNamara, to maintain close surveillance to avoid impulsive action fanned by fury. Following a tense naval blockade off Cuba which went to the edge of full war, a reasoned, rational diplomatic solution was achieved between the US and Soviet Russia. Reasonable and rational in every sense, it was a nonetheless decision made in a climate of high anxiety and anger. The emotional intensity that came with that crisis very likely brought special clarity to the consequences of a bad decision. This kind of rationality is actually tightly disciplined emotional calculation.[3]

In Western culture, reasonableness is the accepted standard of decision making. There is strong prejudice against emotion in formal decision making. It is generally assumed that emotion distorts thought and reason, (in the sense of *sound argument!*). In contradiction to the prevailing bias against emotionally underscored decisions, there nevertheless is evidence that high emotional intensity can be beneficial to good decision making. Indeed, feelings must ordinarily be taken into account when making important choices. Pure logical, rational reasoning can be sterile. The choice to bomb Cuba while missile installations were still under construction would have been coldly rational and wrong.

The alternative to *rational* or *reasonable* thinking is *prudent* thinking. That which is prudent is judged from a ground of shared experience to yield the best, most socially acceptable outcome. Calculation of the consequences is important to prudent decisions. Emotion can be useful for enhancing thoughtfulness as to consequences, for improving decision making and for communicating clearly.

Anger in decision making again illustrates the point. It does not necessarily impair decision making and, in fact, may even improve it as in the case of John Kennedy and the Cuban Missile crisis. A psychological study provocatively titled "Thinking Straight While Seeing Red" examined anger and ability to process information analytically.[4] College student research subjects were cleverly insulted (some were, some weren't, in a standard control group design), then, in a seemingly unrelated activity, asked to evaluate recommendations for improving students' investment habits. Angry decision makers were found to think more analytically than others about issues that were of relevance to them. Their decisions had an edge that produced sharper focus in selecting relevant information. As it did with the Cuban missile crisis, anger evoked enhanced clarity of thinking. A related psychological research study titled "Negative Emotion Enhances Memory Accuracy" found that memories formed under conditions of negative emotion are more vividly recalled and are remembered in greater detail. Anger can clarify and focus awareness. Too much rationality may render thinking sterile and unfeeling. Some anger, disciplined to bring clarity, can improve rational thinking.[5]

Feeling Is Physically Real

Anger is only one of the basic human emotions. Thinking may be variously influenced by emotions other than anger. Emotions like fear, sadness, disgust, surprise, joy or love can distort thinking and influence the quality of decision making. As a matter of common observation most people would agree that love overrides "rational" thought. No amount of argument can dissuade the lovesick swain from his object of affection. Unless offset by earlier experience or training, feelings of fear, sadness, disgust, and surprise may evoke defensive response. The attendant adrenaline rush will overcome reasoned response unless self-discipline is quickly invoked. Practice at self-control is needed to respond rationally to the startle of surprise, the queasiness of disgust or even the tears of joy. Most emotions arouse energy and sharpen mental focus. The reaction chosen is likely to be that which is best practiced or trained. Absence of self awareness of how words shape action in the face of emotion produces inappropriate overreaction. Disciplined emotions are essential to good thinking.

Those human emotions that are wired into the nervous system, fear, surprise, disgust, anger, sadness, joy and love, have special relevance to language and the personal reality map. The words that designate them are perhaps the truest examples of mental reality. There is innate honesty in their expression. Actors and actresses cannot realistically express them without also inducing the underlying muscular and nervous system processes. Real anger, fear or love is fully felt at the gut level. The adrenalin must flow and the body must be prepared for them to have authenticity.

Emotions felt are real. Feeling is expressed by the body, and especially the face. Feelings are difficult to fake. Feelings expressed physically through tears, laughter or anger are almost always accepted and believed. Language used to describe emotional experience possesses a special lack of ambiguity and clarity. The meaning of words for emotion is always clear. There is no confusion about the quality of feeling that attends words like anger, disgust, fear, sadness, surprise, joy and love. Each of these emotions is distinct and must be described by synonyms that have no other meaning. There can be no confusion about which emotion is being described. In language, this is quite unusual. Examples of the semantic prime for feeling and its synonyms are offered here.

Primary Descriptor	Synonyms
Anger	Annoyance, Fury, Rage
Disgust	Revulsion, Repugnance
Fear	Terror, Dread
Sadness	Grief, Sorrow
Surprise	Shock, Astonishment
Joy	Delight, Elation
Love	Affection, Adoration

In language and as expressed through words, emotions are the most naturally and fully shared human reality because emotions are directly, physically experienced. Words that describe (make reference to) external things that are perceived through the five senses are less direct, but because they are accessed through the senses, they evoke only a less intense quality of reality. Emotions felt and things sensed as physical phenomena are experientially real. Everything else is an idea.

Emotions, sensations, ideas in that order describe the natural hierarchy of word classes. Those highest on the scale describe feelings. At the next level are those that describe sensed things. Last are those that stand for essences and abstract ideas. Reason and rationality were invented to deal with ideas, the least real of the language lexicon. Words for feelings and perceptions stand on their own merits.

Ideas, words that have no natural, neurological connection with feeling and sense, nonetheless easily become permeated with emotional baggage. The emotional loading of ideas is conditional and free floating. That quality contrasts with the experienced reality of innate emotions like love or sadness versus that of the perceived world of trees and clouds. Words like government, freedom, independence, labor union, patriotism and loyalty gather emotional overlay only through association. The emotional meaning of most such words is negative or positive, good or bad, aversive or desirable as personal experience has attached emotion to them. Unlike innate, felt emotions, there need be little or no consistency in the emotional content assigned to a given idea from one person to another. Ideas loaded with emotion can become renegade words that hijack reason completely. Abstract ideas that catch fire with emotion are an out of control train. Unlike words for emotions themselves, the emotional meaning of ideas is acquired entirely through association. It can be learned or unlearned. The behaviors that ideas evoke can be wildly inconsistent and destructive.

Over time, good ideas can become bad ideas and vice versa. Social conformity and conditioned association put the emotion into those ideas. The emotion expressed in words used by those liked and respected will be intuited and accepted. Some emotion will come through the process of Pavlovian (psychological) conditioning, whereby feelings become unconsciously and intuitively associated with ideas. Unique emotional associations with ideational words will arise out of personal experience, random rewards and punishments, conditions of comfort or discomfort. Good and bad are inadvertently added to the meaning of ideas. Affective association attaches easily to ideational words. Wars are fought over ideas. Good and bad are generalized as abstract principles and beliefs in words. Words define moral and immoral qualities. Words spawn belief. Fervent belief drives behavior to extreme ends. That is truly irrational.

Beliefs are necessary to civilized discourse and human adjustment. They can come in a variety of forms. When belief is invested in abstract intangibles that describe social morality and immortality it is called religion. When the belief is called natural law and is justified through thoughtful argument and demonstration, the authority is called Science. "Good health requires a balanced diet." "Viruses cause disease." "Lightning is the result of violent updrafts of moist air." "Water freezes at zero degrees Centigrade." These causal assertions are supported by scientific demonstration. They are no less beliefs for those who have never participated in their demonstration.

Belief is established by authority or demonstration, often both together. Emotions can be stirred by the words of a passionate evangelist or an enthusiastic teacher. Social movements are energized by ideals of justice and freedom. The emotions that saturate ideas encode joy, misery, anger, hope in them. Disentangling ideational words from feelings is difficult because the association becomes intuitively set. To strip those words back down to their referential or rational core requires that those feelings associated be identified and examined. That can be very difficult. Evaluations firmly linked to words in the mental map can have stronger meaning than words themselves.

The fact of emotion attached to words cannot be denied. Emotional feelings activate bodily processes. The rich overlay of feeling content that is loaded onto most words can overwhelm their purely referentially symbolic or defined meaning of a word. The effort to be reasonable, rational, and uninfluenced by emotion is made futile. To regain mastery over word meaning, it would be best to be prudent and to sort through the words that describe one's threats and opportunities with concern for the imbedded values and consequences that are identifiable.

Language can never be fully stripped of emotion. It would be foolish to try. Feelings are a part of experienced reality for everyone. Reasonableness is nice but has its limitations. Sensation is gut level reality that everyone understands and appreciates. Emotion is the real driver of human action. To be a functionally rational person one must cultivate skill in identifying the emotional loading of words so they can be dealt with from a ground of considered choice.

11. Loaded Words: Hot and Cool Language

Words in a strict physical sense are no more than sound patterns that have become associated in the mind with objects, events and feelings. Calls for rationality and reasonableness in argument presume that through rational use of words any feeling associated with them can be muted or stripped away. Aside from a certain sterility that might introduce, it may be difficult or impossible to do. Emotion is a primary, visceral experience. The emotional loading that words acquire easily becomes the greater and more stubborn part of their meaning that is firmly and obstinately imbedded into the mental map at a very early age.

Emotional language is exciting and colorful, but it can set communication on a course that cannot be easily controlled or changed. Once spoken, the feeling content cannot easily be muted because the words are so intensely permeated with emotional tone. Emotionally loaded words don't function just as stand-ins for sensory objects, events or ideas. They are permeated with feelings of good and bad that become firmly attached. The feeling content is more than just a secondary association. It is a description of causation and outcome. It communicates conditions that offer penalty or reward. It cues to places of hurt or happiness. It is a map of the social world, an ultimate reality in its own right and a fundamental contributor to an individual's sense of social stability. It should be no surprise that language is such an immensely pervasive part of social dealings. Initiating, redirecting, stopping, shaping behavior in others is most efficiently and effectively brought about through well-chosen words. Words can and do drive the throngs of humans who surge here and there in search of safety, satisfaction, self-expression.

Not all emotional expression can be at maximum feeling intensity. Full intensity pulls up words that express it fully.

Unemotional communication finds other, less intense words. Differential degrees of emotional intensity become attached to different words. Some are hot, some are cool. The youth culture injunction to *stay cool* is not about temperature, it is reference to and recognition of the variable quality of emotions that characterize social word play. Words can be hot, they can be heated, they can be tepid, they can be cool. The feelings associated can become the largest part of a word's meaning.

Rational, reasonable thinking is all about consciously choosing the appropriate words for the social setting. For that choice to be made there must be practice in choice of words at different degrees of emotional loading. Those words that come quick to mind in moments of passion tend to be the hotter ones. Practice in the selection of cool words in heated conversation gives rational choice and control. It is a skill that confers the power to set the tone and deescalate emotional exchange when it gets too hot.

It is instructive to examine alternative ways an event can be described in words that are either loaded with heated emotion or toned down to somewhere nearer their descriptive meaning. Much language works on parallel levels of emotional loading, ranging from incendiary to descriptively bland. Words like *heavenly,* or *fantastic* are loaded for joy or love. They are pushed far beyond the referential meanings of sky or something that is made-up or unreal. Words like *good* and *nice* do the same job without the emotional hype. Words like *faulty* or *polluted* have acquired meaning well beyond their dictionary definitions of flaw, discontinuity or the mere discharge of physical waste. They describe poor character and illegal waste disposal. They conflate to create incendiary words.

Alternative words without excess emotional loading but with similar or same meaning can almost always be found and used to change the emotional level of communication. The availability of alternative, emotionally cool words that possess approximately parallel meaning can mute the emotional tone of almost any conversation. Emotionally muted words inserted into a setting that could become intense can work wonders for improving feelings and relationships.

Many moods and actions can be described alternatively by words that load emotionally on a scale from *very heated* to *quite cool.* The relative weight and intensity of the heat generated can be thought of as an irregular inflection on a common base. Inflection is a ranking of word by case, tense, gender of mood. The suggested inflections that follow make reference to emotional qualities of personal mood and action. They are examples of how words can describe the same thing, yet range significantly from high to low in their emotional loading.

Clear, direct communication in the form of argument or debate can be pointed and penetrating. The words used to argue can be experienced as *attack, confrontation* or *discussion* depending on the sentiments of the participants. Attack carries a high level of emotional loading even though the actual conversation might be graded in tone from angrily aggressive to energetically spirited, to crisp and sharp. What makes any of these qualities an *attack* is the perception of a beholder. Experiencing oneself to be under attack generates its own social script. It starts with the assumption that there is intent to do harm that demands counter attack. It may generate an image of bruised eyes and flowing blood. Still, it need not imply physical assault and is frequently used to describe only very intense verbal exchange. There are alternative terms that can reasonably be used to describe the same quality of exchange without escalating the intensity of the conversation. *Confrontation* can describe an energetic word exchange in a somewhat less volatile way, allowing it to proceed on a less intense level. Mentally converting a spirited communication into a *discussion* unloads the emotional content substantially, maybe even entirely, leaving only the bare social communicative exchange. Depending on the mental and emotional set of the participants and observers, each of these words could be used by different observers to describe the same argument. Choice of emotional level gives parties to the event some latitude in electing the degree of emotional loading injected into conversation. Many seeming attacks and most confrontations can be deescalated to the level of discussion if words are chosen carefully. Discussion, in like manner, will be escalated to confrontation or attack when emotion takes over. Parallel language permits the exchange to be hot or cool depending on the emotional temper of the participants.

The care with which words are chosen can influence the level of accuracy or inaccuracy perceived. A statement may be seen as a *lie,* as *dissembling* or as an *error of fact* depending on how the hearer chooses to interpret it. An intentional lie is assertion of untruth as if it were full truth. Judging someone a liar is justification for discrediting the other's word and accepting nothing said as truth. It is a major social cue that says no one should pay heed to the dishonest person's words. The choice of words to characterize the supposed *lie* will often depend on one's judgment of the story teller's motives. That judgment will shape the ensuing quality of relationship. Worst-case presumption of lying will likely be taken as insult or ill-will, setting the exchange on the maximally combative path. To *dissemble* suggests an intentional inaccuracy in another's words introduced to advance a purpose that need not necessarily be gross or mean spirited. *Dissembling* is talking around an issue in an attempt to distort or conceal a harsh or inconvenient truth. It lacks the emotional impact of lying and can be used to describe the observed behavior in cooler terms. It may sometimes even express admiration for skill at verbal evasion. *Dissembling* is an issue of motive and intent. The emotional intensity is dialed down significantly when the cooler word *inaccurate* is chosen for the challenge. The most generous description of a perceived wrong assertion would simply be to say that it is an *error of fact.* There is often so much ambiguity inherent in sensory reality that almost any report of events observed can be challenged for unintended distortion. An error of fact might arise out of bad data, mistaken interpretation or recall of an event, or overzealous revision of information. It is not necessarily an indictment of personal character. For a wide variety of argumentative exchanges, any one of these descriptors might fit just as well. Consistently choosing the hottest is a choice for maximum conflict.

Relative dominance in social relationships is subject to a range of descriptions that can range from *arrogant* on to *assertive,* to *self-confident* or *self-assured. Arrogance* describes someone who is seen as either overbearing or not sufficiently respectful. It implies superior airs and may be reaction to what is seen as self-praise. It will likely be chosen as the descriptor by one who feels intentionally "put down" or diminished in social status by another's manner of speech. Someone who is seen as *assertive* has likely taken a clear position in an argument or on an issue. The more colloquial but widely used term pushy may soften the description just enough to be used as polite objection to perceived domination. "You're getting a little pushy, Jill", says "back off a little". The person described as *self-assured* is one whose dominance is perceived to be confident or competent for the situation. Description of dominance in social exchange is almost fully unloaded of feeling content if words like *self-confident* or *self-assured* are used to describe it. Clearly it is the perception that counts. One who lacks self-confidence can easily see any self assurance of another as *arrogance.* The eye of the beholder rules. These emotionally commutative words might be laconically expressed as the irregular inflection of the adjective *dominating and be conjugated thus:* "I am self assured, you are assertive, he/she is arrogant."

Personal causality has it own set of irregular inflections. Ascribing *fault* or *blame* to someone points a reproachful finger and suggests personal moral failure. Assigning *responsibility* implies an obligation to perform properly and puts a spotlight on action. Responsibility suggests a relatively formal social relationship in which failure to perform requires some form of response. Assigning *credit* or *ownership for* an action allows a still cooler, more neutral tone to be introduced to the notion of responsibility.

An event involving intervention of an outsider in someone's activities can be described as *meddling* or as *assisting* depending on interpretation of the would-be helper's motives. Meddling is unwarranted or mistaken intrusion, whereas assistance is desirable or useful support. Interpretation of intent is central to choosing between help and meddling. The degree of meddlesomeness revolves around about the meddler's purposes and intentions. Assistance given without strings attached is not meddling.

Few words cut quite as deeply as *stupid*. It is a hot term that suggests totality of ineptness wrapped in bad judgment and uncaring. Anger frequently accompanies the charge of stupidity. It is spit out for emphasis as much as said. For someone to be stupid says they have trouble managing their actions and lives. It suggests that the person can be fooled, manipulated, induced to perform inappropriate actions and otherwise made to dance like a marionette on strings. There are useful alternatives that have far less emotional loading like *inept, awkward* or *unskilled*. *Inept* dials it down, implying lack of knowledge or skill, perhaps without fault, perhaps for not trying. *Awkward* suggests absence of sufficient practice or experience. *Unskilled* offers simple description of ability that may be overcome with effort.

Some contemporary hot words come pre-loaded with emotional freight, positive or negative. *Natural* is not just something from nature, it is everything good, healthy, eco-friendly, virtuous. *Contamination* is the ultimate in sickness and death, a silent creeping villain that those without conscience inflict on the unwary world. *Crisis* is not just a major choice-point, it is Armageddon, Apocalypse Now and Nuclear Winter. *Dreams* are perfection of life and desire. Nightmares are Hell. A Guarantee does not merely confer certain legal rights, it wipes out all risk. *Smart* is the ultimate in good judgment and taste. *Safety* is the absolute requirement in all products, services and schools. There is little room for quiet non-judgmental discussion in the presence of these words.

Some words are employed to inflame, intimidate and manipulate others. Pejorative racial labels are clear put-downs and discounters. These are self-esteem hooks. Certain crude four letter words are general purpose shock dispensers. When freely interspersed in conversation, they operate as attention grabbers. They are offensive more for their intrusion on attention than for their literal meaning. They invite anger and conflict. They get or even demand attention. Indeed, chronic use of emotionally loaded words can arise mostly out of need for attention and acknowledgement from others.

Angry, upset, vindictive feelings are clearly expressed through hot words. They are sometimes the earliest words in children's vocabularies, largely because they yield such interesting, strong reactions from adults. The habit of expressing emotion through such words is easily established. Practiced as an habitual expression, emotionally hot words ride on whatever wave of emotion is felt at the moment. When driven by emotion alone, they can become transparent expression of inner emotional turmoil. People who cannot discipline their feelings enough to carry on cool conversations are a pain. A continuous gush of emotion is not just uncomfortable, it is exhausting and wearing. It is no pleasure to watch the ugly thrashing of an undisciplined or tortured mind as it fires out emotion laden words.

The best defense against the confusion of overheated language can be to recognize the intent and ignore excess emotional expression. One must choose to buy into the game before emotionally loaded words become a hook. Diminished self-confidence or self-esteem, anger close to the surface or fear conditioned by past use of a word sets in place the habit of reaction to hot words. Self assurance and cool response unloads the wellsprings of emotional word play. Those emotional transactions that are repeated over a span of time can become well developed social scripts with psychoneurotic qualities called *social games*. They are described in scripted detail in Eric Berne's classic pop psychology book *Games People Play*.[1] Berne's message is that with training and awareness, the emotional words that initiate and drive these games can be recognized and avoided. Emotionally loaded words initiate the game script. As long as they can set off the game, words that hook emotions will be used liberally. One must fully join the game in order to be influenced by them. Refusal to be drawn in kills the game.

Manipulation with games of hot words is a perversion of language. There is no intent or willingness on the part of the manipulator to reveal personal feelings or improve relationships. Words are used solely as tools of emotional assault when manipulation is the object. Words have no meaning beyond generating response from the target person. Used as gambits as in psychological games, words are mere instruments. The reality map of a manipulator is a description of the fears, yearnings and aspirations of people. It is put together on a foundation of personal fears, yearnings and aspirations that are kept hidden. Words themselves are the manipulator's end reality. They communicate images, feelings and purposes designed to drive the sought behavior. They are the tools of troubled minds, con artists and manipulators. One who recognizes their malignant use need not play the game.

Effective communication without manipulation requires command of parallel language that emphasizes generosity of judgment and cool description of social events. Emotionally loaded words can be replaced with alternatives that describe intense exchanges dispassionately, or at least less passionately, so that a coolly rational and descriptive alternative language can be employed. Emotion will always be a part of social exchange. Feeling content enriches language. Cultivating the use of cool words permits excessive feeling tone to be avoided so that misunderstanding and ill feeling in social exchange can be avoided.

12. Inventions of the Mind

Michael Gazziniga, Roger Sperry's lab assistant in split brain research, concludes from his research experience that the mind is an "interpreter" that cleverly tenders made-up stories to explain events that are beyond its grasp. In his view, the mind cannot help itself but offer up in words the most plausible story it can conceive to rationalize events in play. It is a perspective that unflinchingly debunks the accuracy of unaided, naive human observation. It suggests that much of what we take to be facts may actually be convenient inventions of the mind. There is much evidence from well investigated real world events to support that conclusion.

Most theorizing of how the world works is shared common sense. A naïve, common sense grasp of reality works fairly well, even when distorted in small ways. The average human carries around a word model of how everything works -- or should work. To the extent that ongoing experience fits the model there will be very little question or confusion about what is happening. Experience that comes up against gaps in the model may go unnoticed or may be creatively structured as a best fit to available past experience. The process of invention is seldom challenged when it occurs. Words are found that fit the situation and are accepted as adequate explanation. For the most part, individuals see, hear, smell and otherwise sense what they have words to describe. If an event cannot be instantly identified and explained in words, whatever short term memory there is of the event quickly fades to a crude visualized scene. Sensory details that can not be put in words are lost. The explanation is the event and becomes its memory as well.

Phenomenal reality always seems simpler than it is and is accepted at full face value. For ordinary situations, a quick comparison with the perceptions of others privy to the event is enough to clarify the small uncertainties. Crisis can jumble it all. Events can come in a rush. A comprehensive reconstruction after the fact can be costly in energy and time. If there is upset or pain from the resulting confusion it is yet more difficult. Only if there is real importance attached, like accidental injury or criminal assault, will serious effort at clarity be undertaken. Sometimes, though, an event is so important that the full resources of society are brought to bear in its investigation. When that happens, the full extent of potential for confusion in grasp of what has happened becomes apparent. Such an event was the assassination of President John F. Kennedy.[1]

Around noon on September 22, 1963, as the presidential motorcade passed through Dealey Plaza in Dallas, Texas, gun shots were heard. President John F. Kennedy fell across the seat toward the floor of his open limousine. It appeared that he had been shot. Bedlam ensued.

Because of the echo chamber acoustics of the plaza, most bystanders were unable to locate the source of the shots. A few, who possessed either special training, relevant experience or propitious positioning, were able to fix where the gunfire had come from. Two workers on the floor immediately below the sniper's nest heard the shots directly above and the sound of the rifle's bolt action during firing. Another witness, a police officer and active game hunter, recognized the sound of fire from a high-powered rifle. He observed a flock of pigeons fly off the roof of the building 200 feet ahead and raced his motorcycle to the front steps of the Texas School Book Repository. On entry, quite remarkably, he encountered Lee Harvey Oswald, later identified as the shooter, and asked the building manager if Oswald worked in the building. With confirmation of Oswald's legitimate status on premises, the officer, Marrion Baker, let Oswald pass and began a search of the building. Forty-five minutes later, the improvised sniper's nest, rifle and spent cartridges were found on the sixth floor of the building. For any ordinary shooting event, this would have offered all the evidence necessary to fix guilt and identify the murderer. This was no ordinary event.

Almost immediately, radio, television and newspaper reporters were on the scene interviewing anyone who would talk. Naïve, eyewitness testimony became the first story of the event. By the time reportage of Kennedy's assassination hit the evening news, the source of the gunfire had been described as in front of the limo as well as behind it, and the number of shots was variously claimed to have been from one to eight. Suspicious persons were reported all about the Plaza, some with handguns. A secret service agent was seen rising up in the presidential limousine with a machine gun. Taken as a whole, the testimony gathered by the media on September 22, 1963 would graphically describe the willingness of people to describe an event in detail when they have only the barest notion as to what had happened. Sense was made of the event when there was no sense to it at all.

Based on supposition blended with some of this nonsense, much of the nation, perhaps of the world, "knew" who had to be responsible for this awful thing. The quickest to fix blame for the assassination were those who immediately believed the shooting to have been initiated by the radical political right, orchestrated by an organization like the John Birch Society. Discovery soon after that a communist sympathizer was the shooter demolished that supposition. As for others, there was no shortage of certain bad guys. Communist conspiracy was an easy theory. "One of their own" had pulled the trigger. Conspiracy theory of every kind flourished. For many, it was unthinkable that a lone, personally troubled young man could plan and commit such an atrocity. Lyndon Johnson, Vice President in the morning, President at sundown, must certainly have been a conspirator in the murder. For some, it was entirely logical that the Mafia had to be involved. The FBI and the CIA were accused of complicity. As those agencies scurried to protect bureaucratic turf and reputation they became easy targets of suspicion. An actual eyewitness who, from beneath, watched Oswald firing the rifle believed he was seeing an assassination conspiracy unfold and feared for his life if he revealed his account of it to anyone. The easy conclusion for him and others was that "they" were shooting at the President of the United States. There was, indeed, every possibility that the event was cosmic. In the event that the Soviet Union or Cuba was involved, there might be call for full military response. The darkest possibilities for grand conspiracy were real from the moment of the assassination.

Interviewing the vast number of witnesses to evaluate evidence fully would take the better part of a year. The FBI's investigation alone was enormous, comprising over 25,000 interviews and 2,300 investigative reports. The job of sorting out the facts, evaluating witnesses and arriving at reasoned judgments was assigned to a "blue-ribbon" panel headed by the Chief Justice of the Supreme Court, Earl Warren. The final report was published almost one year after the assassination. That left a lot of open space for speculation. Not surprisingly a mix of theories had become items of faith by the time the Warren report was published. Its conclusion that Oswald was a lone assassin was rejected by many. Controversy continues to the present day. The most significant summary of the Kennedy assassination is a 1,664 page prosecutorial tome titled *Reclaiming History: The Assassination of President John F. Kennedy,* by Vincent Bugliosi. His conclusion was the same as that of the Warren Commission.

The evidence on which Bugliosi's and the Commission's conclusion was based is openly available to the public and has been summarized in other books and documentaries. As a body of evidence, it is as complete a record as was ever assembled of how perceptual distortion and error emerges in the face of a frighteningly dramatic event. The manner in which the word map at hand produces either accurate or spurious understanding is revealed. The way that reports of some witnesses changed and evolved with time go further to show how the words used to describe can become the remembered reality. Language provides ready made causal chains (who's to blame, why did it happen!) as well as words that shape, sharpen and amend memory.

Inventing and revising reality is so commonplace that it regularly goes unnoticed. The mind searches its memory stores for plausible explanation and spins it out. Most simply seize the first plausible explanation that comes to mind and take it as truth. That explanation then becomes the invented memory.

A quick explanation can be defense against frightening, hard reality or self-indictment. Personal interest and prejudice are often served by the explanation chosen. The reputation of the FBI, for instance, was under the spotlight with the investigation of John Kennedy's assassination. The agency had an open file on Lee Harvey Oswald detailing the record of its most recent investigation. If Oswald had been a part of any conspiracy the bureau's image would take a major hit for not having uncovered it. J. Edgar Hoover, the agency's autocratic head, was convinced that there could have been no conspiracy. It was a faith that was in part driven by self-interest. That was all too apparent to many. The Warren Commission had no choice but to rely on the FBI for the greatest part of its field investigation. There was doubt even within the commission over whether or not the FBI was fully committed to find the truth, wherever it might lie. Always secretive and uncooperative with other government agencies, Hoover's FBI may have been reluctant to share embarrassing information with the Commission. It was clear that the agency urgently wanted Oswald quickly identified as the lone assassin so the case would be closed. The message this behavior sent could be read that the FBI had embarrassing knowledge it did not want others to know of. For some this was firm evidence of the FBI's complicity in conspiracy. Hoover's conviction of Oswald's solo guilt was shaped by his self-interest. His behavior shaped the convictions of conspiracy theorists who were convinced Oswald could not have acted alone.

Reality invention of this nature goes on at multiple levels. Families, communities, ethnic groups, as well as public or private institutions all participate in the game of public image construction and revision. For some, it is merely putting the best foot forward, literally, an exercise in impression management.

For others, it may be cover-up or putting a mask on a less than attractive reality. In institutionalized form, it is called public relations. For politicians it can be a game of survival that demands constant posturing and damage control. For CEOs of publicly traded firms, it can mean creative accounting that fashions an image of continuing growth and profitability. For the average individual it can be as simple as the effort to enhance and maintain self-respect.

Invention of fictitious capabilities and events can arise out of unwillingness to be sensible and practical when calculating the possibilities. A head on assault against unfavorable odds may be heroic or foolhardy. Like Pickett's disastrous charge in the battle of Gettysburg, it arises out of invented, unrealistic assessment of capability. Making choices and taking risks based on invented reality is certain to end badly. The dramatic rise and fall of Houston's Enron Corporation illustrates how a wholly invented vision of corporate greatness produced a badly flawed institutional identity that ultimately dashed the financial dreams of thousands.[2]

Like many current day companies, Enron was assembled through merger of existing, undistinguished middle-sized companies. The founding vision was to transcend the humble beginnings of these companies and move quickly onto the world economic stage. The nominal founder of Enron was Ken Lay, a Ph.D. economist with a background of high-level service in the Federal Power Commission. Ken was a classic nice guy boss who employed tough lieutenants to do the dirty work. The core of Enron was built upon owned natural gas pipelines that stretched throughout the US and enjoyed a limited international presence as well. With natural gas as a business base, becoming an international growth company had to be a very long stretch.

Lay was nonetheless out to dazzle Wall Street by seizing control of the world of energy management. The first imperative of the bottom-line dazzle game is to grow, not just big, but consistently. Unfortunately for Enron and Ken Lay, natural gas pipeline management is not your usual growth industry. Natural gas prices, like those of other energy sources, are volatile. Initially, the generation of large profits, the standard Wall Street indicator of fast growth, was not found in the price-volatile natural gas business but from oil futures trading. Enron's small, energy contract trading shop in Valhalla, New York was the secret of its reported profit growth. This almost incidental business center was generating a majority of the new company's profits, quarter by quarter, millions upon millions with its speculation in oil futures contracts. Though such trading, realistically, involves substantial risk, Ken didn't care as long as the hefty profits continued to flow in. Valhalla traders operated under few restraints. Risky deals meant that some trades had to be on the losing end. Discovery of secret bank accounts maintained by the chief of the trading operation set off danger signals. Traders, it was found, had bet the wrong position in the market and the losses incurred threatened to bankrupt the entire company. If an experienced trader on Ken's staff had not stepped in to bluff through the crisis, this could have been an early end of his dream of world energy market domination.

The lesson of this early near-death experience, though, seems to have been lost on Ken Lay and his more aggressive lieutenants. Quarter by quarter profit increases continued to be the unquestioned imperative of management, despite the unsuitability of the natural gas business to that kind of financial performance. Innovation was deemed necessary to maintain the appearance of continuous growth that drives stock price. Jeff Skilling, a Harvard MBA and managing director of McKinsey and Company's Houston consulting office, came forward with fresh strategies. He proposed to use accounting practices as the lever. Risk inherent in the volatile pricing of natural gas would be offset by posting the full value of profits from long-term gas delivery contracts immediately on execution of a contract. This is called "mark to market" accounting. It pretends that all the profits from future years' billings on a new contract are already in the bank. There is no real money, only numbers in some accounts. It was a dangerous ploy. For a time, though, it worked, and for his cleverness, Skilling was appointed president of the company.

From this position he set in motion a series of equally innovative (and unrealistic) ideas. Among them was the practice of hiding enormous amounts of debt in fictitious business entities that were not included on Enron's balance sheet. Heavy indebtedness for a company, as for an individual, signals that what could be profit margins may actually be interest due to a lender. Hiding the debt inflates the appearance of profit. Though these accounting practices might not be judged strictly illegal, they were seriously misleading to investors and stockholders.

Some actual fraud was committed. Skilling invited Wall Street analysts to Houston to "see for themselves" the success of a newly launched trading operation. He set up a phony trading room where scores of employees and temps pretended to execute energy trades by phone and computer. Analysts were impressed and fooled. Skilling felt justified using the sham because he saw it as a preview of the great success that would come later. A bright guy type who solved every problem with words, Skilling apparently saw no difference between a hoped-for future and a fake now.

Large scale trading success was actually achieved by Enron in the electric power market. Real traders who gamed the newly deregulated California market brought the state to its knees with artificially inflated energy costs. Tens of millions in profits from this trading scheme that fed the profit line of Enron also brought unwanted scrutiny to its accounting and financial practices. Media and government investigators went after the company to expose their unethical practices and indict officers. As this controversy broiled around it Enron suddenly collapsed from the simplest of business errors. Ensnared in its own fantasy of profitability, Enron management lost control of cash flow and ran out of money to pay its debts and bills. It went bankrupt!

Enron was only one of several major companies in the late nineteen nineties that seriously strayed from good business practices and went straight into the criminal courts. This was in many ways an era of excess. Brilliant, hot-shot managers like Skilling were confident they could get by with almost anything as long as it was dressed up in the right language. Words were more important, even taken to be more powerful, than business performance. Consistently overstating the benefits of the product to make the sale is the salesman's disease. It can lead to a disaster.

If truth be told, it's likely that a great majority of people invent alternative realities when there is no one to challenge the enhancement. The actions of Lay and Skilling were not so much enhancements as they were visions that lacked reality anchors. Skilling, the master of word play, was a bright guy consultant on the staff of the prestigious consulting firm, McKinsey and Company, where intellect and idea ruled supreme. He was the nearest thing to a pure idea person. As long as the quarterly crisis of making the specified sales and profit numbers could be overcome, all was well. The insufficiency of cash flow to justify investment and the ever mounting mass of debt could be ignored as long as Wall Street was not disappointed. Equally surprising was the willingness of respected, successful Wall Street securities analysts and financiers to accept the soundness of trading-based profits despite their own hard experience in the trading world. A shared belief in the doctrine of free markets and deregulation of energy prices may have provided an intellectual bond that overcame the deserved skepticism. Toward the end, even as problems were coming apparent, Lay and Skilling continued to articulate their vision of Enron's future as the *world's greatest company.* That was not vision, it was wholly invented fantasy.

One might justify the visionary policies and actions of Enron Management as a strategy that could yield self-fulfillment. Childhood fantasies of becoming a physician or astronaut *can* be fulfilled if pursued realistically. Realization of impossible dreams occurs. Even heroic failure may be seen worth the effort. But the reach must be possible. The Enron vision was wholly made-up. It is hard to label the Enron smart guys as heroic. Both were convicted of fraud. Skilling was imprisoned, Lay died before he could be sentenced. The destruction left in the wake of Enron's collapse devastated many lives other than just Lay's and Skilling's.

Much mental invention has potential for productivity. The propensity of the mind to invent explanations for how the universe works, as well as to illuminate its own workings, is illustrated by the wealth of scientific theory produced. Much of natural theory seems solidly founded, though there is ongoing debate over the ultimate laws of physics. In matters of the social sciences, theory is continuously under development and revision. Some corners of artfully invented social theory do seem driven by self-interest than settled science. The social science of economics offers an impelling example of propensity to inventiveness. No theory is more vulnerable to self-interested grand design than is economics.

Economists presume to solve issues of wealth. They labor to explain how wealth is produced, used and distributed. They invent realities that demonstrate how monetary and trading systems work. In their application of supply and demand theory, for instance, some economists favor supply-side theory as the more reliable engine of economic growth. This approach calls for tax reduction measures and other incentives that favor producers so that the supply of product or service will grow. The opposing theory favors stimulation of increased consumer demand with higher real wages and discretionary income as the surer way to promote economic growth. Tax policies and incentives that favor consumers are expected to do the better job of driving growth. Economic benefits flow in very different directions depending on which side of supply and demand is enacted into tax policy. The inevitable "either-or" quality of the central political decisions favored creates its own reality. Demonstrating the real superiority of one or the other is difficult, probably futile. Both points of view reflect hopes and expectations of their respective theorists and their self-interested constituencies.

The biggest of the either/or economic options is communism versus capitalism. Marxist economics and socialism invented a whole new world of reality based on words alone. Marxism calls for the radical redistribution of ownership and economic wealth controlled by the State. Capitalism is a dominantly pragmatic system of private ownership wherein the increase of general prosperity justifies considerable inequity in wealth distribution. Marxist economics establishes the principle of social equity as primary, seeking prosperity through government management of capital resources. Capitalism employs the self-interest of ownership to offset the risks of decisions made by centralized government planners.

Soviet Russia became a major reality test of Marxian economic theory. The Union of Soviet Socialist Republics was created in 1918 by Bolshevik revolutionaries on faith that communism is a superior economic and social system. Soviet Russia came into being with the overthrow of the incompetent and self-absorbed Romanov ruler, Tzar Nicholas. For a nation of serfs who historically knew only oppression and poverty, any reality had to look superior to what they knew. The utopian dream of a government of equals was impelling. According to Marxist theory, government would wither away after the proletariat revolution. Those who labored would themselves regulate their political and economic lives. The new order began with extermination of the bourgeoisie, those who resented loss of former economic privilege and ownership. Dissidents and non-believers were summarily executed. The dream began in a nightmare. It was not an auspicious start.

Government did not disappear as Marx said it would. A new elite of communist party apparatchiks emerged. Party membership in good standing was based on a blend of reputation in past military battles, strictness of belief in Marxist doctrine, and personal political loyalties within the party. Measures of worthiness were entirely subjective, untested against the hard practicalities of real prosperity or popular democratic elections. Leaders were subject to political removal by powers from above in the hierarchy, not from below as in electoral politics. The abstracted words of Karl Marx were the sole anchor of Communist reality. Without pragmatic test, they were insufficient. A maverick named Yeltsin huffed and puffed and blew the government down with another blast of rhetoric. The Russian economy was too weak to withstand even the smallest storm of words.

There are those who do not yet accept the fall of Russian communism as a final test of Marxian economic theory. There are bound to be great risks in an experiment so grand in scope and radical in vision. Whether or not the invented vision of a workers' paradise has any chance of success may never be fully tested. The real world is much too complex to be adequately described by either communist or capitalist economic theories. They are grand abstractions that float above sensory reality.

Much of what is accepted as knowledge and wisdom is invented reality. Attempting to assign causality to crimes lends to invented reality. Certainly, it is a fascinating exercise to attempt untangling the causes of a crime like murder. The practice of forensic investigation as portrayed in crime dramas is a blend of hard science plus experienced intuition and reasoning. The reality of a crime can be reconstructed (sometimes) with these tools. The desired reality in this situation is one that stands up to harsh scrutiny, especially the challenge of a creative defense attorney's alternative scenario. And there is no more hard reality to test competing inventions than a murder.

Criminal forensics is a major form of current day dramatic entertainment. The simulated reality of death and corpses is invested with grim attraction. Police drama captures the puzzle solution process real detectives enact. That process requires reconstruction of violent events from examination of injury and evidential patterns that makes real an event which no one other than the murdered and murderer experienced. Reality is invented in service of justice. The analysis of bodily decomposition under a variety of conditions contributes its own macabre reality. The science behind DNA analysis, fiber comparison, firearms and bullet identification, insect larvae stages, fingerprints and blood spatter have the power to make real that which is hidden in the shadows of small detail. Alternative scenarios about what happened at the moment of death determines guilt and innocence. There is seldom final, complete proof or certainty as to what happened. It is just invention of fact after the fact. Invented reality from police investigation is subject to the same confusion as a presidential assassination.

Courtroom drama is appealing because of the clash of realities it can produce. The object is to make the better case for one or the other conflicting explanations for the set of events and outcomes that constitute the issue on trial. Though murder may represent the higher drama, the more common courtroom controversy comes out of every-day critical events like automobile accidents. Multiple rear end collisions and intersection accidents can be very difficult to sort out for fault and responsibility. Any "between" vehicle in a series of rear end smashes might have come to a stop before being struck and pushed into the car ahead, or may have first collided ahead, then been struck from behind. The extent of liability for damage or injury borne by that "between car" could vary greatly depending on which reality is best supported and argued. Fault for collisions at traffic light controlled intersections can spawn conflicting stories. One car may run the light, another may jump it. When there is a collision each driver invents the explanation that best fits his/her interests. Truck drivers who jackknife may argue they were cut off when the reality was they were inattentive and driving at excessive speed. Drivers who run off the road at night may have been blinded by oncoming traffic or just driving too fast. These can be ambiguous situations that permit considerable range of invention. Significant penalties are incurred for fault in auto accidents. Those penalties urgently drive the generation of plausible alternative scenarios. If the operator of a vehicle cannot come up with a good enough, self-serving accident scenario, a clever attorney may be able to. When making argument for or against guilt or liability, the face of the legal profession is dominantly one of inventing plausible alternative realities for the benefit of judge and jury. For many lawyers, reality invention is a way of life. They are not alone. Invention is everywhere.

Invention of common reality in stories must not be overlooked in this survey. Simulated reality is offered up continuously in the form of movie, television and stage dramas. Much social wisdom is captured in these enacted stories. Roles, social mores and language are taught through them. Quality story design and acting can take on a high degree of reality. Through them, standard behavioral strategies can be modeled by dramatic presentations. Behavior is shaped and changed by storied drama. The power of any good dramatic performance reaches far beyond the uncertainties of the moment. It is teaching with invented reality.

A mind full of words cannot help but generate new symbols. Word invention is creation and recreation. It is science and literature, sense and nonsense, treasure and trash. The fact of literate, technologized, civilized society is that fabricated realities of one stripe or another are almost continuously being generated at all levels. Language is a central tool of creativity. The mental map of one's environment is built with words every bit as much as it is assembled out of neurologically processed sensory inputs. It is part of human coping. Invented reality extends the map into the foggy realm of the unknown. Gross fantasies as well as discovery of new worlds can be the product.

PART THREE:

Words at Work;

Heavy Lifting Required

13. Propaganda; The Language of Manipulation

Propaganda is the nuclear option in word spin. It uses the full intensity of raw emotion to generate its power. Fear, prejudice, anger, all are part of propaganda messages. When the screaming horrors are released from their cage, they must either be joined or hidden from. Emotional bombast becomes the stampeding elephant in the room. No one wants to stop it, everyone gets out of the way. Appeasement will likely be the only response attempted.

The most powerful and irresistible source of propaganda is government. A governmental leader who is determined to impose his mind-map of politics on citizens or the world has awesome resources at his disposal. Any well organized, highly cohesive group can also produce its own propaganda. High minded social movements use propaganda to advance their aims. Hate campaigns are propagandistic. Any effort to shape public opinion with fear, prejudice or anger can reasonably be termed propaganda. One's judgment of the good or evil intent behind any given propaganda effort will determine whether one rides on or gets out of the way of the stampeding elephant.

The term propaganda is a Latin word lifted from the name of the Catholic Church's seventeenth century missionary program, *Propaganda Fide* – Spreading the Faith. In its original use, it was a high-minded concept associated with the spread of religious doctrine. The fervor, even aggressiveness, with which Catholic missionaries may have preached the Church's doctrines to those outside the faith likely contributed to propaganda's association with foreign dogma pressed on a culture.[1]

Propaganda today is firmly associated with war. Propaganda put out by the enemy is instantly seen as distortion. The propaganda of one's own nation connects emotionally even when there is recognizable overstatement. A vast quantity of propaganda was exchanged between the United States and Soviet Russia in the cold war era. The US Central Intelligence Agency supported broadcasts of anti-Soviet propaganda throughout Eastern Europe on Radio Free Europe and Radio Liberty. The US Information Agency operated The Voice of America as the official source of US supplied information about the cold war.[2] Russia focused its propaganda efforts on the great disparity in wealth in capitalist countries and the prejudicial treatment of minority classes in America. Propaganda was broadcast into Cuba throughout the Fidel Castro era by the CIA and Cuban expatriates. In recent times China, North Korea and Al Quaida have all actively promoted propaganda messages to their constituencies and against the United States.

Propaganda is closely associated with Adolph Hitler's 1930s rise to power in Germany. He played on the great humiliation of Germany's surrender and the imposed war reparations after World War I blaming those insults on a variety of scapegoats, particularly Jews. Movies such as Leni Reifenstahl's *Triumph of the Will* were used to stimulate national pride among Germans. Hitler claimed personal credit for restoration of stability of the national economy and spoke to Eastern European and Baltic nations as ethnic brothers who should join with Germany against the world. To foster foreign anti-war sentiment, propaganda directed at British, French and Americans reassured their citizens that Germany did not want war but, rather, their governments were contriving to start it with the Germans. Throughout World War II, Germany sought to demoralize the British and French with radio broadcasts proclaiming German war supremacy and extolling its victories. World War II was a battle of bullets, bombs and, especially, propaganda.[3]

The word *propaganda* acquired its strongly negative English language loading from the very special internal propaganda effort undertaken by the United States in World War I. The First World War saw one of the most intensely organized programs of internal propaganda ever undertaken by any government.

After following a policy of neutrality through the early years of the war, President Woodrow Wilson switched position and took the United States into the war on the side of the Allies. Wilson realistically feared that existing anti-war sentiment would block or impede full-scale war mobilization. To counter anticipated resistance, he established the Committee on Public Information (CPI). The effort was brutally thorough and effective. The postwar backlash to its excesses was appropriately enormous.[4]

Inflaming pro-war sentiment with propaganda was probably necessary to overcome a long history of American pacificism. At the turn of the twentieth century US neutrality toward European nations was a well established national policy. The Socialist Party and Women's peace movements campaigned vigorously against war. Anti-war sentiment was well organized and financed. When war had erupted in August of 1914 Wilson had urged neutrality on the United States. Wilson narrowly won reelection in 1915 on the theme "He kept us out of war". Neutrality prevailed into 1916, despite sinking of the British liner Lusitania with loss of 128 American passengers.

With much of Europe and the middle-east at war with France, Tsarist Russia and Great Britain, there was little chance of maintaining strict neutrality. The German policy of unrestricted submarine warfare on Atlantic shipping was highly unpopular in the United States. Ships and American sailors carrying war material to Britain were continuously at risk from German torpedoes. Remaining neutral was not easy.

The US pro-war propaganda campaign was initially a British import. Great Britain initiated a well orchestrated propaganda campaign urging American support for the war. The British Navy cut Germany's transatlantic cable to the US leaving American newspapers dependent on Britain as the only source of news about the war. Drawing names of 200,000 prominent Americans from the "Who's Who" listing, Britain conducted a covert campaign of mailings concerning the war. Pamphlets and reprints of prominent speeches were sent to the homes of community leaders throughout the US. British propaganda targeted libraries and newspapers with similar mailings. It was a time of written dispatches from "correspondents at the front", and demand for war news was insatiable. Britain provided it, all written from the Allies' point of view. German atrocity stories were especially popular.

Ultimately the tide of opinion shifted toward intervention in the war. Former President Teddy Roosevelt spoke stridently in favor of entry on the side of the Allies. America's financial stake in Allied victory was made substantial with major bank loans and arms sales to Britain and France. In a clumsy move discovered by British intelligence, Germany proposed to Mexico that it declare war against the United States. In return, Germany promised to support Mexico in reclaiming Texas, New Mexico and Arizona as its territories. Overt German hostility exemplified by the Mexico caper was accompanied with intensive submarine warfare in early 1917 that claimed seven US merchant ships. Wilson and the US seemed to have no alternative. Congress declared war in April of 1917.

The Committee on Public Information (CPI) was created for the explicit object of reshaping American public opinion through propaganda. George Creel, a journalist, was named chairman, to be assisted by the Secretaries of State, War and the Navy as CPI board members. The objective of the Committee on Public Information was to mobilize and sustain support for the war through overt use of propaganda.

Creel organized the CPI around the three communication lines of Speech, Publication and Motion Picture propaganda. The speaking division hit upon a highly effective innovation, its "Four Minute Men" speeches. A group of Chicago business men developed the practice as a method for reaching movie audiences in the then standard four minute intermission between moving picture reel changes. Four minute speeches were framed to be given by prominent community leaders. Theater managers were contacted and arrangements made. The idea proved so popular and successful that it became standard throughout the US.[5]

The notion of four minute men served both to exploit the prevailing movie screening format and to evoke the patriotic symbolism of Revolutionary War minute men. In practice it became very powerful and effective communication. The United States of 1917 was a nation in which one in six citizens was a recent immigrant. Speeches in movie houses permitted local citizens to directly address new citizens in their own language. This approach took propaganda into communities where there was the weakest sense of patriotism and delivered it in the person of respected members of the local community.

Speakers were recruited for public speaking skill and were closely supervised. Topical bulletins were published from which speakers could formulate speeches appropriate to their audiences. The four minute time constraint was strictly enforced and speeches were typically delivered in the speakers' own words. A women's division was created to address matinee audiences and young children were competitively recruited to promote Liberty loan drives in the four minute spots. Ultimately, these four-minute speeches were extended into churches, lodges and clubs. Overall, more than 700,000 four-minute speeches were delivered in 5200 communities nationwide.

To support America's involvement in the war, the CPI generated a continuous flow of news releases and war-related information. Pro-war artists created posters that were distributed for display in post offices, public buildings and factories throughout the country.[6] The CPI even had a Bureau of Cartoons. Its large staff of skilled writers and artists created pro war messages for just about every conceivable published media. Millions of war information pamphlets were distributed in the US and around the world. The National School Service published a bulletin that went to schools every month to assist teachers in making their students "messengers for Uncle Sam". A Division of Advertising prepared copy for insertion in space donated by newspapers and magazines. There was a division for promotion of immigrant loyalty and another for communication with factory workers.

Themes of posters and pamphlets included calls for military enlistment, war bond and saving stamps purchase, patriotic teamwork, diligent labor for the war effort, as well as supporting the spread of home gardens, animal husbandry, and volunteer work in support of the war. People were urged to clean their plates of food and cut down on consumption of wheat, meat, sugar and fats. "Food is ammunition" was the rally cry.

Women were important targets in the program to manage the country's food supply. They were urged to conserve food and plant home gardens. Garbage was recycled in some cities. The still active Women's Peace Party was a particular concern to the CPI. A popular song of the Women's Peace Party was "I Didn't Raise My Boy to Be a Soldier". With entry into war, the fear was high that mothers would discourage sons from enlisting if "excessive emotional attachment to their sons" was not rendered unpopular. The CPI undertook a program of actively discrediting women's peace views. One measure was to cleverly recycle "I Didn't Raise My Boy to be a..." inserting "Slacker" in place of "Soldier".

Edward Bok, editor of The Ladies' Home Journal was enlisted by the CPI to publish stories, editorials and advertisements supporting the war effort. Support of enlistment, food conservation and volunteer effort on behalf of the war effort were regular messages. Bok was quoted as saying "The Journal is not a 'slacker' magazine". The covers of its issues were actively slanted toward patriotic messages. Women could not yet vote and were subject to the traditional male view of their place being in the home. The Ladies' Home Journal and other women's magazines of the time were straightforwardly employed to remind them of that place. It was not a reminder that would be passively taken into the post war era.

Movies were a particularly powerful media for stirring patriotic fervor and building an ugly image of the German enemy. Movies were still a new experience and as yet more than a decade away from being "talkies". The product was often little more than filmed vaudeville or theatrical performance. It was nonetheless a highly popular medium from its beginning and exerted great influence on public attitudes toward the war. The CPI Division of Pictures promoted exhibitions of war photos and captured military equipment that toured the country, and produced a weekly movie newsreel called "Official War Review". Hollywood rose eagerly to the opportunity to satisfy the public appetite for war stories. Titles like *"The Prussian Cur", "To Hell with the Kaiser",* and *"The Claws of the Hun"* were greeted enthusiastically by audiences. Thematic "mother-son" and "enlistment decision" movies idealized "good mothers" who sent their sons off to war, while portraying those who discouraged sons from joining the military as emotionally smothering or excessively attached to their sons. Patriotism and duty were vigorously celebrated to offset any lingering pre-war pacifism.

In case any anti-war sentiment did linger, straightforward censorship and intimidation came to the rescue. The Espionage Act, the Trading with the Enemy Act and the Sedition Act gave broad power to the government in dealing with wartime non-conformity. Socialist, pacifist and anti-war mailings were actively suppressed by the Post Office. Offenders were arrested and prosecuted. The Socialist standard-bearer and presidential candidate Eugene V. Debs was imprisoned for three years following his public criticism of the war. Local vigilante groups took the matter further, resorting to active harassment of those deemed insufficiently patriotic. The American Protective League (APL) operated as a shadow police agency, illegally intercepting mail, arresting citizens and harassing suspected "slackers". In every way possible, radical, progressive and liberal groups were targeted. The aim of the propaganda effort was to engineer popular consent for war in the previously anti-war, neutral nation. With the full power of the government behind it, the CPI was a juggernaut. The principles underlying Ashe's yet to come perceptual conformity experiments[7] were intuitively applied to coordinate and homogenize public opinion in all segments of the population. The pressure for uniformity of war support was near maximum. It was propaganda at its most intense. Words were fully mobilized in support of war.

Post World War I was inevitably a time for reappraisal of the war and its propaganda. The enormity of casualties suffered was staggering -- almost twenty million deaths among combatant nations. America counted 117,500 dead and more than 200,000 wounded. In light of such carnage, CPI and European propagandists may have later expressed a bit too much pride in their war work. British and French propagandists published memoirs detailing their campaigns to win American hearts and minds. George Creel, fresh from the propaganda trenches, published his best selling book, *How We Advertised America: the world's greatest adventure in advertising.* His description of the effort as one of "manufacturing consent" for war was taken by many as arrogance.[8] Creel was proud to proclaim his organization's success, describing it as an effort to "weld the people of the United States into one white-hot mass instinct with fraternity, devotion, courage and deathless determination". For it all, Creel insisted that the CPI did not deal in propaganda. That did not stop it from being consistently described by others as the most intensive propaganda effort ever undertaken.

American journalists, among the most independent in the world, reconsidered their own contribution to the CPIs effectiveness and were embarrassed. They were stunned at the demonstration of mass manipulation, much of it accomplished through their own newspapers and magazines. Beginning almost immediately and continuing through the decade of the 1920s, passionate, angry, accusatory magazine and news articles denounced propaganda as dishonest and anti-democratic. One editorial sarcastically queried, "A subservient citizenry, well drilled in falsehoods and hatreds – what could be a finer or more fitting fruit of war fought for democracy?" Another asked if there might not inevitably be "a yielding to the temptation to use these new and vast powers of propaganda for the benefit of those in public office or for the propagation of the views that they hold?" The fear was expressed that "the honest editor or reporter will be as much the victim as the public."

Propaganda was described as a parasite whose instrument is the press agent, its influence pernicious and to be despised. It was said that the war had given the word propaganda, once an honorable one, "a sinister significance, making it at once a term of reproach and the plague and torment of our lives." The war had revealed "a devilish skill of the minority in wholesale, inspired lying and in hypocritical, pious adroitness in untruth." Propaganda was succinctly defined as "a longer way to spell lie", "a subtle and insidious reptile", an instrument of "indifference to the truth", as "poison".[9]

The advertising industry had a different view. World War I had demonstrated the power of clever, skilled communication to sway public action and opinion. Edward Bernays, a pre-war advertising specialist and member of CPI war time staff, promoted propaganda enthusiastically as a necessary support for working democracy. In Bernays' view, propaganda was not necessarily good or bad. "The most effective propaganda', he insisted, " is that which enlarges and presents the truth so that an indifferent public will understand and accept it." He asserted that "propaganda makes available to the public the newest ideas, inventions and products". In his best selling and still published book *Propaganda,* Bernays stated his case thus:

> "The conscious and intelligent manipulation of the organized habits and opinions of the masses is an important element in democratic society. Those who

manipulate this unseen mechanism of society constitute an invisible government that is the true ruling power of our country. We are governed, our minds are molded, our tastes formed, our ideas suggested, largely by men we have never heard of. This is the logical result of the way in which our democratic society is organized. Vast numbers of human beings must cooperate in this manner if they are to live together as a smoothly functioning society. In almost every act of our daily lives, whether in the sphere of politics or business, in our social conduct or our ethical thinking, we are dominated by the relatively small number of persons ... who understand the mental processes and social patterns of the masses. It is they who pull the wires which control the public mind."[10]

His was a distinctly elitist view of democratic society wherein a modern day version of Plato's philosopher king beneficently guides the thinking and action of the citizenry. The ease and extent of this view's comfortable fit to the thinking of politicians and industrial captains of that age should not be surprising. Bernays went on to become a leading figure in the expanding field of public relations, credited by some as its founding father. Crafting the word messages that move public action and opinion became and remains a thriving business that extends deep into America's industry and politics. From humble roots in propaganda, public relations has become industry and electioneering standard. Words rule!

14. Words That Create Markets And Social Movements

Salesmanship uses of words to arouse need and drive sales. The effective salesperson appears to be selling nothing. Selective provision of information, sensitivity to customer response, focusing acutely on customer need or interest all make the sale progress smoothly on to its conclusion. If well done, customers may not even realize they have been sold. On his best game, the effective sales person can get away with the claim, "I'm not here to sell anything."

The teacher from a school of dance brings a troop of aspirant grade school ballerinas to perform for the Friday evening young adults group at church. To the music of lush symphonic recordings, the brightly costumed girls offer cute approximations of Swan Lake and Coppelia ballet routines. Their instructor speaks glowingly of enhanced health, increased self-confidence, reduced TV watching exhibited in her pupils. The benefits obtainable, it is said, cannot be priced.

No mention is made of class openings or costs. Parents in the audience eagerly converge on the ballet mistress to learn if there might be any openings for their daughters in her school. The response is a teaser; "it isn't yet certain, but there may be one or two in next month's schedule". Several parents ask price and communicate together earnestly about how they can fit it into their budget. They urge the master to hold a spot when one comes open. It is offhandedly suggested to these parents that they might bring the child to a sample lesson some evening next week. The parents are sold and the sale is virtually closed, unless, of course, the child throws a total tizzy on being told of the regimen to come.

An athletic looking fellow is speaking today at a men's luncheon meeting about his personal physical fitness regimen. He arrives early and inquires about members. "Who is the group clown? Who is the most healthy and athletic? Who is physically flabby?" On opening the show, he demonstrates his physical strength with a set of elastic cords. He claims that this simple equipment can train "every muscle that a ten thousand dollar weight machine can...and, I can take them with me anywhere, use them anywhere." Cords are stood on, attached to chairs and doors, pulled, twisted. He cleverly calls on members to demonstrate their use. The clown groans, the group laughs. The flabby weakling strains and says "Wow". The resident athlete says "that's a real workout". On conclusion, the presenter asks for questions. The first is "Where can I get that equipment?" The answer is "I didn't come here to sell these, but I can take a limited number of orders to be filled at the factory. A quarter of those in attendance crowd around to place orders. One or two walk away upon learning the stiff price. Most eagerly write checks or provide credit card numbers.

A Tai Chi master offers a demonstration of his ancient Chinese art to the town's sports booster's association. He speaks of reduced pain, greater joint flexibility, enhanced posture, generally increased health that can come from learning the postures. The manner in which energy flow is controlled and directed in the body is explained. He muses on the practices of Chinese community culture where Tai Chi Masters go to the town center to practice, allowing young and old to come and imitate his moves. Then he gracefully demonstrates the art through its traditional, carefully choreographed routines. One of the participants enthusiastically proposes, "Why don't we do this in the park this Summer? Everyone could come and learn! It would be a great benefit to the community!" The group discusses making contact with local merchants and employers to obtain funds to hire the master. The master, who has never explicitly offered himself for hire, modestly suggests that "I may be able to put it in my schedule". In almost embarrassed tones, he explains his fee schedule to the group's leaders.

Just inside the entrance door of the upscale department store brightly lit displays of cosmetics and fragrances present themselves to each incoming customer. These are high mark-up items that generate huge profits. For the proportionate floor space used, the largest staff of salespeople is assigned here. Unusually good commission structures attract and hold the best ones. The cosmetics department is advertised as a great place for employees to build skills for a sales career. It offers basic training for the sales natural.

Customers are urged to sit in comfort and be treated to a free skin or make-up treatment. Fragrances are applied and experienced. The words of sales attendants are soft and confirming. "You have such wonderful skin. It has a natural glow. See how this special formula brings out its full radiance." Even flawed skin is a sales asset. Most customers have blemishes, if not scars, from acne or accident. "We have this miracle crème that fills wrinkles, stretches the skin and covers blemishes." Romantic enhancement gets special emphasis. "If you desire a fragrance for that special evening, Moonlight in Venice is the right choice."

These scenarios involve ordinary middle to upper middleclass sales people and customers. There is no exaggeration or special inducement put forward. People want fulfilling lives for themselves and their children. Given a bright, well rehearsed sales pitch for something that looks attractive, they respond. Ballet training, novel exercise equipment, Tai Chi coaching and skin crème are hardly necessities of living. Neither are Mickey Mouse wrist watches or "World's Greatest Dad" coffee cups. Ballet and exercise are components of the good life. Cosmetics make magic. They are bought because they are presented as enhancements to quality of life. A little puffery is surely involved. The words and supporting images used in promoting the product are designed to make the product appear a necessity. With the aid of an act that is more like entertainment than merchandising the product is subtly and effectively sold. Practice in exercise of the right words is the salesperson's central skill.

Advertising differs from salesmanship largely in its scope and distance from the audience. It aims at a mass market using words as if they were precision instruments. The craft of advertising carries the word magic to breathless heights. Ads must live in a highly emotional zone on the edge of language. Power words are continually evolving, being invented, losing effect or being replaced. Some are truly lasting. They are firmly identified with the products or services they once trumpeted. "We are bullish on America". "It keeps going and going". "We bring good things to life". "You are now free to move about the country". These are simple, direct phrases that use the power of their words to identify one specific company or product. Merrill Lynch, Energizer Batteries, GE and Southwest Airlines are enshrined in words by the cleverness of these ad lines. Ads go out of their way to attach a quality or characteristic to a product. An auto isn't just safe to drive, it makes life high adventure. It's not just a soft mattress, it's made for sweet sleep. It isn't an investment opportunity, its hard working money. It's not a TV documentary, it's a penetrating look at a changing world.

Advertising is word play. Some call it wordsmithing and portray it as a process of crafting words to fit the desired purpose. Good wordsmiths carefully test the effect of their words on the market and product. They know that the meaning of a word changes with use. They are aware that the context in which a word is used can change its meaning. They are attuned to the subtleties of language. Marketers recruit small groups to test those subtleties. Clusters of individuals sometimes randomly selected, sometimes screened for selection, become sounding boards for newly crafted words and phrases. Group participants may be paid or rewarded with gifts. Sessions will generally be at least an hour or more in length. The wordsmith probes reaction to words under test for as much depth as possible. He/she zeros in on meaning and emotional association. The smallest nuance is examined for its possible influence. Misunderstandings, secondary meanings and alternate uses of target words are identified. If the group is chosen well and the test is carried out thoroughly, the process can be the equivalent of a simulated test of the product in use. Once the words that advertise it are right, the product is right. Words are ultimate tools of advertising and sales.

Some advertising words are virtual standards. Advertising copy writers make heavy use of what they call power words. Words like *free, easy, new, proven, incredible, ultimate, shocking, best* or *breakthrough* appear with high frequency in advertisements. These words are tested attention getters that advertising copywriters trust to do the job. Their utility inheres in the emotional power of language to portray an appealing image that is instantly understood. Advertising works by successfully communicating an opportunity for self-reward to the reader or listener. It sends the generic message "Here is something you want and need".

Much advertising in the current market place is through television and radio broadcasts. The word *broadcast* used in this sense is metaphor on the planting seeds by casting them broadly onto the ground. Some seeds will germinate, some will not. Some waste of seed is tolerated to gain efficiency in planting. Advertising is broadcasting almost in the original sense of that word. It is cost efficient, impersonal and indirect. The advertiser never knows in advance where the message will connect and where it will not. Words are cast outward to take root where they will. Finding words that will germinate in the largest number of minds is the art of the advertiser.

The vast amount of advertising routinely broadcast does not permit formula words to keep their attention getting effect for long. Wants and needs change. There can be too much broadcasting. Over statement of the message and over use of supposed power words dulls effect. Words change their meaning with intensive use. The most skillful ad writers know how to invent new words and invest old words with new meaning. They don't just write or design ads. They create new language. They add to and reshape language culture. Advertising is a culture in its own right with its own language. It works with *mass media,* it *brands* products and it uses *hype* to capture attention. These terms are, in themselves, examples of both newly created words and old words with new meaning.

The emergence of mass markets for mass distributed products in the twentieth century founded the mass media industry through which advertising is conveyed. The concept of humanity as the working masses is credited to the economic philosopher Karl Marx who used it to contrast workers with capitalists. In the same way that Mediterranean (the Sea) originally meant *middle* (medi) of the known world (terra) the new word *media* is a stem broken from words like *median* and *mediate* that are rooted in old words for *middle* or *center.*[1] The Mediterranean Sea effectively connected the medieval world and unified it economically. Mass media is a jargon term that is handy for categorizing the variety of channels through or along which advertising messages are communicated between source and audience. It connects the seller with the buyer.

The marketing (advertising) term *branding* is another twentieth century invention. It is employed to describe the process of establishing a distinctive word descriptor that may be supported by a distinctive image termed a logo. Word and image identify a product and its owner. *Brand* in old English meant a piece of burning wood. That meaning evolved from an earlier meaning, *burn.* A *brand* in the old sense was a source of heat used to make a mark, as in branding an animal or person. Cowboys brand cattle. That is, they sear a mark of ownership into the animal's hide with a red hot iron. In other times, criminals were similarly marked with a brand. One who is convicted of a crime is still spoken of as *branded a criminal.* Merchants have long marked their products in some distinctive way that permits them to trade on a reputation for quality. With the rise in mass marketing, terms like *brand leader* (best selling brand) and *brand manager* (product executive in charge of the product line) have come into the language. The term *Brand X* is conventionally used to identify a competing product.

The term *hype* is used to describe excessive claims in advertising. It is a fractured word taken from words like hyperbole and hyperactive, where the root *hyper* is the Greek word for *over* or *beyond*. *Hype* has come to mean almost any kind of excess in word or action. *Mass media, brand* and *hype* are all words and/or meanings invented in the twentieth century by the advertising industry.

As the practice of marketing has advanced over the past hundred years the names of products themselves have proliferated. Language has been extended with invented proper nouns, many transformed into verbs and adjectives. These are new words that formerly referenced a branded product. Kleenex and Frigidaire are now generic terms for facial tissue and refrigerator. Words like *ecosystem, profiteer, stagflation,* and *biodegradable* are all twentieth century inventions. These four were invented from older words. *Ecology* and *system* combine to describe the complexity of life and biochemical interactions in nature. *Profiteer* uses the standard capitalist term profit with a suffix that suggests that profit is a kind of piracy. *Stagflation* is put together from the words stagnation and inflation to express the difficulty of comprehending the contradictions that modern economics faces in explaining financial markets. *Bio* is the stem of biology hooked onto degradable and used to suggest natural breakdown of substances or materials. The flood of new words surges forward using just such inventive devices as these. Marketers, the makers of advertising language, are in the forefront of that word creation.

Evidence of the fascination of marketers with new names can be found in many places. The marketing magazine *Brandweek* featured an article titled *"What's in a Name? Study Toasts Top New Brands"*. Thirteen hundred *Brandweek* readers were surveyed by advertising agency TippingSprung to identify new brand names that have demonstrated the greatest marketing appeal. Anheuser-Busch's flavored malt beverage *Spykes* was singled out as tops among alcoholic beverages. The name had such great appeal to the under 21 market that the product had to be pulled from the shelves before government action forced it off. As a name for running shoes, *Tailwind* was voted best. The connotation of running with a tailwind at your back gives it special spin. Among new airline names, *go!* got high honors as did *Aloft* for the best new hotel brand.

Enjuvia, a new menopause drug was singled out as head of the pack, and a new insulin brand, Exhubera was rated close behind. From a list of new names for ice cream flavors, *Bohemian Raspberry* was voted number one, *Karamel Sutra* second and *Jamaica Me Crazy* third. Martyn Tipping, partner in the agency that conducted the survey, is quoted saying "marketers struggle with choosing between a product or service name that doesn't have to be explained and ...building a brand that is ownable, distinguishable and unique." Among wordsmiths, creating new names is a high urgency (and high profit) pursuit. Many of the names thus invented for branding will eventually become household words in use.[2]

The power of words used in advertisements arises from multiple sources. The simple power of suggestion is one. The strong associations that exist between words and word-like sounds is another. Humans find the meaning of words in the context of other words. This is especially so with new words. Synonyms and antonyms that substitute for well known, simpler words are learned as members of a set. Words that have multiple meanings or that just sound similar to other words can capture a variety of associations, making them the source of puns. The ubiquity of word association is demonstrated in the widely used multiple choice examination used by many teachers. A question followed by a set of alternative answers is answered by selecting the best answer – the answer that associates most closely with the question is correct. Other answers may be cleverly written false associations. Multiple choice tests demonstrate the process of word play that goes with learning new word associations. In advertising, the best association may well be the punning or even a false association. Advertising is supreme word play.

Advertising suggestion may be simple and direct, like a perfume called "moonlight and roses" raising romantic images. Or it may be indirect like *enjuvia,* clearly intended to echo the words *rejuvenate you.* Much suggestion inherent in the invented ad implies that a product or lotion will please or be beneficial to the customer. A medication quickly relieves itching, pain or other discomfort or a lotion makes one irresistible. The implication itself can initiate buying behavior. As with so many other suggestions that swirl about in the social environment, it is easier and more efficient to respond to directions offered than to test all possible alternatives. Flowing with the advertiser's suggestion usually, perhaps often enough, makes life easier or more fun.

In practice, some suggestion is influence for the sake of influence, only slightly different from propaganda. Some may be for the good of the person or community. It is in the nature of self-interest that advertisers emphasize their contribution to the greater good wherever they can. To differentiate its effort to sell advertising as a public good from that of manipulative propaganda, the US Advertising Council emphasizes on its web site its long history of serving the public interest.[3]

In truth, the difference is very small. It would be naïve not expect a significant element of self promotion in all advertising. Twentieth century advertising history offers ample demonstration of orchestrated influence to reshape the broader culture by reshaping fundamental habits of health. The marketing of soap is a case example of broad cultural redesign through advertising.[4]

As American involvement in World War I wound down in 1919, Lever Brothers Company placed an unusual advertisement in national magazines and major newspapers. Alongside the picture of a fully uniformed American soldier, the lead read "For the first time in history soap is a part of a soldier's equipment, and every man in the United States Army is *compelled* to use it." In extra large boldfaced uppercase the soap was identified as LIFEBUOY HEALTH SOAP. General John "Black Jack" Pershing was quoted by the ad as saying "The clean soldier is more courageous, never discouraged...". Advertising Lifebuoy as the soldier's soap marked the beginning of the era when cleanliness was advanced as a national, social imperative.

In the decades just before World War I, cleanliness had begun to be scientifically related to good health. The fifty years between the American Civil War and World War I saw a seismic change in knowledge and attitudes toward disease. In the period immediately following the War Between the States, Austrian-Hungarian physician Ignatz Semmelweiz discovered that childbed fever in new mothers could be sharply reduced by the practice of washing his hands with chlorinated lime between patient examinations. Louis Pasteur demonstrated that microorganisms would grow in a nutrient broth exposed to the air thereby demonstrating the ubiquity of germs. German scientist Robert Koch demonstrated experimentally that anthrax outbreaks in cows started from endospores embedded in the soil. Germ theory of disease transmission was firmly founded by researchers like these over the last decades in the nineteenth century. Former folk theories that "explained" the causes of disease continued to prevail for much of the following century. Germ theory would be accepted slowly. In the post World War I era Lever Brothers and their soap making competitors put the awesome power of advertising fully behind its spread through the sale of soap.

Soap has been used for at least four thousand years. Prior to the twentieth century soap was an item of household manufacture that used wood ashes and rendered cooking grease as its base. The utility of soap is in its ability to dissolve dirt and oil in a water base. Soap cleanses the skin of germs. Manufacture and commercial sale of soap became common in the late nineteenth century, about 1875 to 1900, with the earliest promotion of Proctor and Gamble's Ivory brand. Early use of manufactured soap was largely limited to the wealthy. For the general population, personal hygiene remained as primitive as the old fashioned outhouse. A variety of measures to bring about sanitary reform would emerge at the turn of the twentieth century. Few would have more effect than advertising soap.

Lifebuoy soap was advertised as early as 1900 to be a "Wonderful cleanser that not only ensures perfect cleanliness but also insures freedom from infectious disease". In that same era Lehn & Fink marketed the disinfectant *Lysol* as a protector of the home against germs. Soap was healthy, and was promoted also for skin care. B.J. Johnson Company's Palmolive Soap promised to maintain skin "as velvety in texture as a rose petal". Woodbury's facial soap moved the advertising message up a notch with the slogan "A skin you love to touch", subtly investing soap with sex appeal. Its advertising campaign was designed to educate women in the care and improvement of their skin. Over a five year span of advertising, sales of Palmolive increased from only half a million to over two and a half million dollars annually.

Lifebuoy continued to press its health theme in ads. An ad showing children on the seashore under the watchful eye of a lifeguard asks "Isn't health worth guarding too." In a series of "make the best first impression" ads, lifebouy cautioned readers against offending others with B.O. – body odor. Soap and romance were linked. Palmolive pictured a housewife with a gift of flowers cradled in her arms followed by the caption, "He remembered – That Schoolgirl Complexion". Lever Brothers Lux Toilet Soap was advertised with a continental styled illustration over the lead line "From France The Gift of Smooth Skin". Prestigious endorsements by experts and celebrities were employed. Camay soap claimed it had been thoroughly tested by sixty-nine leading dermatologists. Hollywood actress Bette Davis informed women "how to protect daintiness" with Lux soap. Health, beauty, romance, all were themes of soap ads of the 1920s. Soap was selling briskly, but soap makers' production capacity was nowhere near full. It was judged that the market could absorb yet more soap.

The answer came with establishment in 1927 of an industry wide *Cleanliness Institute.* The Association of Soap and Detergent Manufacturers formed the institute for the explicit purpose of cooperative sales promotion. The association's president summarized its aim as one of promoting the public welfare in cooperation with school and social agencies. Brief cleanliness sermons in print were widely published. Ads suggested that personal slovenliness brought career failure with the theme, "you can't keep a clean man down." They asked how neighbors would judge your children if they weren't clean with the tag line "There's character in soap and water". Cleanliness assures career success; "For Health and Wealth, use SOAP and WATER". It was suggested that the husband's position depended on the size of the weekly laundry in ads that urged women to be sure their husbands went out in a clean shirt every day. A coupon ad offering a free booklet on cleanliness was one of the most successful such campaigns ever conceived resulting in distribution of over a million booklets.

The Cleanliness Institute published the Cleanliness Journal, a sixteen page booklet with articles on all aspects of cleanliness. It was distributed to sixty-five hundred leaders in public health, social service and home economics. Cleanliness campaigns targeted school children through the public school system using pamphlets and posters. Cleanliness was made the mark of those who were morally superior, possessed better character and were more attractive. Clean people, ads suggested, have more self-respect, exude more confidence, and are just overall nicer. The Cleanliness Institute was the ultimate in building popular culture through advertising.

Soap and detergent manufacturers went on to invent the soap opera, an icon of the radio and early television era. Along the way, they helped bring the ceramic fixtured bathroom into the house as the shrine of cleanliness and personal hygiene. Taboos concerning reference to sex were tested and banished by promoting beauty and sensuality as acceptable elements of home making. Soap manufacturers advertised their own products to assure that demand for soap would be synchronized with production capacity and inventory levels. Mass markets provided the context for it to come together as the American way of life. Advertising works miracles!

Advertising in its most basic form straightforwardly communicates the availability of a product or service. In a competitive market, it may have to detail price and special features. Basic commodities like food or fuel may compete almost wholly on price and availability. They are necessities purchased regularly enough to set a price pattern into the memory of buyers. Small changes in cost are quickly seen and reacted to. Advertising reflects these realities. Ads for them are simple, direct and price oriented. They are informative.

It is in the luxuries and non-necessities of life that advertising can become creative and culturally influential. Upscale personal grooming items, specialty food, stylish clothing, jewelry and new automobiles all employ high quality ad writing skill. Pharmaceuticals and related personal hygiene products drive the perpetual search for better health and wellbeing. Invention of words for these purposes is high art. These are not just invitations to a purchase; they are elements of the culture. They change the meaning of language and the identity of their users.

Automobiles in the age of ads are not merely a means of going somewhere, they are a special environment. "Every part, every feature, every detail of (this auto) is ingeniously designed to bring comfort, safety and peace of mind to the driver." (Honda) A tooth brush is not just for oral hygiene, it promises that "a healthy smile can lead to a healthy life." (Phillips) A cell phone with contract wireless service supports a heroic way of life because it is "Road Warrior Tested, Multitasker Approved." (Palm Treo/Sprint).[5]

Advertising slogans come down to earth like wisdom from on high. A new electronics gadget isn't just a purchase, it represents "thousands of possibilities, get yours!." (Best Buy) An advanced pharmaceutical represents "Hope, triumph and the miracle of medicine." (Bristol Meyers/Squib) A grocery store is not just a place to buy food, it offers "All the Ingredients for Life." (Safeway) Computers are the miracle of the new age. They are "New World, New thinking." (Lenovo) The computer user is "Empowered by Innovation". (NEC) Computer applications are "Solutions for a Small Planet." (IBM) Computer systems consulting isn't just offering useful ideas, it is "Powered by Intellect, Driven by Values". (Infosys) Purchase of running shoes is a clear necessity "Because Life is not a Spectator Sport." (Reebok) It is said of the psychological power of a body fragrance that "Between Love and Madness Lies Obsession." (Calvin Klein).[6]

The effectiveness and power of advertising is unquestioned. Ultimately, the complaint with advertising power is that it may have too much effectiveness. Advertising has created and continues to drive a thriving consumption economy. Society is saturated in advertising as well as in the goods and services it promotes. The charge can reasonably be made that western society is drowning in trivial commercial noise and the junk it promotes. Excessive, non-biodegradable packaging wrapped around disposable product stuff is choking the ecosystem. Is it really all too much? Ultimately, how much reality can be squeezed out of the language of advertising? How much out of any language? So far, the end does not appear in sight.

The currency of advertising is in the words chosen for the message intended. Words are employed to channel and shape the actions of others. The hot button word that will set the target person(s) into desired motion is as urgently sought after as the gold and silver forty-niner prospectors once searched the mountains for. There is wealth to be had in its discovery.

15. Rhetorical Language: The Words of Politics and Public Policy

Politics is the battle to influence public policy at all levels of government. Political rhetoric sways votes. Winning at politics requires skilled, or at least clever, use of words in constructing the appropriate rhetoric. For the active, position seeking politician, words are a critical, indispensable tool. To some, this is cynical. Actually, it is entirely rational and reasonable. Politics is about the priorities of public policy. Public policy debate is the language that hammers out the priorities of a nation. It is not necessary to buy the policy position emotionally to promote it well. Carrying out the public's will is the proper object of elected politicians. The language of public policy debate represents the vigorous debate among the variety of cultures that make up the political and social landscape of the nation. Politicians are the debaters.

Within every political culture there are words that distinguish the ideological fidelity of adherents. Those loyal to its principles speak their chosen power words with force and sincerity. Firm opposition to sexual transgression and abortion are the mark of one cultural identity, rejection of prejudice and injustice the mark of another. Issues of pollution and climate change have a large vocal constituency. The right to bear arms and own high fire power weapons is vigorously asserted by one politically powerful lobby. Taxes and government regulation of the economy are vigorously rejected by another ideological cabal. Conflict between cultures is acted out as a war of words, firmly, rhetorically and theatrically declaimed with maximum conviction. Each campaign has a set of slogans and passwords that are real and vital to their special culture. Those of another culture are dismissed as empty rhetoric, hollow, without reality, used solely for dramatic effect. Political culture campaigns are wars of words. Opposing orators regularly and vigorously accuse one another of political theatrics as if only they were innocent of them.

Strong adherence to sharply defined and differentiated viewpoints like these is rarely found among more than about ten to twenty percent of voters. Thus, the loyal core of an ideological subculture rarely represents only a small part of the voting population. The culture wars are fought out between opposing political positions that depend for support on a limited, loyal constituency. Each core group campaigns for the votes of a large, ideologically uncommitted political center. Political theater is enacted for the benefit of that center. The object is to capture as many of these votes as possible. Merely trumpeting the rhetoric of a culture's power words is not likely to gain much ground in the political center. Outside the center of that culture, the full force of standard rhetoric is lost. Engaging in nothing more than an ongoing war of hot words is likely to leave the uncommitted voting middle to judge which set of political slogans it dislikes least.

With the rise of professional public relations and political polling firms the methods of public relations have come to be systematically applied in the national political campaigns, particularly so in campaigning from the political right in recent decades. The object of this rhetoric is to translate ideological positions into words that appeal to middle ground voters. The success of right wing political rhetoric in making these translations offers a particularly clear illustration of the word play that characterizes American politics.

In the early 1970s, the core movement of political conservatism began to organize and focus on ways to rehabilitate achievement of goals for limited government, tax cuts and roll-back of social welfare programs. Words acceptable to the political middle were tested and scripted by political pollsters through a well financed, sharply focused campaign of focus group research in service of conservative objectives. The work of building that language fund is documented by Frank Luntz, conservative political and corporate pollster, in his book *Words that Work.*

Luntz claims credit for proposing phrases like *death tax,* to stand in the place of *estate tax, personalizing,* to replace *privatizing* of Social Security and *energy exploration,* to replace *oil drilling. School vouchers* for finance of private education he renamed *opportunity scholarships.* For those positioned and committed on either side of these issues, there is no ambiguity about what is under discussion. The political basis of word meaning is understood. The clear object of this rhetorical dry cleaning of language is to make ideological positions palatable to the less polarized political middle. Luntz and his polling organization carefully tested and confirmed that, when his recommended language is used, a significant shift occurs in acceptance of many of the positions that his clients promote. In doing so he demonstrated that politics is often more about the words employed than the issue at stake. How this happens can be illuminated through examination of issues and their words that Dr. Luntz has spun.[1]

When called an estate tax, revenue collected on estates is clearly a concern only to the very rich. Estate taxes fall on a limited proportion of tax payers, and are seldom paid on the full estate. At their most onerous they prevent the very wealthy from passing all of their wealth on to heirs. Small estates, in the mere low millions, are exempted. The nominal tax rate is about half the value of those inheritances that are *in excess* of five million dollars (as of this writing).

A variety of legal devices are available to avoid estate taxes, trust funds especially, and the typical taxed estate is assessed only a small fraction of the full rate. The percentage of US estates actually taxed *in any way at all* in a given year has never exceeded 3% of all deaths, and is typically only in the 1% to 2% range of all estates that are passed through inheritance. In application, estate taxes are only a nuisance and a disappointment for beneficiaries of inheritance. Taxation of estates should be of no concern at all to most voters were the full facts communicated. By combining two of the most negatively loaded words in the language, *death* and *taxes,* estate taxes are branded as something approaching evil. A high proportion of the political center supports repeal of the estate tax when they are so labeled.

The greatest inconvenience of taxed estates falls on family small businesses and farms. If valuable enough to be taxed, a going small business might have to be sold. With foresight and sound legal counsel, this can usually be avoided. The personal economic loss of the estate tax is seldom severe. The real issue is the ideology of ownership rights. The contest is between the ancient custom of passing ownership on to one's heirs versus the social inequity of financial advantage passing fully only to those heirs. The question is, should accumulated wealth be inherited, or should it, in some part at least, be redistributed. It could reasonably be said by proponents of the estate tax that elimination or reduction of estate taxes might justifiably be labeled the "millionaire's wealth preservation act". Arguments are plentiful on both sides. Most are historically complex, emotionally hot arguments. The philosophical and legal issues that pertain to estate taxes are so complicated that Luntz' blended use of death and taxes simply overwhelms the argument. Power words do the heavy lifting of persuasion.[2]

Bringing about a change of national mood toward Social Security benefits was also undertaken by Dr. Luntz. Within the US, approximately one person in five receives a Social Security check each month. Anyone who has worked forty quarters (10 years) in a lifetime is entitled to income from the Social Security fund after age 65. One of the largest core political cultures in the nation is made up of Social Security beneficiaries. There is no clearly identifiable block of those *opposing* Social Security. It is old age insurance and everyone not already old wants to think they will become old. The greatest opposition has always come from that small proportion of those who are wealthy enough to have no interest in or need for Social Security. Many in this class would prefer, for purely economic reasons, to invest their

Social Security tax monies privately to enjoy a larger return on their money. Privatization of retirement investment would offer the choice of investing FICA payroll taxes in personally held investment accounts. *Privatize* is not a particularly impelling political word. Replacing *privatize* with the word *personalize* is therefore recommended by Luntz.[3]

Education has become a political and ideological battleground. Education acculturates the young to the word play of reading, writing, speaking and calculating. Although it is regularly said to be in need of reform, public education is an American icon. Attitudes about education of the young are keen and political constituencies are powerful. The political debate over education policy is spirited.

Education in the US became a major industry during the first half of the twentieth century. Teaching became a profession. In early decades finishing eighth grade was enough to demonstrate basic literacy. Graduating after twelve grades of secondary education was the goal of the upward mobile. Teachers were unquestioned authority in their classes. There was no hesitation in identifying good students and poor students. The only dress codes had to do with formal or informal standards of clothing. In its early twentieth century conception, education provided the melting pot within which a variety of social and ethnic cultures were commonly acculturated.

The social climate shifted in the second half century. Public education became a political battleground of fighting over what should and should not be included in the teaching curriculum. Traditional educational practice covered the patriotic basics in acculturating the young politically. Multiple political cultures shattered those old standards. Every social and political culture sought to shape the education system in its special ideological format. Diversity became the watchword.

Modern education now places high priority on preserving diverse political, social and ethnic cultures. For students, finishing twelve grades is the minimum for employment and attending college is the path of upward mobility. Assignment of any grade that could block that mobility has become a judgmental and therefore controversial act. Students themselves want less authority and restriction in their pursuit of learning. They demand freedom to adopt any style of dress current fashion may dictate. Parents just want good jobs for them when they graduate.

The cost of funding education has escalated from incidental in the community a hundred years earlier to where it is now second only to military expenditures. Taxpayers are in rebellion. Teachers join unions in self-defense of the fierce political pressure they face. Public education is limited at every turn by political and legal constraint. Students and their parents, from poor or affluent backgrounds alike, want out. Some merely drop out, some seek remedy in the courts, some demand new legislation, some change residence into a more congenial community. Some are caught and cannot escape.

The answer for many of Frank Luntz' clients is school vouchers that allow tax money to pay for private education. Vouchers support culture specific student teaching. Vouchers also may eliminate unionized teachers' jobs. Vouchers have thus generated a political storm. Debate is over quality of education and community control. Words fly. Frank Luntz' approach to redefining the argument is to rename vouchers *Opportunity Scholarships*. It is one of his more creative attempts at word play.[4]

Oil is black, dirty and dangerous. It can partly be rehabilitated as Texas Tea, but no one wants an oil well in their back yard – unless, of course, they own it. In an age of militant environmentalism, burning oil is a major contributor to air pollution and global climate warming. Though the inherent negatives of oil can be easily enumerated the presumed economic threat of an oil shortage is also worrisome. There is the fear that in the absence of sufficient oil resources, quality of (economic) life may be threatened. It is argued that a minor environmental intrusion onto government owned land preserves should easily be tolerated to avoid the possibility of broad economic disruption. To support argument for drilling in national parks, Frank Luntz recommends that *energy exploration*, not *oil drilling* be the object. *Energy* is the object, and *exploration* lacks the hard bite of *drilling*. *Environmentalism* nonetheless has a vast constituency of its own. The alternative description applied by those opposed to exploration is *environmental destruction*. It is a politically charged word on its own terms.

Environmentalism is a cause that has deep historical roots, a militant wing and a record of vigorous political debate.[5] It is a cause that came to full maturity with the twenty-first century. Nineteenth century environmental causes centered on the natural wonders of the US. Protection of Yosemite Valley and the California Redwoods was brought about by John Muir, a nineteenth century naturalist, with the help of President Teddy Roosevelt. Muir established the Sierra Club, committed to defending natural resources from exploitation by private commercial interests. The communities of those interests were miners, loggers, ranchers and farmers concerned about preserving commercial rights to their use of federal land. National Parks and preserves were an important economic resource to them. Muir and the Sierra club sought to represent the inherent rights of nature by removing them from private use. The debate pitted national economic growth against nature, placing abstract natural beauty in competition with real wealth.[6]

Rachael Carlson's book *The Silent Spring* appeared in 1962. Carlson detailed losses of living species, especially birds, from insecticide poisoning. DDT and other agricultural chemicals were indicted for widespread assaults on nature. Ultimately, DDT was banned, though not without controversy over the loss of an inexpensive, easy form of insect control to increase crop yield. Rachael Carlson's message brought about a variety of green organizations promoting earth-first policies for the promotion and practice of ecological policy. Politics responded and the struggle to balance the interests of industry and nature was renewed.[7]

During most of this history, political lobbying was the field of contest. Political pressure groups used the ballot box as leverage, economic interests used money contributions to political candidates to push back. The intensity of the contest heightened in the decade of the 1990s when the evidence of permanent climate change from global warming emerged. In 1988 the Intergovernmental Panel on Climate Change – IPCC - was commissioned by the World Meteorological Organization and The United Nations Environment Program to study the problem on a global scale.[8] A more than thousand page report, *Climate Change 2001,* published by the IPCC, detailed an assessment of possible consequences and adaptations required by climate change. The conflict escalated to the level of world economic growth versus the health of mother earth.[9]

The IPCC report, inevitably speculative in many ways, was roundly criticized as propaganda by its opponents. Organizations labeled *Competitive Enterprise Institute* and *National Consumer Coalition* became the *Cooler Heads Coalition* that raised objection to its conclusions. "Cooler heads" dismissed IPCC and its global warming claims as *junk science.* The UN was accused of trying to pin the cost of world wide natural disasters on "deep-pocket" Americans. Environmentalists countered that the US Government was hiding evidence linking hurricanes with global warming.[10]

Labels used in the climate change battle were chosen to have very specific emotional association. "Cooler heads" suggests that global warming is the issue of the hot heads. The cooler heads message is that competitive enterprise offers superior goods and services and that sensible consumers do not want their flow interrupted. Drastic shifts to avert global warming demanded by environmentalists would disrupt those benefits. The argument rages between those who fear that efforts to control greenhouse emissions will limit or stunt economic growth and those who predict that it will bring about catastrophic environmental change. Words hurled by each position represent the reality maps of those who use them. Words *are* the reality of the core cultures that are in opposition about global warming. They operate from wholly different language and culture based views of the political, economic and natural world.

The war of words between hotheads and cooler heads is transparent enough to permit identification of motives behind the positions taken. Cooler heads are those with entrenched economic positions that could be jeopardized by radical action to reduce greenhouse emissions. Oil interests are primary in this group. Oil industry investment policy since 2007 has nevertheless acknowledged that the industry is in end game status. It emphasized limited new investment in refineries, preferential development of the most easily recovered oil reserves, application of technology to keep old fields pumping oil at the maximum and urgent accumulation of profit to guard against any sudden change in energy technology. In purely investment terms, this is rational capital management. Those who have capital and wealth are fearful of being caught by change that wipes them out. Oil capital is not uninformed concerning the limits of oil reserves. They are probably the best informed of any group. Their argument is that oil is still the best energy choice. It is the appeal to status quo. Those who are more threatened by collapse of their investments easily reject claims of an energy or ecological crisis that *might* be coming.

The "hotheads" in the environmental wars tend to be young. They have cause for concern that climate change may occur and have serious impact on their future quality of life.

Intellectuals and academics join this group through their investment in rational problem solving methodology. They argue that the science of climate change is well demonstrated, the product of sound science, that it makes sense and deserves to be examined. In their view action to avoid climate crisis urgently requires new social, political and engineering solutions. Those with advanced education may also benefit economically from the vast money flows that would go into creating advanced technical solutions to global warming. It is in their economic (good jobs) interest to campaign for immediate radical action. A considerable investment of self interest prevails on both sides of the argument.

Frank Luntz' efforts to find words that support partisan legislation have gone far beyond estate taxes, social security, education or the environmental issues. He put a positive spin on a variety of proposed 1990s cultural issues put forward by conservative congressmen and senators in their 1993 "contract with America. A *"Taking Back Our Streets Act"* included provisions to finance prison construction by cutting social services spending. A *"Personal Responsibility Act"* proposed denial of welfare payments to minor mothers for dependent children born while the mother collected welfare. The *"Job Creation and Wage Enactment Act"* cut the capital gains tax and relaxed regulations on small business.[11]

While there is nothing new in generating word spin for political ends, these titles were clearly chosen to smooth the way for passage of class specific legislation. It is the "putting the best face on it" approach long used in product advertising. Using a professional pollster to craft language and test it on the voting public is simply the logical progression of national, televised political advertising that began in the 1950s. Driven by advertising and public relations, passage of legislation has evolved into a quest. It is the pursuit of the ideological, sometimes represented as a noble cause. The words used to promote that cause are critical. Discovering those words that have the desired effect on behavior is the quest of professional spinmeisters like Dr. Frank Luntz.

Those who spin language are not always, probably not even usually, mere cynics who dress it up in clever words that obscure self-interest. Real fear and ambition become articulated in the argumentative rhetoric. The principle that drives Dr. Luntz' political spin is the same as that driving all polarized argument: The best available argument will be made that advances and protects one's personal interests. The object of political and social rhetoric is to convince unaligned voters that their interests are somehow in parallel with those of an ideological culture. Argument between parents and children over money allowance or auto use, argument between management and labor over wages and benefits, argument between husband and wife over spending, argument between neighbors over kids and pets, argument among politicians about anything, it is all the same stuff. It is self-interest dressed up in words generated by the ever creative word play capability of a highly literate left brain. The object is to find words that have the right spin, or as Frank Luntz put it, to discover "words that work". That is something the speaking left brain seems to do well.

16. Economica: The Words Of Wealth And Welfare Policy

American politics of the twentieth century was an ongoing conflict over how best to maximize wealth and still advance social welfare. The language in contention centered on issues like taxation, business regulation, living standards of the poor and elderly, provision of good jobs, and protecting the rights of labor. At times it has been characterized a class struggle between rich and poor, at others as a philosophical battle between the rights of ownership and the power of the State. Fought out in two, four and six year cycles on the election ballot, advantage has tilted back and forth between the political right and left. The contest is balanced politically by the wealth that finances political campaigns versus the power of the ballot owned by the employed masses who work for wages. The language of the ongoing political skirmish is economics. The invention of economic theory can be traced back to the words of political economist and Scottish moral philosopher Adam Smith.

Smith invented much of the language that became the foundations of social theory *and* market economics. He is generally taken to be father of modern economics although his philosophy was more about politics than a description of economic laws. Smith laid out his thesis on political economics in the dauntingly titled *An Inquiry Into The Nature and Causes of the Wealth of Nations,* published in 1776. His most radical departure from prevailing eighteenth century thought was his challenge to the belief that land was the basis of wealth. The wealthy of that time were those with large agricultural land holdings. The industrial revolution was in its barest infancy. Steam power applied to manufacture and transport was at its earliest stages. Whether he envisioned it or not, Smith anticipated nineteenth century post-agricultural economy that would be labor intensive, not land intensive. It was a revolutionary shift in vocabulary.[1]

Smith's published thought set the foundation for expanded free market capitalism. He affirmed that individual self-interest in the pursuit of economic gain functioned like an "invisible hand" that automatically regulates the production and pricing of goods." He argued that rising demand raises prices, inducing producers to add labor and increase production. In the reverse direction, falling demand drives down prices and forces both producers and labor out of the market. The notion that prices were regulated by the interplay of self-interest and competition in a free market was an intuitively impelling, radical idea that literally invented capitalist economics. It was an idea that in time would elaborate into the increasingly comprehensive complex of theories and principles that makes up the modern discipline of economics.

Smith was neither a capitalist nor a socialist. He was a remarkably insightful economist and social philosopher. Of central importance to Smith's recommendations was his critique and rejection of guild and government protection of private monopolies and wages. For Smith's invisible hand to operate perfectly, it must not be unduly or artificially restrained by government or monopoly interference. He warned that monopoly was bad management practice and argued for a laissez-faire, hands-off policy by government. His views, though, were not so extreme a limitation on government's role as some have since made them out to be. Smith recognized that narrowly specialized work would discourage education among workers and saw the need for public education to offset ignorance among the working poor. He accepted the need for government institutions that the free market could not support adequately, and saw the need for an independent judiciary to mediate disputes. Smith was a man of the enlightenment, a product of the age of reason. His thinking was broad ranging, intuitively profound and balanced. It was also greatly influential for public policy, producing, among other things, near full implementation of free trade throughout Europe in the nineteenth century.[2]

Modern political economy focuses on how government can and should be used to further one economic interest over another for the benefit of all. Smith was not mute on this matter. He was astute enough to recognize that protecting the economic privilege of private property is a fundamental purpose of civil government. "Civil government," he wrote, "so far as it is instituted for the security of property, is in reality instituted for the defense of the rich against the poor." He observed that the job of police and magistrates was to maintain the economic status quo in every society and that free, fair elections of public officials are the best remedy available to the less economically advantaged. He observed that corrupt states can rig elections to maintain privilege of the powerful and that genuine political reform rarely comes easily or quickly. Limited private charity may hold back the swelling demand for a better life for the working poor, but eventually significant social change must be accepted by all. Government, chartered to maintain economic stability that assures social and economic privilege for the few, must ultimately be the instrument of social reform for the many. Smith's words went beyond capitalism to establish the foundations of Socialism. He anticipated government as social equalizer. He favored taxes that would rest more heavily on the wealthy than on the poor. Citizens should be taxed "in proportion to the revenue they enjoy under the protection of the state." He recommended taxes on the wealthy to redistribute income to finance public services and provide income maintenance for the working poor.

In the context of national and international trade and finance, Smith's political economics defines the methods used to protect and advance the economic interests of a nation. Import tariffs protect industries and jobs. Government fiscal policy promotes one interest group's privilege at the expense of another's. Taxes encourage one form of industry and discourage another. Through implementation of tax and legislative policies government becomes a protector and extender of special privilege. Political economics is the arena where the struggle takes place to balance the multitude of these clamoring political interests. Word play is the fulcrum of that balance.

The words of Adam Smith set the foundation for the great economic conflicts and debates of the nineteenth and twentieth centuries. There is no good reason to expect those conflicts and debates to cease just because the twenty-first century has arrived. The words that talk of wealth building, distribution and redistribution are as relevant as ever. This grand debate must continue indefinitely.

The Emergence Of Ideological Economic Debate

The nineteenth century, fully engaged with the growth of steam powered industry, spawned great fortunes side by side with masses of minimum wage laborers. The reality of capitalism as a system of economic growth clashed with visions of a more equal society. Philosophers of socialism and communism constructed those visions as an alternative to capitalism. The languages of socialism and capitalism became the battleground of politics. The words of each ascended to the level of iconic and ideological. Private ownership was defined as the enemy of social welfare; taxation as the enemy of economic growth. Each system argued its principles as not only in the best interest of all but also founded on soundest philosophical and moral ground.[3]

Capitalism dominated politics through the nineteenth century until it was battled to a political standoff by organized labor. The communist socialism of Soviet Russia tested State ownership and management of production until its collapse from gross economic inefficiency. The words that economic ideologues placed their bets on proved weak foundation on which to construct ultimate truths. The more advanced present day political and economic systems of the world are a pragmatic balance of political tension between some form of social welfare and some degree of market capitalism. Political debate continues nonetheless as a struggle to discover those words that build public support for one or the other of these old economic ideologies. Clothed in the rhetoric of the political right and left, the debates of capitalists and socialists continue to rage.

For capitalistic ideologues socialism is evil and immoral because it steals the hard earned, just reward of the capitalist's labor and skill. Socialism rewards sloth, not hard work, it reduces all of society to its lowest common social denominator and fails to provide the valued goods and services that customers demand. Socialist output is shoddy, poor in quality. Capitalists point to the power of a free market to create wealth and satisfy consumer wants. Maintenance and growth of wealth requires that government not interfere with the free market by regulating it. Government agents are vilified as bureaucratic meddlers who prevent citizens from satisfying their economic wants. Taxes are implicitly bad for the free market because they encourage growth in government bureaucracy and discourage investment that creates jobs. Taxes are the great enemy of ownership. They extract money to finance the government agencies that control and limit ownership rights. There must overall be minimal government interference in all business dealings so that the market remains free to work its distributive magic. The free market must be supreme. The rhetoric of the capitalist right is captured in words like these.

Socialists, though, are not far behind in the force of emotional words brought to bear for their position. From the socialist's view, capitalism is unrestrained greed that lacks concern for the public good. Socialists look to government for enforcement of fairness, honest dealing and respect for the public interest. Where necessary to protect the public interest, government must take ownership of public services to assure fair access and prices.

In the clash of these visions, there is rarely reconciliation. Blending market capitalism with social welfare objectives is a fight. Political solutions come hard. The battle is often taken to the streets. In contemporary Western culture, the battle between these polarities is most often acted out as labor-management conflict in the form of a laborers' *Strike* where both words and actions become heated.[4]

Labor unions were formed in the nineteenth century in response to mechanization of production. Early labor unions were more like guilds than collectives. Former independent artisans who could not afford the capital investment required to own powered machines became shop employees. Joining their skill with the machinery of production required a partnership. As guild members, skilled workers were on a par with owners. Without machines, their skill went unused and unrewarded. Without labor applied to the operation of machines the owner's capital was unproductive. There was incentive to work together.[5]

As the industrial revolution expanded, machinery amassed in factories that were themselves gigantic machines. Factories needed hands, not skills. Unions as collectives of unskilled laborers were the response to fragmented, unskilled tasks offered by the factories where any healthy body would do. Employers could hire, fire and replace at will. Collective action was required to level the playing field. A core of committed labor leaders found it beneficial to be part of world wide socialist movements. They fashioned a socialist labor movement that ideologically stood in opposition to capitalist exploitation of unskilled labor. On the world stage, labor-management conflict became a war of words between contesting ideologies.

Labor unions of the nineteenth century lacked legal legitimacy. A labor strike was still a criminal action. Labor strikes were at that time legally defined as constitutionally forbidden *restraint of trade*. Strikes were an act of civil disobedience, carried out in defiance of the law and subject to forceful police and military response. Unions, of necessity, became standing economic armies waging war against capitalism. Socialist economic philosophy was a useful and convenient philosophical battering ram in the fight against the sometimes brutal tactics of capitalist plant owners. Brutality generated a spirit of cohesion among striking workers that carried the movement forward despite its extra-legal status. *Solidarity* was (and still is) the battle slogan of union organizers.

FDR's National Labor Relations Act of 1935 made labor strikes legal. Unionization in the United States expanded rapidly even though strikes were temporarily prohibited through the course of World War II. The end of the war unleashed a torrent of pent up demand for goods. Employers, fearful of violating the new labor laws and of losing market share in a lengthy strike, became easy marks for unions and their organizers. In a climate of economic growth, union strikers were almost always victorious. Solidarity born of the pre-1935 era emboldened workers to press for maximum gains. Unionization for a time became the norm of American industry.[6]

Unions have long been portrayed as rabble rousers, disrupters of social accord or angry bullies. Striking members carry derogatory signs and shout obscenities that shock and offend. From the outside it is difficult for the on-looking public to decide where the greater justice lies in the battle between unions and management. Are the rights of workers in need of greater defense to maintain living standards, or are employers being bullied into paying excessive wages that drive up prices? The words that shroud strike conflict rarely offer useful facts. One is asked to take sides in favor of capitalism or socialism, on behalf of the oppressed little guy or in favor of economic growth. Choice is buried in a blizzard of emotion-laden word play. Loyalty trumps fact on both sides while onlookers express disgust and dismay at the bitterness of battle.

Polarization of the issues as socialist versus capitalist, labor versus management, is largely driven by self-interest aided by personal and cultural loyalties. Sides are taken, excesses occur, politics or the courts decide the winner. The fundamental issues go unexamined for it. The limits of ownership, the responsibilities of the individual, the clarity of language used are ignored. Winning is the sole test. The battle of words over how to fairly distribute wealth generated by industrial productivity has gone on for just over two centuries with little evidence of any acceptable solution. A limited part of the electorate may take one side or the other. Most wait out passage of the conflict, offended by the blustering of organized labor while skeptical of management words and intentions.

Business' Dilemma With Clarity Of Words

Business, operating behind the screen of anonymous public relations messaging, enjoys little credibility for its words. The paradox of business' public image is that Americans, though skeptical of corporations' words, still endorse the free market system that provides business freedom to game the system. Barely a month passes without a new corporate scandal hitting the news. Public opinion of Corporate America plummeted when major scandals were exposed with criminal prosecution of corporate executives. Recurring reports of executive pay in the tens and hundreds of millions paints a picture of unlimited greed. Public pronouncements couched in business double speak suggest intentional dishonesty. Lack of concern for public and shareholder interest is the message. The challenge to public relations firms that serve corporations is to reverse or modify these images. They work the trenches of PR with words as their only tools. Despite their best skill and effort it is difficult to portray corporations as inherently honest and truthful. Few corporate communications are written for clarity and transparency. They must satisfy requirements of law pertaining to publicly traded stock companies and still enhance the corporate image. Words from the corporate PR department typically are obtuse and twisted. Corporate reports are among the more impenetrable.

By way of example, a typical "disclosure" line from one annual report reads:

"The management . . . is responsible for establishing and maintaining an adequate system of internal control over financial reporting. Internal control over financial reporting is a process designed to provide reasonable assurance regarding the reliability of financial reporting and the preparation of financial statements for external reporting purposes in accordance with generally accepted accounting principles. Because of its inherent limitations, internal control over financial reporting may not prevent or detect misstatements.[7]

It is an obtuse and evasive statement. One must have the training and credentials of a corporate lawyer or accountant to read further. Care is taken not to claim accuracy or honesty. The impression offered is that the barest legal necessities are being satisfied. Where questions are raised, the response is likely to be that the data on which the report is based are as accurate as they can be. Financial analyses included in it are good as any other companies are. Errors of record can happen. "Trust us; we know what we are doing."

Most of the formal press pronouncements that describe business activity are pretentious, stale and widely distrusted. Claims of professionalism in management, reliance on factual data and control of financial matters will likely be deeply discounted. It does little good to point out that clarity has been sacrificed in favor of the safety of report formality. There is the danger that clarity might be misunderstood. It is safer to use well-worn, ambiguous, legally safe words. From the viewpoint of corporate officers it may be just as well that it is difficult to pierce the veil of verbiage in their annual report.

The contradiction inherent in most business communication is that clarity of communication may be legally risky. "Reasonable assurance regarding reliability" suggests little more than the likelihood that the numbers are added up correctly. Claiming use of generally accepted accounting rules says "we do it the way everyone else does it." Asserting that the internal control that exists "may not prevent or detect misstatements" all but admits that mistakes and approximations have crept into the data. Efforts of corporate officers to screen themselves from liability add to the perception of fundamental dishonesty. Words are carefully selected to defend corporate management, not to inform readers. The smokescreens raised around the activities of a company result from concern for being distrusted and misunderstood. That concern is self-fulfilling when clarity is sacrificed for safety behind the screen. Evidence that clarity need not be sacrificed is annually demonstrated in Warren Buffet's personally drafted annual reports. They are so highly informative that knowledgeable investors eagerly seek out copies.

Concern for profit over the general welfare is often carried to obvious extremes when production and development of new products is limited to those that assure only the highest profit. Pharmaceutical corporations produce only those blockbuster drugs that deal with the most feared illness and disease. Pricing of the drugs reflects demand driven by hope. Justification of high drug prices is based on the value of a new drug in providing relief from feared scourges. Illness or disease that lacks a paying customer base rarely gets noticed. Profitability is a practical but socially shallow foundation for allocating money and talent to medical research. The pursuit of financial gain, not public health, is the first priority of profit oriented pharmaceutical companies.

That is hardly surprising. Financial gain is what pays corporate officers large salaries and bonuses. Publicly traded companies see their successes and failures reflected in stock prices. Purchasers of equities (stocks) want return on their investment in the form of regular dividends and increased stock value. The innermost line of defense of this market system of rewards and payouts is the doctrine that an unregulated free market assures the greatest economic good for the greatest number. The story of political economics throughout the twentieth century has been one of raw socialism (government ownership of production resource) pitted against raw capitalism (unregulated free markets).

Capitalism versus socialism is a battle of words that has at times risen to the level of a shooting war. For those who take a side in this battle, the words that define it quickly come to define their lives. The ideology in which one is immersed settles all open metaphysical, materialistic and political issues. Words are not just the minds of the ideologically committed. Words are their personalities, their purpose in life, their absolutes. Remarkable things, those words.

PART FOUR:

Non-Sense;

The Ultimate In Word Play

17. Abstracting The Size Of The World; Words For Numeration

Not long after mama and dada, the earliest words a child is likely to learn are numbers. Laboriously articulated to the delight of parents, the first "won, too, tree" sequence signals entry into the world of words as pure ideas. Later, the fun of number manipulation or the pain of number confusion will follow. Numbers won't just be words. They will be a part of personal reality throughout life.

Numbers are widely taken to be hard, objective reality. If something can be counted and numerated, it is concrete, reliable, real. One need not be concerned about the meaning of 60 – unless you are not sure that is inches, centimeters, pounds, grams, feet, meters, or birthdays. It has to be something. Unless, of course, it is zero, then it is nothing. Which makes the point that a system of numbers begins with the definition of two symbolic entities, zero and one, which is to say, nothing and something, the semantic primes of numeration. These two numbers are the beginnings of the purest form of intellectual abstraction. Any system that entertains the concept of *nothing* would have to be.[1]

Words for quantity and counting depend on the brain's remarkable capacity to discriminate unitary entities out of the visual background. These entities are perceived to have boundaries that contain them as they move or change shape. The normal infant brain sees them as independent of other things in the visual frame. It takes an interest in them, smiling or grimacing and following them as they move about. At about age two when attention is called to the hand, the child's ten fingers are identified as capable of independence of action. When an adult or older child applies the words of the standard number sequence to the fingers, a sensory foundation for the decimal counting system is revealed to the infant's mind. Everything then becomes countable; people, toys, dogs, steps, years of age. Thereby the capacity for abstract thinking is set in place.

Elaborated into a system of mathematics, counting allows anything to be numerated. The gallons of a milk cow production, the bushels of wheat required for a winter's supply of bread, the number of men required to raise the roof of a barn, the arc of an artillery shell aimed at the target 1000 yards distant, the tons of nitrogen needed to send a rocket to the moon and return . . . . .

Mathematics in all its various forms is a magnificently flexible, adaptable system of abstraction that fits just about anything that needs to be described with quantified precision. Though its precision is entirely unreal, ideal and imaginary, counting stands as one of man's greatest achievements of imagination and is the foundation of all science. When words that describe purely imaginative, abstracted no-things become central to practical affairs the potential for confusion and self-delusion greatly increases. Avoiding bewilderment requires that mathematics be applied with high discipline.

Much of that discipline begins with definition of the terms of debate. The words of quantity demand exactness in their use because the language of quantity is only loosely anchored to sensory phenomena. "Real" numbers, for instance, are defined as integers, as whole numbers, or numbers with decimal places that do not extend to infinity. Real numbers that can be expressed as a ratio (x/y) of two integers are rational. Those that can*not* be expressed as a ratio of whole numbers are irrational. There are also imaginary numbers that result from calculations using negative values. Imagination is very much at the foundation of numbers. Numbers can never be physical things; they are forever extraordinarily philosophical, abstract ideas. They are probably the purest expression of the human intellect at play.

The nature of reality with numeration gets very muddy. The binding of numbers to physical reality comes about only when they are used to represent *some thing*. Numbers are overlaid onto physical reality as we perceive it. Sixty sheep, sixty dollars, sixty years, sixty stories, all have utility as descriptions more or less of *some thing*. Numbers that are not overlaid on things are not something in any physical sense. They are ideas. For those who love ideas, numbers are as real as any idea can be.

Numbers are used in "countless" ways. Mathematicians often engage in pure number play. The result of that play can be exceedingly practical when applied to real problems. Isaac Newton's calculus, one of the most widely used forms of mathematics in engineering, physics and economics, has been and continues to be a huge challenge to students. Calculus is basic to building bridges, firing rockets, designing computers, navigating in space or forecasting weather. Calculus, an imaginative and powerful use of numbers, does the job with efficiency and accuracy. It is the language of motion in physical space.[2]

Probability, the quantitative science used to forecast the future, is similarly a powerful problem-solving language. In constrained systems like the play of cards in poker or bridge, the probability of all possible card combinations can be calculated with precision. The probability of any sequence of coin tosses can be exactly determined across a series of fifty-fifty chance flips of heads or tails.[3] The best known model of probability is the normal, bell shaped curve, often used by teachers to compare the performance of students with one another. The normal curve is founded on an expectation of randomness in the measures of some quality or event. IQ, height, weight, daily temperature, rainfall, gas mileage, tire wear, can all vary around a central mean over a range from more to less. The normal curve is used as the probability model for the high to low distribution of a large number of measurements or observations. Its use is based on the idea (assumption) that the cause of variation is a wholly random sequence of yesses or nos, positives or minuses. In reality, actual distributions, even of very large funds of data, only approximate normal curve, high in the middle, low near the edges of the bell's rim. The normal curve of random distribution is a mathematical fiction built on some very simple, strict, and some say, unrealistically artificial assumptions. As used to predict a wide variety of phenomena the language of probability can be made to sound very exact. By its nature, real distributions are always approximate and often crudely so. Numbers fit physical reality only as far as the items they reference are physically precise and even then physical reality can be very imprecise.[4]

Numbers themselves have no inherent accuracy. This is true of numbers in general and of number concepts in particular. Ratios calculated as averages and percents can be especially confusing. For instance, if you purchase a new flat screen TV for $1000 with 10% off, then are offered an additional 10% price reduction if you make your decision *now,* the final price is not 20% less than $1000, or $800, rather it is $810, which is 10% off $1000 = $900, then 10% off $900 = $810. Think you've been scammed? Not at all! It's just the way percentages work. The words of numeration are inherently slippery.

Percents of percents, widely used in reporting and analyzing financial reports, can be treacherous. Company profits appear in published reports in the most positive form possible. When last year's profit of 2% net is matched against this year's 4% profit it can be claimed to have doubled from year to year. For an investor with a 6% standard, doubling is failure and is altogether unacceptable. Percentages permit differences to be focused on with simple, round *index* numbers. The percents themselves may then be further summarized in percentage form. Considerable distortion can result. The language of numbers is full of traps like these that can confuse and confound.

Despite the ambiguity that may pervade them, numbers can drive public action and social policy in powerful ways. For example, a research study of 16,000 women, aged 50 and over, reported in the March 4, 2004 issue of the New England Journal of Medicine, had very positive words for the effectiveness of estrogen in reducing colorectal cancers.[5] The ten year study was actually very complex, and the absolute numbers of cancers over that time span were quite small considering that the group studied numbered in the thousands. Cancer was ultimately diagnosed in 72 women in the placebo (no estrogen) group and 43 of those receiving estrogen. Because of this very large study population, the difference in these numbers greatly exceeds the probability of chance and can be confidently accepted. That however, may not be the entire story. Estrogen treatment was also associated with more serious cancers, those that had metastasized when discovered. That was not so good.

A paragraph summary in the news or a sound bit on television cannot begin to do justice to results of a study like this. Participants began to drop out after the first year, and only 70% of the 16,500 beginning group were still active in the study at the end of ten years. This loss in subjects was masked by reporting an <u>average</u> five year participation rate for all participants. Any time such an average is used, an underlying range from low to high must be assumed. The typical person hearing of the study might think this was a five year study. In fact, it was a one year study for some, a ten year study for others. It is very difficult to know what that means to the results.

A research design as expensive as this could not have been undertaken without some confidence in the likely outcome. It would not have begun without a fairly strong expectation that estrogen would reduce colorectal cancer. Every major research project chases the best experience and hypotheses of medical experts so that best guesses can become cloaked in science. Health research is a huge business employing tens of thousands of highly trained researchers. The results are big news to the media and are certain to drive recommendations of doctors and the hopes of patients. So, what should the average individual make of this study?

A battalion of highly credentialed experts stands behind the report. It is Science with a capital "S" and is presented in boiled down form as if the facts are clear and unambiguous. For thousands of women the message is read as "go to your doctor and have estrogen prescribed." For pharmaceutical companies it is interpreted as a signal to invest in estrogen production, create an impelling new trademarked name and gear up for the sales surge. And what should one make of the possibility that estrogen may increase the virulence of some cancers? Pharmaceutical companies should perhaps prepare for a jump in estrogen damage suits once trial lawyers catch onto the meaning of the full NEJM report. All of these outcomes are driven by prevailing confidence in the "hard reality" of numbers.

A study of this kind offers an abundance of impressive numbers that suggest something significant is being accomplished. The scientists who "crunch the numbers" talk statistical jargon that only other scientists fully understand. Much of this report in full form would be incomprehensible to the general population. Even a good many doctors may not grasp the full meaning of the results. The limitations of a substantial (thirty percent) drop-out rate and the need to trust participants to self-administer medication according to instructions are accepted as methodologically tolerable and necessary. Problems of a complex research design are assumed to be solved by the huge research population and by random assignment of participants into either medication or placebo groups. Researchers make their living working with this kind of complexity and randomness. They learn to accept approximations and estimates that might disturb others. Whether that is seasoned thinking or complacency with the language of numbers may be subject to debate.

To understand such research, medical and otherwise, it is essential to know that reducing physical events to the numbers always involves over-simplification of real events. It requires *encoding* counts of things and measures of events into numbers that can be manipulated quantitatively. Much is lost in the translation into number code. Much if not most of the complexity of cancer as a disease is ignored by the research design described above. The large number of participants limits the amount of medical, personal or family history that could be gathered and coded as part of the study. Even so, the uniqueness of each individual could never be adequately expressed as a set of numeric codes in the computer. Numbers are cold, impersonal representations of simple, easily observed differences among people. They are never real. They are forever ideas, abstractions, fluid and elusive.

The attempt to quantify human behavior at the level of mental ability creates its own special distortions. Intelligence, so called IQ, cannot be measured in the absence of developed language skill. Until the emergence of universal elementary education in Western nations, it was neither necessary nor practical to measure IQ. In the early decades of the twentieth century it became an experiment in evaluating human ability. The first IQ tests applied were essentially vocabulary knowledge quizes. High IQ meant facility in word use.

On America's entry into World War I, 1.7 million inductees into the American Army were tested for intelligence. Tests were loosely used to place soldiers in jobs deemed appropriate to their ability. Measuring language ability was assumed to be the equivalent of measuring overall general ability. Because language skill is so great a factor in intelligence as it is tested, performance of Eastern European immigrants and American Blacks tested in 1916, using English based IQ tests, was consistently far below that of schooled Caucasians. Widespread knowledge of differences in measured IQ fueled the prevailing view that despite being language-disadvantaged, low IQ measures of non-Caucasians reflected genetic inferiority. The practice of eugenics, the sterilization of low intelligence populations, was driven by the notion that mixing genes would "mongrelize" the language superior Caucasian population. Adolph Hitler took this idea to extremes.[6]

Mastery of language, because it disperses valuable knowledge of improved agriculture and industrial methods, is highly correlated with wealth. A liberal (language intensive) college education in the first half of the twentieth century was almost exclusively accessible to children of the wealthy elite. Intermarriage of college educated males and females preserved and consolidated wealth. Any theory that kept the poor, unlettered rabble in their place was certain to be popular. Measured intelligence was a handy bludgeon for that purpose. Factors in the socio/cultural environment were heavily discounted. Measured IQ was an easy justification for prejudice. That it seemed scientifically objective and unbiased because it was represented as a number made it more justifiable yet. Social status was buttressed by numbers.

Poor language ability continues to be a barrier to economic progress in all cultures. Recognition that exposure to language use in very early infancy is fundamental to language development now drives public policy that starts classroom education as early as age three.

Intelligence is not the only form of measurement applied to the human mind. Mental metrics designed to measure personality and character traits followed intelligence testing as a popular psychological tool beginning in the 1930s. Early efforts were directed at diagnosing mental illness to better understand and treat it. Delusions, hallucinations, withdrawal, all the various forms of *madness* found in the human population came under the scrutiny of psychological tests that reduced mental health to a number.

After World War II many employers began to test job candidates to assure that they would not bring problem behaviors into the work place. Theories were spun to explain why strong, dominant personalities make good managers, aggressive, outgoing ones are top salesmen, while careful, exacting ones make good bookkeepers. Most entry level positions, from which future managers, salespeople and bookkeepers would be promoted, were selected for their passivity and cooperativeness. Employers are most comfortable with people who will work comfortably under hierarchical authority. That people can and do grow and change was largely ignored. That may not be a major issue. There is question as to just how reliably permanent these measures are. It can be demonstrated that personality test results do vary with time and circumstance for the same candidate. Those who understand what qualities are needed by their job can choose to shape their answers to fit the desired personality profile. Measures of people qualities are not necessarily all that fixed or reliable. They are often rubber numbers.[7]

Human beings do not lend easily to quantification as digitized data for easy prediction or manipulation. Employers, marketers and political pollsters all make extensive use of data in targeting their messages and predicting how consumers or voters will behave. The most accurate prediction is achieved when relevant questions are asked of those who are willing to answer candidly. Much opinion polling, though, depends on use of averages, statistically constrained sampling, and good guesses. Communities or voting districts are characterized by religious affiliation and average age. Gaining access to data on purchases made, favorite TV shows or movies, make of car and number of children may improve these guesses somewhat. Those who make decisions based on numbers are always working with rough estimates, approximate categories and calculated probabilities. Anything that improves them is a win. The better their data, the happier they are. It's not unlike forecasting the weather where most people expect error. An overgeneralization maybe, though it is the kind of cautionary attitude that weather forecasts deserve. It should be applied to all forms of quantitative measurement of human skills and attributes.

The coding process itself can introduce distortion in measurement. Coding observations into quantitative data requires reduction of a lively thing or event into a simple number. The NEJM estrogen study illustrates how numbers can be organized and manipulated in some very creative ways to yield the anticipated relationships within them. Those relationships must then somehow be translated back onto the realm of sensory experience. At either stage of translation, there may be error or distortion. Limitations of time and cost on the amount of data coded means that only the most salient, easily accessible observations are encoded. Other observations that might be numerically coded as data must either go unrecognized or ignored. In pursuit of useful knowledge, quantitative analysis of data elements ignores the vast richness of nature. The universe of coded data is greatly constrained by cost and practicality. It is impossible to code everything. The scope and amount of information that data analysis can yield is limited only by those data elements coded as well as by the accuracy of observation and the coding. Computers don't care what they process. The working maxim is GIGO, garbage in, garbage out. And garbage *can* produce statistically significant results. If there is enough randomness, it almost certainly will. Numbers don't know what they are doing. There is no inherent reality to them.

The end product of the coding process effort is stored data. In the early days of computing, it was common to hear talk of gathering data on everything about everybody so that all decisions would be scientifically accurate and, thereby, *free of troublesome personal judgments.* The computer was expected to be the ultimate controller of human destiny. There is still concern on the part of many people that anyone with access to credit, medical or personal records could know everything about them. Human beings are vastly more complex than the few numerically coded records on a computer. The greater problem with access to such records is that they could yield a distorted picture. Indeed, it is common in human affairs for trivial events to be grossly overblown by coding and measurement. The strongest argument against easy access to personal data is *not* that our individual lives will become too intimately known. Rather, it is that a grossly oversimplified, quantified record will lead to serious misunderstanding or even defamation. Numbers fail at nuanced description of the complex.

Vast computer banks of encoded data are now regularly processed with statistical analysis called *data mining* on the assumption that there is a wealth of information to be extracted from data stored in electronic form. In the pre-computer era, data was stored on paper documents in file drawers. If you did not already know the value of the data you wished to examine, it was probably too costly to access it. The power of the computer to process electronically coded data into some form of statistical summary creates expectations for production of instant wisdom. Data quality is always deserving of question, especially so with giant, general purpose data bases. If the coding process is not very strict, the reliability of the data can be quite low. There may be more error than information value in it. Even when carefully measured and coded, there is question as to its inherent value. There may be built in biases and distortions that generate uncertain, even wrong-headed conclusions in analyses. There is always the likelihood that important or even critical variables have not been recognized and thus are not coded and available in the data base. Data is not information. It is just coded observation of events observed and thought to be significant.

The human mind entertains vastly more richness of observation than any data base ever could. With practice, it can perceive and execute complex, elaborate patterns like answering quiz show questions with lightning speed, a trick that was modeled on computers at great cost.[8] As with modeling language structure on the computer, adding a level of intuitive judgment to the scheme of computation is very difficult. Many skills may never be programmable for representation on a computer. The complex, dangerous job of driving a car involves sensing the speed, observing the movement of other cars on the road, watching for and reacting to road hazards, controlling the location of the car in the road and moderating its speed. The athletes on a basketball or hockey team are continually observing the location and movement of both teammates and opponents with relationship to ball or puck and net. No quantified variables are recorded or coded for use in performing these actions. The complexity of patterns that must be managed is boggling. Only skill and practice is sufficient for the demands of safe, high-speed driving, or a tightly choreographed, furiously paced competition for game points. Measurement of the variables involved with these circumstances would be impractical to the point of silliness.

That begs the question: what about the fact that computer simulations of these skills and sports can be designed through skilled application of mathematics and observed variables. The answer is that simulations are totally different from the game itself. The simulation is displayed on a two dimensional surface (screen) where no one crashes, falls, fights or gets injured. Experienced in simulated play, computer games are nothing like the real thing. The simulated game is a computerized map of those variables identifiable and measurable in real play that game designers can quantify and display as action images on a visual screen. Designers of simulations are constantly testing their simulation for realism. The gap between the real and the simulated presents limitless opportunity for upgrading the game to still higher levels of realism. They are a marketer's dream.

The current version is regularly replaced by a new, updated one. The market is forever being renewed because the technology can never fully mature. There is likely no end to that chase.

The extent of seeming reality in some simulations can be remarkable. Those used for space and aircraft flight training, for instance, can be designed for play using the actual control devices and consoles used in flight. Flight simulations may also be supplemented with hydraulic shifting and lifting of the simulation capsule. Flight control responses of pilots and astronauts can be trained under a variety of simulated conditions, setting in place the necessary decision processes and reactions before the real job is to be performed in the air or in space. It is never the real thing, though, until life is at risk.

What is of serious concern is the gap between real and realism that numbers try to bridge. Scientific decisions, especially medical ones, are based on scientifically quantified and tested variables. But humans are not all put together alike. The cause of one person's complaint may be irrelevant to the same complaint of another. The pharmaceutical industry operates on probabilities – the likelihood, that is, of a pharmaceutical helping or not. Or, it may hurt. Knowledge of biochemistry – the real workings of chemicals in the human body – may suggest cause and effect that justifies use of a given pharmaceutical. Individual human body chemistries are not all identical. Physicians rely on the probabilities asserted by pharmaceutical companies, prescribing, trying and erring when dealing with the pattern of symptoms they hear and see from the patient. The more useful scientific words a physician has available to explain complex symptom patterns, the greater the accuracy of treatment –but only up to a point. Intuition must then fill the gaps. There is clearly something beyond routinely identifying and measuring health related variables. In many such domains, experienced human judgment is superior to quantified science.

Elemental science based on numbers has moved man and civilization forward in dramatic fashion. It has disciplined and shaped the intellectual capabilities of mankind. Science and mathematics are powerful things. Some scientists and philosophers believe that a unified, mathematically based theory of science will eventually explain everything. Maybe so, but at his best, man is still a long way from that place. Human intuition and judgment remain central and indispensable tools of intellect. It must never be forgotten that numbers are no more than a very high form of intellectual play. They are symbols for nothing and something. Before numeration can become a useful tool, you must first know what *nothing* and *something* are.

18. Science; Empirical Abstractions

The foundation of science is language, the first mind map of nature. Language begins with sensory experience that elaborates into a mind map of word constructs. Social exchange shapes the mind map to where it becomes common sense. Critical questions challenge common sense to produce science. From this process, defined variables and data elements emerge as the basis of testing. Numbers quantify experimental tests. Methods and instruments that advance scientific, quantified testing are invented. A rigorous mind map based on well-defined variables and data elements takes shape. If the process is carried out with skill and discipline, it can yield remarkable results. It is a special art and skill that requires controlled use of intuition and feeling combined with rigorous scientific method.

Humans sense things first, investigate them systematically later. Application of scientific method must overcome native prejudice and the authority of raw sensory reality. In the practice of science, emotion must not be allowed to unduly distort or overwhelm method. Science must be awarded priority over intuition. In Anglo-English words, the status of science is expressed in ways that emphasize rational thinking. Intuition is indispensable to research and discovery but hard, quantified, rational science gets the final credit. This comes from a strong historical preference for reason and rationality arising out of the seventeenth century Age of Reason. Science is the exercise of reason in creating and clarifying word based knowledge. A prejudice for science, rationality and reason may, though, obscure the need for balance between method and sound human judgment.

The words *rational* and *reasonable* come from a common Latin base word meaning to reason, to think, to count. They describe special qualities of thinking, decision making and argument. In an earlier chapter it was observed that rationality includes good thinking, clear argumentation, dispassionate reflection and overall care in choosing a point of view or course of action. Irrationality is characterized by impulsive, emotional, and generally ill-considered actions and speech. Rationality is "cool reason", irrationality is hot emotion. One who is rational takes time to stop, observe closely and carefully, consider the situation and compare it with the best available counsel and experience. Rational people are cool cats, irrational ones, hotheads. Rationality is good. Irrationality is to be guarded against. The rationality of science is presumed to be inherently better than the passion of search for the answers to life's vexing problems.

Logic is a form of systematic, rational argument that is the foundation of scientific theory. It brings the rigor of mathematics to scientific method. Though the rigor of logic lends a certain prestige to the practice of science it has only limited utility in formulating scientific experiments. Logic and logical reasoning are concepts that evoke a sense of clarity and accuracy of thought. Like rational thinking, logical reasoning means cool judgment and cautious calculation. In a pre-computer age, logic and math were useful tools of philosophers and scientists who labored to discover the workings of physics and metaphysics. Complex logic and calculation required systematic, deliberate work. In science, application of good method is everything. Rationality is good science. Logical reasoning is good thinking. The esoterically abstract methods of eighteenth and nineteenth century logicians imparted mystery and awe to science. Logical reasoning was not just good, it was near magical.

A dispassionate judgment of logic must take into account that formal logic is only as good as the quality of the definitions of words or symbols used in the logical structure. The words employed in logic need *not* be directly referential to sensory phenomena. They can be purely abstract. Logic that uses abstractions can develop "true" but nonsensical results. Pure logic is pure abstraction. Truth is in the correct application of logical method not in achievement of practical results. There are huge pitfalls in the use of symbolic logic. Nonetheless, logic can be useful in important ways. It is very useful as the basis of modern mathematics and computer science. That does not make the language of logical abstraction any less problematic.

Further evidence of prejudice in favor of reason over emotion can be found in the term fact. Once used to simply mean *an act accomplished,* the meaning has been extended significantly. A *fact* is now something established and unarguable whether it has been accomplished or not. Facts are hard, facts are firm knowledge, facts are facts. Facts arise out of good thinking and good science. Facts are what science is about. Facts are about accuracy and veracity. The word fact used in the English language has a hard edge of finality to it that is special. Facts go with rationality, logic and science. Facts are what science and knowledge are built on. Without fact, there can be no theory. Good scientific thinking requires hard facts. If it isn't a fact, how can you trust it?

The extended meanings of *rational, irrational, logical* and *factual* include significant preference for all things scientific over those that are emotional and intuitive. It is generally overlooked that mathematics and logic are severely limited as to the range of problems they can be applied to. The vast proportion of scientific theory building is based on experienced intuition. Scientific method is a tool. Science is its product. Complex philosophical arguments required a bias for simplicity and precision in thinking through math calculations and logical syllogisms. The prestige of philosophers and scientists gave weight to the words they wrote. Their writings formed the meaning of these words. This is the way the meaning of words emerges with their use. The language of western culture is full of embedded prejudice for science based on mathematics and logic because of their very special status in the eighteenth and nineteenth centuries. Math calculation, once a tortuous and tedious task, is now relegated to calculators and computers. Logic, once taught as basis of every scientist's training, is now rarely taught except as a tool of computer programming.

The result of all this history is established status behind words favoring systematic, scientific judgment. It is a preference that downgrades those many decisions that should properly be made impulsively or automatically. When a child runs from the curb in front of your automobile there is no wisdom in stopping to consider the situation coolly. It is a crisis condition! You must hit the brakes without thinking. Only an instant reaction will do. Nor does the play of sports call for lengthy analysis. When the long ball is blasted toward the warning track, the fielder does *not* pull out a calculator to determine with calculus the baseball's likely trajectory. From experience, he visually estimates the ball's path and demonstrates his skill at intuitive calculus by catching it. Intuition is not scientific, and thus suspect. Science is good; emotion is suspect. Scientific rationality enjoys unwarranted preference as not just a *good* quality but *the best* as well. It is unwarranted prejudice

The language of science and logic continues to celebrate science as a superior and preferred mode of thinking. But rationality, logic, reasonableness and facts rarely dominate human decision making. Intuition always plays a major part in human judgment just as it does in an infant's discovery and use of words. It almost always plays a role in shaping facts. More often than not, science is brought to bear demonstrating what is already widely known or assumed. Great mathematical problem solutions are rarely born out of routine calculation. They come in a flash after extended consideration, or when a missing piece of the puzzle is suddenly fitted in place. Much irrational, below-consciousness processing precedes the great "ah-has" of science. Good scientific theory is not so much built as it comes together in a rush of intuitive insight after the lengthy trial and error of mental struggle. Until it is later disciplined by scientific method, the process will be a messy, intuitive, emotional one.

Science comes in many different packages all of which contribute significantly to the richness of language as well as improvement of the human condition. The ways in which science can be applied is illustrated variously. Invention of the periodic table of natural elements is one, emergence of the theory of evolution out of natural science and historical geology another. Marketing surveys, opinion polling, and the examination of the still poorly understood workings of diet and nutrition are also scientific processes. Each of these endeavors has required invention of its own special language in support of its science.

The periodic table of physical elements was historically long in coming.[1] Alchemy as it was practiced in the middle ages was about turning ordinary matter into silver and gold or about discovering the elixir that would confer eternal life. The economics of supply and demand were as yet unformulated. It was not appreciated that if gold were easily producible from base substance it would no longer have great value. Certainly there must have been costs in pursuing alchemy. The laboratory hazards of poorly informed and dangerous chemical experimentation may have foreshortened many lives. The effort was nonetheless productive in that, over a long span of human history, the basic physical elements of nature were identified, one by one, until they were seen to form a complex pattern.

The discovery process probably began in pre-history. Metals, along with mercury, carbon and sulfur were known to early man. Gold, silver, copper, iron, tin, and lead were extracted with carbon and sulfur and made into tools or ornaments. It was not until the nineteenth century that these metals were identified as elements themselves. The Greek philosopher Aristotle, six centuries before the common era (BCE), pondered the problem of the earth's physical makeup. He concluded that *earth, air, fire* and *water* were the natural elements of all matter. Then he added a fifth unearthly substance called *Ether* as the stuff that makes up the greater universe beyond earth. For more than two millennia, these words were the mental map that described the foundations of the natural world for educated men. The world would have to wait until alchemy was transformed into chemistry for that map to be revised and updated.

Arsenic, antimony, bismuth and zinc were isolated by chemists of the middle-ages (approximately 1250 through 1550), though it was not yet understood that they were elements. Some things were wrongly or fancifully labeled elements. A mysterious substance called phlogiston was put forward to explain combustion by fire and oxidation. It was a widely held but hopelessly wrong addition to the mental map of chemistry. As late as the eighteenth century, chemistry had not yet left its age of alchemy. The practice of alchemy nonetheless had by then discovered phosphorous, hydrogen, oxygen, nitrogen, chlorine, and tungsten, all good, new, scientifically useful words. Major advances in discovery of new elements and formulation of sound method as foundation of chemistry would have to wait until the nineteenth century.[2]

As the science of chemistry developed and the characteristics of known elements were published within the community of scientists, imaginative insight into relationships among elements began to discern system and pattern. The Russian chemist Dmitri Mendeleev is credited with envisioning and forming the periodic table of the elements sometime in the 1860s. He looked at the fragmented knowledge of chemistry and intuited their underlying structure. It was a brilliant insight that would become indispensable to the study of physical and chemical phenomena. Its existence has contributed to the discovery of other elements of nature. It has wide applicability to physics, biology and engineering. It is a powerful mental map.

The periodic table of the elements became the model of how to advance scientific knowledge. Concepts, constructs, ideas, elements, call them as you please, are identified, defined, measured and studied. Useful applications are sought and measurable relationships among them explored. Theory that explains natural phenomena and advances knowledge is adduced. Science in all its forms proceeds on this model. Nature is deconstructed into cleanly identifiable, definable pieces that become the basis of shared, useful communicable knowledge. Science expands language and culture. Theory weaves the words of science into usable knowledge. New theory replaces old.

Charles Robert Darwin, the English naturalist, embarked on a five year, round the world voyage of the HMS Beagle in 1831. The Beagle's mission was to survey world coasts and harbors to produce marine charts for war and commercial use. Largely as an afterthought, Darwin was added to the crew by Robert FitzRoy, the captain, who sought intellectual and social companionship to offset the mind numbing isolation of a long sea voyage. Almost rejected at first by FitzRoy for his political views, Darwin was chosen for his relevant interests in geology and botany. To further his geological knowledge Darwin took with him a newly published text by the leading geologist of the age, Charles Lyell. Voyaging with a sense of the vast contexts of geological time, Charles Darwin would see natural processes in a fresh way. He would uncover and envision evolutionary processes and ultimately formulate them as theory.[3]

In South America and the Galapagos Islands, Darwin observed differences in birds and sea tortoises that suggested a process of adaptive change to be at work in their development over time. He experienced an earthquake on the geologically active west coast of South America that visibly raised a bed of mussels above the high tide line, demonstrating the process of continual geological change. In the high Andes he found fossil trees and seashells that measured the extent of the mountain range's rise. In the South Seas he confirmed that coral reefs had formed as ancient volcanoes sank into the ocean. His theological schooling was challenged by the evidence of his experience on the voyage of the Beagle, while his reputation as a natural scientist was enhanced through letters and specimens sent home to London as the voyage progressed.

On return to London as an accepted gentleman scientist, Darwin was exposed to the full range of scientific theory and knowledge then in play and invited to present findings of his voyage to both the geological and zoological societies of London. Fossils collected were identified by experts as long extinct species. Bird specimens collected from the voyage were examined by leading scientists with unexpected results. Mockingbirds Darwin had classified as interbreeding varieties were discovered to be separate species adapted as a result of isolation from one another. The widely held religious belief that each species of biological creature was a "special creation" of the almighty deity came open to challenge. The Galapagos Islands bird specimens Darwin had first identified as entirely different families were examined and found to be species of finches adapted to differences in available food supply. It was evidence of natural selection that was hard to dismiss and a discovery so significant that it was reported in the newspapers of the time. Evidence of natural selection accumulated in support of evolutionism. Darwin found himself building a bridge between conventional religion and modern science that he would have to cross.

Darwin's actual and intellectual voyage of discovery illustrates the way in which reality maps develop in ongoing experience. The prevailing language provides a starting point that has been built up out of generations of human experience. The human mind faced with novelty invents explanations out of existing words. Old words are given added or new meaning, new words are invented. The reality map changes to fit social and scientific experience. Throughout the actual voyage, Darwin pursued his natural curiosity with the best intellectual tools available. Beginning the intellectual voyage, he struggled to reconcile discrepancies and contradictions. The end result was his landmark publication, "Origin of the Species." The title alone speaks to his passage from the doctrine of special creation to that of natural selection. The discovery of the genetic code of life, DNA, ultimately verifies the thread of continuity that runs from the smallest virus to the most advanced form of life, man. DNA demonstrates that the building blocks of life are the same in all living things. The option to accept or reject such radical evidence continues to vex many.

Science goes far beyond chemistry and physics in search of knowledge. Hard sciences yield close to exact answers on many practical issues, though only as long as they stay above the sub-atomic level. Then they can become very fuzzy around the edge. The social sciences, psychology, political science, anthropology, and linguistics, for instance, are characterized throughout by ambiguous, indistinct ideas and issues. Yet they deal with matters of urgent concern for humanity. These are sciences in the sense that every possible effort is made to bring discipline to the definition of their central ideas and to assure that those ideas are examined rigorously using statistics and accepted research method. Research doctorate degrees in the social sciences require rigorous training and are likely to bear the title, Ph.D., Doctor of Philosophy. As domains of science they are, indeed, an extension of the most rigorous methods of analysis and synthesis employed by history's great philosophers.

Fundamental to social science research in every field is the disciplined use of language to assess the shape of individual mental maps. Personal, group, face-to-face or phone interviews elicit verbal response from research subjects. IQ tests, personality inventories, and questionnaire protocols put questions to individuals to "measure" their characteristics, qualities, abilities, attitudes, or intentions. Design of question formats is carefully thought out down to choice and order of specific words as well as phrasing and format of questions. Words are the fundamental tools of much if not most social science research.

Among the most visible and familiar of questioning approaches used are surveys of voter intention conducted in advance of elections. These are called polls to echo the attempt to predict subsequent voter behavior at election polling places.

Straw votes to test the political wind have been in local use through most of US history. The first organized effort to forecast a presidential election was in 1916 when Literary Digest Magazine correctly predicted the election of Woodrow Wilson as President by mailing out post cards to readers, automobile owners and telephone subscribers. Success at forecasting the election results of the following four elections seemed to verify the method used. For the 1936 presidential election, though, despite polling nearly ten million people, the Magazine's prediction went seriously wrong. It predicted a landslide for the Republican candidate, Alf Landon who ultimately won only Maine and Vermont. Pollster George Gallup made his professional reputation by correctly predicting the Roosevelt landslide using science based sampling that surveyed a much smaller but much more representative population of voters.[4]

The 1936 presidential election came at the depth of the great depression. Economic circumstances were dire nationwide. Those who could afford a Literary Digest subscription, an automobile or telephone service were least distressed by the times and most likely to be registered as Republicans. The population polled by the Digest was not representative of the electorate at large. Gallup, applying the social science methodology of stratified demographic sampling achieved the quality of representation that The Literary Digest, despite a much larger fund of data, failed to achieve.

American society, despite the melting pot ideology, is not all that homogeneous. It is rife with subcultures that have special beliefs, words, customs and politics. Within subcultures there will usually be opinion and attitude differences as a function of gender, age, education and income level. Political issues that fuel strong passions may split many different ways. Severe economic circumstances can produce major change in attitude. Polling must take the variety of those passions into account when forming a representative sample from which to make predictions. Passions are expressed in words.

The words used to question people must be carefully considered and weighed for cultural variation in meaning. They must represent the common core of language. Issues must be framed in simple, non-inflammatory words. The order in which questions are asked will change responses. Words vary subtly in literal and emotional meaning. When emotionally loaded issues are surveyed, special care must be taken as to the sequence of related questions. The way a question is framed can make a major difference. For instance, while more than half of Americans in 2006 considered medically induced fetal abortion to be murder, two-thirds said that government should not interfere with a woman's access to abortion. And, while three-fourths of those polled said there is too much power in the hands of a few big companies, three-quarters still accepted the view that the success of American business has a lot to do with the strength of this country. Ninety-two percent of a polled population sample agreed that it is important that the president and congress deal with issues of environmental quality, while fully two-thirds rejected the need to sacrifice economic growth to achieve improvement in the environment.[5] Word disconnects of this nature are common in opinion surveys. Contradictions are inherent in the mental map.

Beyond the central importance of the words used, much of the science of opinion polling turns on sampling method. The size of the sample can vary substantially depending on the importance of the information obtained and the closeness on which issues divide. Most national electoral polls make use of from one thousand to two thousand interviews. At these population levels, there can still be as much as plus or minus 3% error in the prediction obtained. Extraordinary accuracy of plus or minus 1% can be obtained with population approaching ten thousand people. Reasonably good results can sometimes be obtained from only a few hundred people when the sample is rigorously chosen to represent known and well defined population demographics.

Polling science is about disciplined use of words and careful concern for representative inclusion of important personal and cultural differences. Science requires use of the best, most complete mental map of the subject at issue. It disciplines the application of measures, then verifies results against the best knowledge of other scientists. Words are always its most critical tools.

Science modifies and expands the language and adds new meaning to old words. It enriches the mental maps used to grasp and deal with the physical world. The special status accorded science in the language has unquestioned merit. Humans judge on the basis of feelings and values. Despite its lesser reputation and prestige, emotion continues to dominate most human thinking. The average person is a natural, intuitive scientist. Cause and effect are sensed when things occur in immediate sequence or just together. Trained scientists know the hazards of naïve and untested observation. Simple sequential or simultaneous events that appear to establish cause and effect can always occur by chance. Systematic testing is required to establish cause and effect. Naïve, first impressions are nonetheless hard to resist. Diet and nutrition are complex issues that fall victim to much speculation that passes as science. They offer an example of applied science mixed with emotionally doctrinaire hypothesis making.[6]

Dietary policy examines the broad mix of foods available for human consumption and looks at the consequences of variation in diet for health and well being. Diets are concerned with the balance of fats, proteins, fibers and carbohydrates that make up the typical dietary intake. Dietary scientists recommend a mix of food categories that are thought to provide the desired balance. Diets are the larger picture. Nutrition looks at the molecular level of food intake, studying the effects of specific nutrients on health and well being. Nutrition is the close-up picture of food intake. Most of the core science involved with nutrition is biochemical and involves laboratory experimentation. The hypotheses that drive dietary science are most commonly generated by the medical field of epidemiology – the statistical analysis of disease epidemics. In many ways, laboratory experimentation and epidemiology are a very odd coupling of scientific paradigms.

Dietary science is focused on the causes of the so-called major diseases of civilization; heart disease, diabetes, cancer and obesity. The possible causes of these diseases are taken from national records of mortality (variation in rates of death by a disease) and correlating those disease rates with cultural diet. The usual epidemiological study of causality will opportunistically examine the proportions of fats, proteins and carbohydrates eaten by the average person in a national grouping to see if there is a relationship with disease. Statistical analysis of this kind is correlational. Death or obesity rates, for instance, are analyzed for indication of a positive or negative association with one or another category of food. When a statistically significant correlation is found, resources are quickly brought to bear in a battle against the "epidemic". Correlational research often assumes a cause and effect relation that is false. The cholesterol hypothesis on based on such science. Good science concerning the cause of heart disease has been bypassed in the rush to win the war on heart disease.[7]

The difficulty with correlational analysis is that it very rarely qualifies as real science. It offers no assurance that a disease is *caused* by any given category of food. The real cause may work through intermediary variables and thereby represent only a second hand association. Real science is concerned with cause and effect. It does not settle for mere correlation. Matters of life and death, though, don't easily permit the cool heads of science to continue looking for the underlying causal mechanics while the epidemic rages. The tendency is to seize the first hypothesis that offers satisfying explanation. Urgently advocated and enacted as a solution, the hypothesis can easily become the final statement of knowledge. Science is not fully invoked to clarify or confirm. It there are competing hypotheses, science may be bypassed for argument between adherents to competing positions. Much of current day Western dietary knowledge is little better than a rhetorical battle of words. Any of these words have become invested with so much emotion that they are the science. Rigor of method has been forgotten.

Current day medical policy concerning prevention of heart disease focuses on control of blood cholesterol. Cholesterol is thought to cause fatty build up in the arteries. This is believed to block blood flow and cause heart disease. Cholesterol is found in dietary fat. Therefore, dietary fat must be avoided. The principal alternative to fat is carbohydrate. A "heart healthy diet" is high in protein and carbohydrate. The science underlying this logic is epidemiological and has been challenged as bad science. A close reading of evidence put forward from competing sources suggests that there is, at best, a very small correlation between cholesterol and heart disease. There is question as to whether the small correlation is a worthy foundation for recommending avoidance of dietary fat and prescription of drugs called statins that chemically reduce cholesterol in the blood stream. Statins, unfortunately, can damage the liver, cause muscle cells to break down and create chronic gastrointestinal problems. If dietary fat is avoided in favor of a high carbohydrate diet the result can be obesity, another possible cause of heart disease. Reducing cholesterol by avoiding fatty foods may result in diabetes brought on by obesity from excessive carbohydrates. The worst offender among carbs may be ordinary sugar.[8]

Medical policy concerning diabetes and obesity favors avoidance of sugar and starch in the diet. This means that fat and protein are increased to meet calorie requirements. Diets high in fat have been shown to safely, comfortably and reliably reduce body weight. Such diets are vigorously, even angrily rejected by the medical establishment as ridiculous and dangerous. Nonetheless, diabetics respond well to a reduced carbohydrate, high fat diet. The standard medically therapeutic diet for diabetes continues to be low fat intake because of the concern over high cholesterol when fat is consumed. The alternative, a high carbohydrate diet, promotes the symptoms of diabetes and can produce obesity. Patients are caught in the cross fire of the diet wars.

Research at the biochemical level suggests that the causes of the chronic diseases of civilization may be much more complex than just measuring good, bad and total cholesterol, avoiding dietary fat and using pharmaceutical statins. The role of insulin in regulating the availability to body cells of fat and sucrose, and storage of fat in adipose tissues, appears to be critical. Better science is needed to fully understand those causal factors that may underlie heart disease, diabetes, cancer and obesity.

Nutrition has become the ordinary man's science in the twentieth century. Concern for molecular level nutrition was brought about by diseases such as scurvy, pellagra, beriberi, rickets and anemia. Lack of specific nutrients at the elemental level was identified as the cause of these diseases.[9] Because it seeks to identify the molecular elements of a healthy diet, the periodic table can be used as a rough model for nutrition. Those elements of nutrition, the vitamins and minerals identified as "essential", are the foundation of nutritive knowledge. The government publishes recommendations on the essentials of good nutrition. Recommended daily requirements for basic vitamins and minerals are printed on pill bottles and cereal boxes. One cereal builds its advertising message around addition of 100% of these recommended minimums to the average portion of its flakes. Need for the minimum has in most cases been identified only through emergence of troublesome or obvious symptoms when an element is missing in the diet. The legend of scurvy eradication through use of vitamin C in citrus is regularly retold. British sailors ravaged by scurvy on their long sea voyages were found to recover fully and avoid further disease through the simple measure of carrying a generous supply of limes onboard. Ultimately, vitamin C was chemically isolated and identified as the critical factor in avoiding the disease.

Nutrition has become folk medicine driven by the dietary word wars. Masses of advertising literature circulate offering improved health with the use of one supplement or another of vitamins, minerals or natural organic compounds. Scores of books are written and eagerly read on the subject. Good mothers and housewives inform themselves on the nutrition needs of husbands and children. Common foodstuffs are analyzed for the presence of the various elements of nutrition and cataloged for convenient reference so that sufficient presence in the diet can be assured. The not so subtle hint that there may still be nutritive elements missing from the standard list comes in the form of a claim for the miraculous curative benefits offered by one exotic (and costly) natural nutritive compound or another. Retail nutrition stores in almost any shopping mall and on the internet operate as an extension to retail pharmacies. The invitation to improved health through better nutrition is everywhere.

The suggestion of nutrition hype-advertising is that every disease or malady is curable with the right nutrition. Indeed, one standard dictum of medical practice is that the best medicine is always good nutrition. A belief in the possible efficacy of miracle compounds advances, even though some nutrients are known to be harmful. Excess dosages of vitamin A can be seriously toxic, excess of vitamin D in artificial form can result in kidney failure, excess Vitamin B6 can cause nerve damage and too much vitamin E can thin the blood dangerously. Balanced dosage seems to be the critical issue. Nutrition is in no way a well-founded science founded on a base of comprehensive theory. Individual metabolism and nutritive need may differ substantially. Need for specific nutrients may vary greatly from person to person which means that some recommended minimums or maximums may be approximate or even arbitrary. The evidence of sound nutrition is sound health and the experience of personal well being. It is not until symptoms of ill health occur that it becomes apparent something is missing.

The evidence of good or poor nutrition from experience can be so subtle as to thwart discovery of missing elements in one's diet. This means that the human body itself becomes the experimental laboratory of nutrition science. In present day practice, each person is his/her own scientist experimenting to find out which nutrients seem to make a difference in good health and which seem irrelevant.

Some form of personal nutrition self-diagnosis may indeed be a good answer. Animals are known to seek out foods that offer missing nutrients in their diets. Human appetite and taste are shaped in part, at least, by a need for nutritive balance in diet. Indeed, if appetites were not overwhelmed by the large quantities of refined carbohydrates consumed, humans might discover how to tune their tastes to establish nutritive balance. There still is much mystery about nutrition. Understanding of how elements interact – that is, block or enhance one another

– is limited. Balance may be far more sensitive than anyone knows. Much of nutrition is no more than pop-science. Direct personal experience of the benefits of various foods and a dietary balance may be the surest measure of good nutrition. The world of nutrition is more complex than just adhering to the list of elements with recommended requirements or searching out miracle cures.[10]

Names of nutrients are yet another set of words that expand the individual world map. Without them, the most detailed descriptive category available is that of food names, vegetables, meat, cereal, and so on. The chaos and uncertainty attending nutrition has parallels with the early uncertainty in the chemist's search for the natural elements. There simply is no way to know what important elements of nutrition are yet unidentified. Individual differences in nutritional deficiency or need cause difficulty in describing the field of nutrition with scientific precision. Each individual is, in a real sense, a scientific study in nutritional need. Though the numbers that specify minimum requirements of individual nutrients may assist in defining the ideal of good health, the final specification of recommended requirements for good health can never be more than approximate. The personal scientific observation that goes with nutritional experimentation can increase self-knowledge and probably improve health. The emerging and only partly formed science of nutrition provides words that expand the mental map of good health. They help build and enrich reality.

Our modern world would be inconceivable without the fruits of science. The methods of science enrich all of life by expanding language and clarifying its words. Science is no more than disciplined methods of observation, accurate measurement, and recognition of opportunity for analysis and explication of the physical environment. Science without informed intuition is likely to be barren. Science without method is superstition. The words of science must always be rigorously tested and challenged. The progress of science is never finished.

19. Philosophers At Work: Caution - Language Under Construction

Philosophy is a sea of words so abstract and theoretical that they can sound like madness or so common sensical as to seem trivial. Philosophy can begin with the notion that all mental experience is a dream world with no material substance behind it. At the other extreme, it can assert that sense derived knowledge of the material universe (which includes ourselves) is the ultimate object of all human thought. All is ideal, or alternatively, ideas are merely useful tools for distilling sense out of our physical existence. That leaves a vast middle ground in which philosophers have eagerly played with their words since the beginning of recorded history.

No doubt philosophy as a mental activity exists outside and before the written word. It is the written and recorded word that makes philosophy a social force. Philosophy is the written record of philosophers' thinking. Thinking through and writing down the words applied to philosophical discourse fixes thinking in concrete form where it can be grasped, developed and challenged to become a part of working language. Philosophy produces new language at its outer boundaries.

The study of philosophy and the thinking of philosophers follows the growth of language in its most abstract forms. From its earliest record, philosophy is a process of creating, revising and recreating mental maps of the world that fit the social, political and technical structures in place at each stage of time. Philosophers are the mental map inventors and mechanics of their eras. They are the ultimate spinmeisters, wordsmiths, propagandists and general purpose language makers. Words are their special tools.[1]

Only very limited consistency can be found among the many and various philosophical schools of thought. Every philosopher has his (rarely her) own take on what is a good, useful, truthful, fundamental description of mental or physical reality. Philosophical concepts can be so varied as to be chaotic. It is difficult to understand how philosophers have had such great influence on their eras given the complex verbosity and variety in their published thinking.

Much historical philosophical writing is little more than linguistic curiosity. The social products of philosophy in the examination of political, economic, and psychological processes, plus the technical products from mathematics and physics, have nevertheless brought about immense changes in the modern world. From early philosophical thinking about thinking, philosophy has introduced a steady flow of change into language, creating ever more detailed, nuanced and complex mental maps of the experienced world. Philosophy, the knowledge discipline, is the story of developing language, of the cultures that produced and revised it, and of the way new words are invented.[2]

The formal academic study of philosophy often begins with and centers on the Socratic dialogues of Plato. He is credited with founding in the fourth century BCE the first institution of higher education in the western world, the Academy. The other two best known philosophers of the era are his teacher, Socrates and his pupil Aristotle. Socrates is reputed to have devised the dialogue, an organized discussion of opposing ideas which is the foundation of philosophical method. Aristotle invented natural philosophy positing earth, air, fire and water as the elements that make up earthly nature. This crude mental map of earthly matter became and remained the western world's most widely held theory of physical nature for more than two thousand years. These ancient Greeks were very influential thinkers.

Using Socrates' method of dialogue with a variety of audiences, Plato put forward the philosophy of the academy. For him, sensory experience is unreliable and inherently distorted. It is likened to shadows on the wall of a cave, inexactly and crudely read by the average citizen. The remedy is philosophy, the systematic examination of these rough approximations offered by experience that mentally distills the ideal out of mere sensation and achieves a clear vision of the true. Plato maintained that true reality can be found only in the unchanging universals of the ideal. Platonic reality turns common sense reality on its head, making words that stand for ideas reality, dismissing sensory experience as illusory and fantastic.

Through an extended series of Socratic dialogues Plato employed ideas to evaluate experience toward achievement of increased clarity and understanding in use of language. This permitted him to construct an elaborate mental map of the thinking mind. Mind is the tool that defines and uses words to achieve clarity as to what is real. With Plato, words are reality, perhaps for the first time in recorded history.

Greece in Socrates' and Plato's time was a complex culture of mythology and superstition. The average citizen perceived gods and demons all about in nature. There was no empirically tested natural law to explain the working of the natural world. The citizens of Athens, perceiving it with their unaided senses, were heavily burdened with crude shadows of reality. The philosophy of the Academy was antidote to the confusion of minds captured by myth. Systematic, skeptical examination of those shadows could build a mental map of carefully defined words disciplined in their use. For Plato, a well designed, precisely drawn mental map was the route to escape from the shadows of superstition. Platonic philosophy was the beginning of language used to test and correct sensory experience. Plato's map was a powerful innovation that reigned alone and supreme. It was a tool for examining how one can know what one knows. That was great novelty in itself.

Plato's philosophy extended to politics as well. Perhaps not surprisingly, Plato's view was uncompromisingly elitist. Only the wise philosopher who had mastered universal ideals attainable through Socratic dialogue was fit to judge and rule society. His political State was exclusively secular, ruled by rigorous exercise of abstract intellect. This view was probably shaped by Plato's distress over the fate of his mentor, Socrates, condemned to death in the democratic tribunal of his fellow Athenians. In their view, Socrates was a heretic and troublemaker. Philosophy was an incomprehensible bore. Common sense ancient Greece style prevailed in the citizenry's dealings with Socrates.[3]

Across the millennia since Plato's time, secular philosophy was kept alive by monastic scholars while myth and religion dominated the common man's language. Christianity was invented as was Islam and other religious canon. The organized Catholic church exercised major influence in standardizing the use of the written word in Western society. Producing a written book was a tedious process of hand scripting on vellum or engraving wooden blocks for a crude printing press. When Gutenberg's invention of movable type made publishing commercially feasible the written word in all its forms became easily and widely available to scholars. With commercial printing, the flowering of arts during Europe's Renaissance era and the founding of major universities came together as foundation for the seventeenth century age of reason.

Isaac Newton was born prematurely in 1643 to his widowed mother in a small English hamlet. Newton's education began in the village school and continued with some interruptions until his admission at age 19 into Cambridge's Trinity College. The natural science of Aristotle was still the academic standard, but Newton chose the alternative course of contemporary natural science developed by Copernicus, Galileo and Kepler. Applying this newly invented language of the stars he conceptualized universal gravitation and described the three laws of motion, putting in place the foundations of planetary mechanics. He invented the reflecting telescope, developed a theory of color and studied the speed of sound. Any one of these would have been an exceptional accomplishment. His achievements in mathematics were similarly prodigious. Almost simultaneous with Gottfried Liebnitz, Newton developed The Calculus. Supplied by his culture with an intellectually rich fund of ideas, Newton created a new language of science. Summed together, the life work of Isaac Newton is credited with putting in place all the elements necessary for the scientific revolution that followed. Like many other great minds, he suddenly appeared on the world stage as a scientific genius without forewarning or fanfare and overwhelmed it with his words.

Newton was perhaps the world's greatest natural philosopher. Yet he was a distinctly peculiar man as well. He never married and was apparently a life long virgin. His dispute with Liebnitz over credit for invention of The Calculus was contentious and bitter. He overturned the Church's Aristotelian earth-centric natural science and put the Sun at the center of the planets. Yet he was a deeply religious man who wrote extensively on religious issues. He was himself split between commitment to a fully rational view of nature, and to being intensely spiritual, even occult in his approach to religion. It is fitting that in using mathematics as the lever, his work as a natural philosopher split natural science off the main trunk of philosophy to develop as a distinct domain of knowledge and language. Precision of method and words was thereby introduced into at least one corner of philosophy. Those philosophers who specialized in love of pure word knowledge would thereafter have to go their way without the company of natural science.[4]

Born less than a decade before and contemporary with Isaac Newton, John Locke took philosophy in yet another direction. He developed economic and political theory that would later contribute to Marxian economic theory and the breakaway of American Colonies. His was a middleclass puritan English family. Like Newton, he early showed strong academic promise, sufficiently so, that he was sponsored by a member of parliament into what was arguably the best preparatory school in the realm. Upon graduation and admission to Oxford University, Locke found little attraction in the classical curriculum, preferring modern philosophers. In succession, he received his bachelors, masters and medicine degrees from Oxford. For a time he practiced medicine and surgery as a household member of the Earl of Shaftesbury. Again, like Newton, he never married and lived out his life as a bachelor.

Locke was a liberal political and economic thinker early in the age of reason. Unlike his contemporary Thomas Hobbes who considered man a brutish species that could live in harmony only under the strong hand of a sovereign king, Locke considered humans to be naturally reasonable and tolerant. Locke's political structure called for a social contract under which men would give up some of their freedom to government in return for maintenance of basic social order that is secured through a system of checks and balances in government. He defined (material) property as a natural human right conferred by the application of labour in its creation or acquisition, and exempt from appropriation by government. His practical philosophical interests ran to the development of economic price theory and monetary policy.

Locke contributed substantially to the philosophy of human selfness. He saw the self as a conscious, thinking, feeling, experiencing thing that is fixed in a physical body. He saw the mind as an empty cabinet waiting to be filled by the experience of life. He cautioned against exposure of small children to ugly or disturbing superstitions. He considered man naturally capable of the best character and behavior. He was no Platonic idealist in matters of philosophy. He was a bedrock empiricist who held implicit faith in the human mind to map its world accurately on a ground of its own disciplined experience.

Although Locke's empirical view was in direct contradiction to Plato's notion of universals he accepted the need for abstractions that simplified thinking about classes of phenomena. He held serious reservations about the power of reason alone to search out truth. He believed in the power of sensory perception aided by reflection in the mind as the primary source of man's knowledge. He saw ideas, some of which might be quite complex, to be objects before the mind, created by the mind but ultimately traceable to sensory experience as their source.

In developing his philosophy of knowing, Locke found it necessary to examine the uses and functions of language. He assigned names to the individual elements of sensory experience. Words, he maintained, signify ideas. Ideas emerge because it is necessary to classify the great number of individual elements of experience using general terms. Ideas permit quick, efficient communication of experience. He saw problems in defining terms when they have no certain point of connection in nature, especially so when the ideas are complex. He complained that ideas that have no existence in real things, abstractions and essences, can be no more than mere chimeras. Locke was among the earliest philosophers to draw a clear distinction between abstract ideas and sensory reality.

Locke's influence on the founding fathers of the United States of America was profound. Implementation of his social contract in the Declaration of Independence and Constitution of the new nation was near full. His notion of natural ownership of property by application of labour became a centerpiece of Marxian communist thought. Locke reshaped the language of his time in significant ways that have had vast impact on the modern world. His words have become our words.[5]

Fast forward a hundred years to the eighteenth century, the age of reason. Immanuel Kant was born near Konigsburg, East Prussia and resided there throughout his life. His early education was strict, focusing on study of Latin and religion. He was a sufficiently capable student to be enrolled in the University of Konigsburg at the age of 16. There he studied the rationalist philosophers of the age and was introduced to the mathematical physics of Isaac Newton. He made a career as a private tutor in the local area and built his reputation through writing and publishing philosophical treatises. The quality of his written philosophical product gained him a broad repute as a philosopher. On the strength of that standing, he was appointed Professor of Logic and Metaphysics at the University of Konigsburg.

As was customary in that time, Kant wrote an Inaugural Dissertation in defense of his professorial appointment. Among the themes of his dissertation was the distinction between thinking and sensation. Challenge to his dissertation principally rested on observation that he had failed to examine how thinking and sensation are connected. Kant responded by withdrawing into the search for this connection. After nearly a decade of work, the published result was his *Critique of Pure Reason,* a ponderous, difficult to read tome. Philosophers since have come to judge his Critique as one of the most important philosophical works ever written.

The age of reason was an era in which philosophers believed that any question could be answered with the application of reason because all logical arguments were necessarily grounded in experience. Kant's Critique was a rigorously developed argument setting out the limits of human reason by discriminating between arguments with intuitively grasped words set firmly in time and space as opposed to those working with transcendental constructs (such as in mathematics) that lack any intuitional foundation. Pure reason is a game of symbol manipulation that establishes nothing in the real world. Philosophical analysis that provides substantial answers is rooted in human intuition. Mere use of symbols within an established system of rules does not generate meaning. The meaning of words themselves must always be intuitively grasped before reasoning can generate sensory truth. Pure reason is one universe, intuitively sensed phenomena, anchored in time and space, are a separate one. For Kant, thinking and sensation are inherently different things. Kant's moral philosophy rejected sensory experience in favor of reasoned thinking as its ultimate foundation. He argued that moral behavior arises out of consideration of one's own ultimate interest. Knowing what is right becomes the imperative of moral rightness. Rightness is not relative to occasion or situation. It is one's duty to do what is right for the sake of rightness itself. One must behave in a consistent, rational and principled manner in all things.

Kant's definition of rightness was couched entirely in the abstract. He made no effort to offer concrete specifics that would determine what is consistent, rational and principled. In his insistence on moral rightness Kant was applying something like the Golden Rule. Rightness is determined by the general axiom "Do to others as you would have them do to you." Once rightness is determined, it is an exacting standard in Kant's scheme. Ethical behavior requires that one play strictly and always according to the principles established. There are no ends that justify means. Principle is absolute. One might be justified in observing that such a moral code had as much to do with the formal strictness of Kant's upbringing and rational training as with reason alone. Certainly, much of his thinking and writing has the quality of a secular theology. Kant's imperative of personal duty is offered only in the abstract. Each individual must determine what is right for him or herself, but one's standard of rightness and duty is presumed to be intuitively obvious. Kant found rightness and reason in wholly separate domains.[6]

The Englishman Jeremy Bentham was a practical man who had little use for rightfulness and duty. In contrast with Emanuel Kant he proposed that moral rules be dispensed with and replaced with the rule of good feeling. Conformity to rules brought no happiness for Bentham. He expected humans to differ greatly in what they take for good and bad. His solution to ethical behavior was to propose practical utilitarianism as the standard of social policy. Ethical action and behavior was that which resulted in the greatest good for the greatest number. For Jeremy Bentham it is only necessary to determine what produces harmony and goodness in social relations. Harmony and goodness will bring about a society of happy citizens. Happy citizens are the measure of a moral society.[7]

Bentham's life spanned the eighteenth and nineteenth centuries beginning at the end of the era of Enlightenment and ending as the Industrial Revolution commenced. He was a precocious child who began reading at the age of two. He began the study of Latin at four. He was enrolled in Queens College, Oxford at twelve, took his bachelors degree at fifteen, and earned his master's degree at eighteen. Bentham was trained to practice law though he never did so. He found British law confused and overly complex. He had strong interest in social reform and focused much of his writing on proposals for reform of the legal code.

As a philosopher of law, Bentham's reputation has since come to enjoy the respect that he was not given for his theory of utilitarianism. While he has enjoyed substantial influence in legal and ethical philosophy, Bentham has never been held in high regard as a philosopher. Many of his arguments are judged to be logically flawed and his definitions poor. Perhaps that is because he undertook to put so much in writing. It is estimated that he wrote at least five million words. Only a small part was published in his lifetime. Editing and publishing those that were not put in print during is life was a labor that continued well into the twentieth century.

In matters of social reform, Bentham was a thoroughgoing radical. He was an early proponent of equal rights for women, animal rights, separation of church and state, divorce, free trade among nations, abolition of slavery, abolition of physical punishment of criminals, and decriminalization of homosexuality. He proposed an inheritance tax, pensions for the aged and health insurance for all. Even in the twentieth century he would be thought a wild-eyed liberal by some. Social conservatives of his time must have been positively spastic with distress.

Bentham's philosophy of utilitarianism stands in clear contrast to Kant's strict rule of duty. In his published *"The Principles of Morals and Legislation"* he writes that:

> "Nature has placed mankind under the governance of two sovereign masters, pain and pleasure. It is for them alone to point out what we ought to do, as well as to determine what we shall do. On the one hand the standard of right and wrong, on the other the chain of causes and effects, are fastened to their throne."

His ethical maxim for assurance of social fairness is stated thus: "the greatest happiness of the greatest number is the foundation of morals and legislation." He proposed a felecific calculus for establishing the greatest happiness for the greatest number. Bentham's student, John Stuart Mill, took his ideas forward to develop the unfinished philosophical product of Bentham's thinking. In doing so he produced what would become the foundation of future liberal state policies.

Directly and indirectly Bentham added a rich fund of new and redefined words to political philosophy. As a philosopher, Bentham may have been a dilettante. Nonetheless he had a clear intuitive grasp of the qualities and policies of an open, liberal society that would come with social reform wrought by the industrial revolution. His advocacy of regular elections, population balanced electoral districts, expanded suffrage, and the secret ballot was fully consistent with his "greatest good" principle. The intuitive foundation of his philosophy was that not reason, but rather, suffering, human or animal alike, must measure the extent of justice or injustice. He was, certainly, a child of the Enlightenment.

The nineteenth century marked the beginning of the industrial revolution that ushered in a period of intense economic and social transition. The printing press was in place, books, pamphlets and tracts of all sorts were widely available, secular philosophy was rapidly pushing aside theology as the core of higher education. The emergence of nation states in Europe offered increased political stability. Revolution was in the air. America had just broken political ties with Great Britain and revolutionary fervor had swept France. Karl Marx, a philosopher and life long revolutionary made it his personal mission to bring about truly fundamental economic revolution. He sought to end the long tradition of private ownership of real property.

Before Marxist political economics, redistribution of wealth occurred only through war or a related form of force. Commonly one family, tribe or culture armed itself and stole from another. The relative stability of the new European nation states protected private ownership under the King's or Emperor's law. Secular government supported secular education. Scholarship was no longer limited to theological study in monasteries. Religion was losing exclusive ownership of the word as reality. Universities had moved into that territory. Words were being used to describe social and secular ideology rather than moral and spiritual ideology. Philosophers of this age vigorously practiced the use of words as full blown reality. Their mental maps of the world were exploding into new realms and dimensions.

In the company of other philosophers of the age, Karl Marx modeled the world around him with a new repertory of power words invented and defined by other philosophers. He was deeply impressed by human adaptability and saw humans as driven to transform nature through a process he called *labour,* borrowed no doubt from John Locke. Labour to Marx was the capacity and instinct to transform nature to make it more hospitable for man. In Marx's eyes the labour of a proletariat class of laborers was exploited in service of a bourgeoisie capitalist owner class. In consequence, the proletariat labor class had become alienated from its spiritual nature creating a conflict of interest Marx labeled *class struggle.* This conclusion led him to radically reinterpret previous political and economic history. In the Communist Manifesto, co-penned with Friedrich Engles, Marx dogmatically states that "The history of all hitherto existing society is the history of class struggle."

Marx's thinking anticipated the twentieth century development of psychology and social psychology. He asserted that relationships arising out of prevailing systems of material production generate the political and economic structures that become man's mental reality. Man in Marx's view is fundamentally an economic creature. Human consciousness that arises out of the struggle to transform nature becomes false consciousness when man is alienated from his product by the capitalist system.

Marx was a prolific and continuous spinner of philosophical treatises. Like many philosophers of that age his purpose was to produce rational arguments that arose straight out of defined premises to yield logical truth. The reality against which he tested his logical argument was the social and economic inequity of the time, with all the history that preceded it. He accepted his observation and evaluation of both as sufficient guide for his arguments. Those arguments, though, were based on wholly abstracted ideas, far removed from any reality anchors themselves. Marx was not a pragmatist. He was most at home in the ivory tower of philosophical dialectic.

The difficulty of Marx's philosophical argument was the disagreement among those who interpreted and attempted to implement the political and economic measures he proposed. Though Marx unequivocally called for implementation of communism as the remedy for laboring man's spiritual alienation, his principal disciples, Lenin, Stalin, Trotsky and Mao, read very different meanings into his prescription for that implementation. The debate has not yet ended. Economic scholars and philosophers continue to contest his meaning. Marx firmly believed he had reality squarely by the horns with the Communist Manifesto. His words were lofty and abstract. It is now clear that when abstracted words are taken as reality, that reality becomes subject to highly personal interpretation.

The words Marx used to model the nineteenth century social and political world were very real to him and eventually to many others. Lenin's Soviet communism was undertaken with the sure conviction that Marx's words were as good as fact. The twentieth century saw a series of tests in use of his theories, ideas, and philosophy. Putting it to use, though, has revealed how tenuously they were linked to intuitive or sensory experience. It is more than a little difficult to discern what a "dictatorship of the proletariat" might be in practice. There is a lot more to its implementation than exhorting "Workers of the world, UNITE".[8]

One result of socialist and communist rhetoric has been to keep private ownership and concentrated wealth on the defensive for well over a century as Socialist/communist styled nations popped up here and there. With the passage of time most have moved toward limited private ownership and open markets. Traditional free market countries similarly have moved toward managed or limited markets. Global trade and global markets offer a distinct edge to private ownership operating in free markets. There is no single state to restrain the wide open competition. The question of private versus public ownership is not yet fully settled. Many maintain that there has to date been no adequate test of Marx's political and economic proposals. The rhetoric goes on.

Across the Atlantic Ocean in America, nineteenth century philosophy was following a less revolutionary path. It progressed in a more quietly and powerfully intellectual way than did its European counterparts. The absence of public rhetoric may have kept it from becoming a major influence on twentieth century philosophical culture and thinking that European philosophers exerted. Americans, though, are natural pragmatists and tend to lack interest in philosophical argument. Philosophers are rarely their heroes.

Charles Sanders Peirce was born in Cambridge, Massachusetts, September 10, 1839. His father, Benjamin Peirce, was a distinguished Harvard Professor of mathematics. Charles graduated Harvard with a Masters degree in Chemistry, awarded summa cum laude. He was self-taught in logic and mathematics from the age of twelve and throughout his life exhibited a dominating interest in the philosophy of logic, mathematics and language. Over a span of some thirty years, Charles worked on and off as a member of the US Coast and Geodesic Survey under the sponsorship of his well connected father who himself performed assignments financed by the US government.

Much of his Geodesic Survey work was in the field of astronomy. Charles was a creative thinker and problem solver who made significant theoretical and practical contributions in his work. He developed theory and practice related to the use of the pendulum swing as a measure of gravitational force and originated use of the wavelength of light as the standard for the length of a meter. His original scientific work was of sufficient quality to bring him international recognition as a scientist and election to the National Academy of Sciences. Sadly, he was never able to form himself to the work demands of government bureaucracy. His extraordinarily broad and varied interests led him to devote a great part of his working time to writing papers on philosophy, logic, mathematics and language. So focused was Peirce on the issues that really interested him that his assigned government work went neglected and he was ultimately asked to resign his geodesic survey post.

Peirce made his mark as a philosopher with a vast quantity of writing that was unrelated to his paid government employment. His output was prodigious. It is estimated that he left as many as 80,000 pages of his work unpublished in his lifetime. Though respected as a scientist and logician Peirce was unable to establish himself in the hierarchy of academicians. A few well-placed detractors may have blocked his efforts to gain a tenured university chair in philosophy or logic. He did hold an untenured position as lecturer in logic for a time at the newly established Johns Hopkins University, and was recognized for his special grasp of philosophical issues by a limited company of friends and philosophers. Among them was William James who held Peirce in high esteem as a scientist and philosopher. Though Peirce enjoyed a reputation as an intellect of first rank among some of the leading scholars and minds of his era, he nevertheless went largely unrecognized as a philosopher. His writings on pragmatism were widely read and accepted, and it was not until after his death that he came to be generally recognized as a founder of philosophical pragmatism and one of the most important American philosophers of his time. Charles Peirce and William James are jointly credited as founders of the American pragmatic movement in philosophy. Of the two, Peirce is generally considered to have contributed the greater depth of philosophical thinking.

For Peirce, *pragmatism* was part of a larger consideration of the human thinking process. *Belief* was established habit of action that is invoked in known circumstances to set appropriate behavior into action. *Inquiry,* on the other hand, was a process of formulating and testing meaningful questions that would explain those circumstances that are outside the boundaries of prevailing belief. Peirce was a practicing scientist whose experience with the methods of science gave him confidence in its power to resolve disputes and problems. Inquiry was a process of clarifying meaning through dispute. The problem of meaning was central to his examination of the human thought process. Concern over meaning led Peirce to examine the way signs (symbols and graphic representations) are employed to stand for a sensory experience or event. His theory of semiotics, the meaning of signs, anticipated twentieth century linguistics.

Peirce's logic, though, was much more than Aristotelian premises and syllogisms. As an accomplished mathematician, he fully appreciated the application of logic to problems of mathematics. He went beyond the search for the extremes of absolute truth and untruth by introducing probability into the logical process of truth determination. He anticipated computers by recognizing the possibilities for modeling Boolean algebra in electrical switches.

Peirce's pragmatism dealt with the way signs and their meaning produce behavior. He was an early cognitive psychologist with his grasp of how language guides and shapes behavior. Thought for Peirce was directly connected with action, prediction and purpose. Thinking is not a sterile mental process that goes nowhere. It results in something. He rejected the notion of pure ideas. Every idea, every word, every thought has a real object. Thought is pragmatic. Peirce contributed hugely to the language of philosophy by clearly connecting thinking with doing.

Modern day Systems Theory follows Peirce's formulation of sign theory in designating coded symbols in a computer as mere data. Data cannot become information until it has been associated with meaning that relates it to human purpose. Whenever a human mind with human purpose relates coded data to those purposes, it is demonstrating Peirce's pragmatic maxim. Meaning emerges from the practical uses that are associated with objects, ideas, and words that constitute thinking. Through that association, symbols become informed with meaning.[9]

Pragmatism as the central intellectual object of current day philosophical thinking no longer drives much academic or scholarly interest. The ground of thinking and language used in modern times is nevertheless full of Peirce's pragmatic notions. Though the exacting definitions of many of his philosophical terms have changed or been forgotten, the core ideas were absorbed into common language. The notion that language is a mental map that guides action in the physical, sensory world is fully compatible with Peirce's pragmatism and he deserves credit as its source. It has provided much of the philosophical foundation for this book.

Most of twentieth century philosophy has tended toward pragmatic thinking and action. William James summarized the best nineteenth century knowledge of human psychology and Peirce developed the outlines of philosophical pragmatism. Twentieth century language has evolved and been tested in use sufficiently that it adequately supports interpretation of most ordinary, raw sensory experience. On the threshold of the twenty-first century the various empirical branches of psychology, personality, social, cognitive and neurological, are actively exploring and identifying sources of human sensory misidentification and distortion. The powers and limitations of sensory perception are better understood than ever previous. Some citizens still experience life through the haze of middle ages superstition, some employ less than fully informed judgment, some live in a personal fantasy world. The opportunity to think, talk and write with a reasonable degree of clarity exists for those who will accept language discipline. Those who have achieved that state are perhaps modern day philosophers whom Plato would nominate as society's kings. Its heroes, though, are its scientists, those in the physical and life sciences particularly. They take us to the moon, to the edge of the universe and into the heart of the atom.

Philosopher scientists are once again building word maps in an attempt to describe the mysteries of physical matter. They are looking into the makeup of the atoms that are the foundation of those familiar physical chemical elements that are used to create health and wealth. Earth, air, fire and water are far in the past. Now there are protons, neutrons, mesons, positrons, muons, pions, bosons, photons and more, extending into a near baffling variety. Particles are "seen" using sophisticated electronic measurements that capture the result of high energy particle accelerator collisions. These events are far outside the limits of those intuitive sensory observations that most language is founded on. It would not be too great a stretch to describe particle physics research as fanciful interpretations of shadows on the cave wall.

A multitude of theories have been formulated to account for the behavior of those particles that up to now have been experimentally discovered and "observed". There is the standard model that describes fundamental electronic forces using bosons. It is based on correspondence among those collider experiments that are most widely accepted and understood. There are phenomenologists who base their work on quantum and effective field theory. There are lattice theorists and most ambitious of all, string theorists who seek to develop a unified theory of quantum mechanics and general relativity to produce the so called "theory of everything". Philosophically, that could be the equivalent of transforming base elements into gold.[10]

Like generations of philosophers before them, particle theorists invent words for things and events they *think* they can reliably observe, then spin theories around the words in hopes of better understanding and predicting what is happening. Particle theorists are the new generation of natural philosophers who seek increased understanding of their physical universe using their newly invented words. Whether those words reflect reality or not is yet to be judged.

20. Non-Sense Language: Abstractions And Essences

A very large part of language is non-sense. That is, there is no direct sensory experience that the words can be related to. Proper names are generally specific and straightforward because the mind intuitively structures experience into patterns that identify things or qualities. Shapes, edges, textures, colors, movement against a fixed background are used by the brain to isolate perceptual elements. One points and says "that's red" or "that's a dog" or "that's a tree" and a child will "see" it. Within the natural order of the brain, the thing or quality represented by the experienced pattern is intuitively grasped. The brain then goes beyond patterns that establish physical things. It organizes the welter of perceptual details encountered into convenient chunks that have the appearance of similarity or coherence. As with stars in the heavens, "things" are perceived and given word names just because they seem to go together.

Words are assigned to stand for all kinds of things, including those that have no direct sensory reference. Modern biological science, for instance, began with the invention of natural word categories called species, genus, family, etc. These categories classified living things according to their similarities and differences. Species are recognized by their ability to interbreed only within the species. That is probably the most precise definition of a category of living things that biology has to offer, and it is still by no means exact or easy to establish. Biological levels are not always clearly defined or even agreed on. They were invented for convenience in dealing with the immense complexity of life forms in nature. They are words that catalog sensory stimuli that are of interest.

That convenience carries over to just about everything that has perceptual difference or similarity. Categorical words are invented by the mind because the appearance of group membership seems natural. Something causes pleasure or pain, helps or hinders, entertains or irritates. A word is assigned as its category name. The reference can be an experience, not a thing or quality. As such, it is not likely to be well defined. Plato called them ideas. Present day psychologists call them essences. It is convenient to call them all abstractions. They are, literally, all non-sense.

The most impressive language trick of all is to make up words that have no physical reference whatever and put them across as real. Remarkably, it is relatively easy to do. Mythological creatures of every sort abound in the vocabulary. Santa Claus, Spiderman, Zeus, Prometheus, Angels, Demons, Heaven, Hell, all have reality for some. They can be made real by imagery in movies, picture books, and costumed human pretenders. Many of these images look and act like living human beings or places we know or have seen. They are images of types or qualities, sometimes carried to extremes, sometimes remarkably common. Other than for impersonators or concocted pictures they lack true sensory or phenomenal reference. They are non-sense.

Then there are ideas that are not in any way sensible. They are pompous, emotion laden words like freedom, equity, peace. These words can be defined only by other words. It is useful to think of these as pure *ideas*. Justice, truth and evil are good examples of pure ideas that deserve examination. These ideas have emotional power of their own. They can easily morph into ideologies that drive major political or social movements.

Justice is a word rich in history. Almost two and a half centuries ago, Plato offered a definition of justice proposing that social order is correctly based on social status and ruled by reason. A just society was one where soldiers and merchants were benevolently ruled by philosophers. It was a community where everyone accepted assigned social status and lived in harmony with one another under the leader's wisdom. Plato's presumption that one like him ought to be the rightful ruler of the populace clearly shaped his view of justice. It was a view that has not always enjoyed wide popularity despite its continuing prevalence among elites.[1]

The Latin word *justus* means upright, equitable. In the religiously intense middle ages, to be *just* was to be righteous in the eyes of God. The old English *right* meant *good, fair, proper, fitting,* and *straight.*[2] These words tend to go round in circles defining one another, the most experientially tangible of the group being the positive word *good* that references an experienced feeling. The emotion of feeling "good" can be real enough. When feeling itself becomes the reference anchor, justice will likely be Benthamish utilitarianism that is entirely in the eye of the beholder.

The metaphors that define justice are derived out of words like upright, fitting and straight that probably go back as far as antiquity. When land transport and travel were on foot or by animal, the road that was *even* and *straight* was good and desired. Rough terrain was hard on man and beast alike.[3] Upright, fitting and straight are terms that describe good building construction. In pre-technological times, the most difficult form to achieve was the straight edge or the straight line. Straightness is simplicity that pleases the eye and allows for a clean fit to other straightness. These are the metaphors on which the intuitive modern day definition and meaning of justice rest. They stand for moral goodness, fitness and uprightness of character.

Aside from moral righteousness, justice also means equity and equality of status or privilege. Or, it can mean appropriate punishment in retribution for unjust action. The loosely related multiple meanings of justice are jumbled together in a mix that invites confusion and permits extension. Justice as a noun has come to mean a system of laws or the magistrate of a law court. It would be appropriate to say that justice makes reference to some form of common social agreement that is the foundation of social order. In philosophical terms, that is called a *social contract.*[4] The modern Anglo-English meaning of *fairness* approximates the meaning of justice as acceptance of those rules of relationship that are agreed on among equals. In establishing a ground of fairness there are not necessarily any exact rules that regulate actions. The rules are formed out of a context of history and expectations for what will be in everyone's best interest. Justice in these terms is a complex social calculus of the greater social good.

The problems of defining justice are many. Contracts, social or otherwise, are made up of agreements among those who make up the community. Small, isolated communities ruled by local leadership may easily come to agreement, at least among a majority. Mass society spawns multiple communities with wide differences in view. Only the most basic principles can be widely agreed on, and there will still be isolated pockets of disagreement on those. The rights of ownership, for instance, are firmly enshrined in Western law, but are challenged by socialists and overridden by thieves. For the dedicated socialist, property never stopped being theft. It is perfectly proper and right to take what you want.

Justice is widely invoked in modern society on behalf of the poor, the down trodden, and the socially marginal. Justice for those constituencies is equality and equity. It assumes that no one should be thought intrinsically better than anyone else. Extreme economic marginality should be offset by income redistribution. This definition of justice requires that the poor and socially disadvantaged be housed, fed and cared for medically. They should be equal before the law, even when they flaunt the law. The rich, the powerful and the intellectually adept must be humble. No one should stand out above others.

In matters of retributive justice, justice should be swift to satisfy the aggrieved, but blunted to avoid brutality and to account for the possibility of erroneous accusation. Retributive justice may pursue the ends of rehabilitation, deterrence or maintenance of personal security but may not be used for payback or revenge. Punishment can be authorized and carried out only by established, legitimate authority. The nature and severity of punishment must fit the crime and the criminal. These are requirements that are impossible to define or to meet with any full consistency. They must be applied judiciously by someone of experienced and thoughtful judgment.

This helps only a little in defining justice. Certainly, at its core, justice is permeated with the notion of social order and its preservation. The exact format of that order or the proper way of achieving it is never finally settled. Justice in its modern meanings is so confused, inconsistent and, as a legal system, so often unworkable, that it is difficult to comprehend, much less to defend. A long history of philosophers' definitions of justice is filled with contradiction. There is no certain definition. Justice is literally a nonsense – not sensed – word. It is experienced as wrongful treatment or behavior and formed out of ancient metaphors that are often inappropriate to modern times. It makes reference to the attempt to bring order to a social world that can be too complex and too morally loose to ever control fully. Diverse languages and cultures defy agreement. For most there is no such thing as a *just* world and probably cannot be. The universal cry for justice is a cruel joke. Still, no one doubts its desirability. It is an essential construct.[5]

Truth is no less problematic. Truth is defined variously as correspondence with objectively sensed reality or as honesty in one's word. It can mean consensus agreement, or sincerity with good faith slipped in somewhere between those extremes. The archaic word *troth,* used in traditional marriage ceremonies, means loyalty, faithfulness. For some, truth is exact and final knowledge. Truth as consistency of action with one's words is a very weak use of the term as contrasted with truth denoting the ideal of some ultimate reality. Common sense meaning of truth is agreement between word and sensory reference or word and action. When it is abstracted as an all-inclusive finality, truth becomes something far beyond sensory reference.

There is also mathematical truth, represented in the truth tables of Boolean Algebra. This is the logical form of truth determination used by computer scientists as the foundation of programming language. Truth is determined by logical arguments that use the digits 1 and 0 to represent True and False. This is the truth of logic, which, like proof in mathematics, assures nothing more than logical consistency within a closed system of relational rules.[6] Extending the meaning of *truth* or *proof* to mean an ultimate demonstration of fact is a metaphor on mathematical proof that takes these words past the bounds of sensible meaning. To be clear on the matter, it is reasonable and feasible to demonstrate the fact of natural phenomena. It is nonsense to claim final and undeniable knowledge of anything. In the end, all is word play.

Evil is a word that helps point up a distinctive emotional character of many ideas. They tend toward intense feeling content. They are final, ultimate pronouncements of believed reality. Delivered up out of the core of one's being, the word evil says "bad as bad can be". The word evil probably came forward to Old English from a Saxon word that meant arrogant or overreaching. The meaning in Old English was something bad or vicious. With usage, the implication of something harmful, criminal, or a source of disease was added. In the eighteenth century it came to mean extreme moral wickedness, a definition that matches the modern, intuited meaning, although present day usage may or may not always require an immoral element. Evil is a terrible, incomprehensible, near magical happening. Even today, the source of disease or personal bad fortune is attributed by some to evil persons or spirits. There is often an element of superstition in the meaning of evil. The emotions that go with evil reach down into the gut. Clearly, evil is an idea loaded with feeling content. Like all genuine sensations of feeling, it has its own undeniable reality. In objective terms, though, it can never be fully or finally defined. It is an idea. It is non-sense.

A new term has recently been set aside to describe non-sense words like these. The word is *essence.* It is socially useful to discriminate essences from ideas. Essences lack the level of abstraction that characterizes ideas. Essences have the appearance of reality because they seem to be based on identifiable, underlying, sensible factors. Because they seem tangible or even concrete, they are easily accepted as natural and treated as phenomenally existing things. In fact, they are wholly abstracted from experience by perceptual organization in the mind. They too are non-sense, but can be more insidiously so than are ideas. They are mere appearances, not facts.

Essences are of interest because of the mischief some have brought about. Concepts like race, gender, intelligence, and personality are recognized in current psychological literature as essences because of their social significance. Perceptual essentiality as a social issue is recognized through the mischief that some essences create. Words like race – black vs. white – or gender – men vs. women – have introduced deep rooted, difficult problems into social relations. Essential categories create the appearance of real differences that are, in fact, superficial or arbitrary. Substantiated as words they take on the undeserved quality of referential words.

The notion of essentialism is taken from the ancient philosophical notion of essence. It was a mysterious, inner quality presumed to give something the character it has. If this seems vague and circular, it is just that. The essence of something is established by the word or words used to describe it. It is a made-up, poorly defined quality, though not all such made-up qualities are necessarily negative. Some kinds of made-up qualities are useful. Essentialisms like occupation, personality, or culture, for instance, make it easier to relate to others in casual social encounter. Some people even locate most of their personal identity within these essences. They believe they are their occupation, intelligence or personality. These are words that represent assumed personal qualities. Referencing them as *essences* is descriptively useful because they are intuitively experienced as inherent, deep traits. The words themselves are said to be experienced as *essentialized* phenomena.[7]

Race is a controversial word for good reason. Historically it was used to describe and justify human groupings on the presumed basis of genetic heritage. Certain groups were judged racially, that is to say, genetically, inferior, others as genetically superior. Skin color or language was taken as true indicator of race. Culturally, the objective basis of racial classification today is likely to be shared language skill. Because language skill can be measured and quantified it has been widely assumed that alleged racial differences are based on differences in natural intelligence.

Race is not a fact. It is a description of apparent distinction related to some observable physical or social characteristic like skin color, distinctive facial features or speech usage. Race is an invented category that allows easy, superficial dissimilarity to be claimed. As a matter for serious research by social scientists, race is an instance of psychological essentialism. It is an invented group category that is used as *if* it is based on real, observable, measurable human characteristics.

Science and social policy have corrected themselves in recent times. It is clear now that the transmission of an advanced language through rich cultural tradition gives those with the deepest and longest language tradition a significant edge in their intellectual development. Genetics does differentiate people in some ways. There will be those of any culture or "race" that are born with weak mental capability, while others of the same genetic lineage exhibit exceptional intellectual skill. Certain specific diseases are in part transmitted genetically. Physical and intellectual characteristics can be systematically introduced into any species through selective breeding. Neo-Darwinian psychologists theorize extensively about how various human characteristics have been shaped by environmental factors. Most genetic characteristics seem quite malleable across various peoples, nationalities and races.

Other common instances of psychological essentialism are qualities like gender, ethnicity, disability, class, or politics. Education and culture are others, all created out of social perceptions.

Education is a category permeated by essence. Education is variously defined as a special "textbook", a teacher in the classroom, a campus with buildings and athletic fields, a tax proposal on the ballot, a political platform. One can observe students in the classroom reading, raising their hands, answering questions, reading books. The physical plant called the school stands concrete in view. A document on the wall authenticates a specified level of education for one who has followed a course of educational study. These are only the symbolic trappings of education. Because they are observable and tangible, they are easily seized on as education itself. Education at its core is an essence. It is acquisition of a complex set of skills, mostly through observing and copying the actions of others. The skills themselves may be technical, intellectual or social. The words *technical, intellectual* and *social* are themselves essences.

Education is a package of intuitively understood essences for abilities that are dependent on language acquisition. It is practice with common tasks, use of common language and social interaction with others. The prevailing format of current day education has not been designed to support the mastery of a complex skill packages. Schooling is shaped by other imperatives. One is the practical need to distance children from full involvement in the tasks of the economy, originally those required by farming, but also child labor in factories and mills. Immersing a child in real, economically purposeful work prevents exposure to social culture and saps developmental energy. Schooling as a process developed as a kind of laboratory where practice of social and intellectual skills could occur while economic production was put on hold. Nonetheless, education will likely come about through schooling on its own as long as there is sufficient exposure to language and culture. The richer the better.

The other major force that has shaped education is the care of children for their working parents permitting specialists to provide a scholastic culture where intellectual skills can be mastered. Custodial control of children emerged as a central priority of education when they were put in the care of surrogate parents. The result was to shape education as a semi-regimented custodial process where teachers and students are left to their best devices to produce learning. In these circumstances, learning is a secondary, not the primary product of education. The essential learning objective of education has been lost in the welter of competing essences that surround it.

Then, there is the essence of *culture,* a word that has been used often in these chapters. Culture in fifteenth century Old English meant tilling the land for planting. Soon after, it acquired meaning that included education, mostly higher education. The nineteenth century's age of reason expanded culture to mean the intellectual life and advance of society. Used in these pages, culture means all the technological, linguistic, social and religious customs that define civilization. The particular focus of culture here is on language as encoded culture. Technology, law, and religion all depend on words to preserve and pass on the culture they represent to each new generation. Culture is a word defined by other, alternative, supportive words. It is identified, established and defined primarily through its existence as a word. It is an essence.

The most powerful quality of culture in political terms is its positioning as a fault line between religious, ethnic and linguistic groupings created by differences in thinking and behavior within culturally identifiable groupings. Because people understand their phenomenal worlds within the context of language culture, significant cultural differences can prevail across different languages. In his book, *The Clash of Civilizations,* Harvard Professor Samuel Huntington looks at culture in the context of global politics. His view is that war is most probable at the boundaries of the world's major civilizations because of the inevitable essential cultural friction that exists where they meet. Cultural differences offer opportunity for misunderstanding that can escalate to conflict.

Though there is certain truth in this observation, it is not necessarily culture that creates conflicts. Rather, it is failure to appreciate and accommodate inevitable cultural and linguistic differences. Invested with such richness of meaning as Huntington gives it, there is the suggestion that culture is a real and observable thing and that inter-civilization conflict can even be pointed to as objective evidence of culture. It is not that easy. There are alternative explanations for conflict between groups, cultures and nations. Culture is an intellectually constructed word that stands for a complex basket of observations, not all of which are necessary to its meaning. It is a very useful and potentially powerful essential word. If there were not a word for culture, it would be difficult or impossible to think of culture. That would be a loss. Carefully defined, the word culture as a complex concept may allow civilizations to better understand the causes of war.

Nonsense words are at the center of much debate over social and political policy. Abstractions in the form of essences and ideas can be useful to advance of social debate when words are carefully defined and respected for their inevitable ambiguity. In a complex society different communities will define them differently. Disagreement will occur as intuitively grasped meaning changes from group to group, community to community. At the boundaries of these communities, the words may not be understood because of differences in intuitive grasp. The words are the same but the intuitive understanding that supports them will not correspond. Misunderstanding, argument, even conflict will prevail.

Language depends heavily on ideas, essences and abstractions for generality and efficiency of expression that necessarily sacrifices accuracy and precision. Essences and ideas are fuzzy words that quickly lose clarity in use. They are non-sense. They are also wonderfully useful, made-up categories. The traps that inhere in them must be appreciated. Care must always be taken never to think of them as having underlying substance.

PART FIVE:

Beyond the Senses

21. Is It Redundant To Say That Words Are Mystical?

Words as abstractions without sensory reference have only traveled part way on their full path. The philosophy of mysticism propels them much further. Almost any word can be searched for meaning lost from earlier times. Words as hidden stores of ancient wisdom are the focus of the mystical arts. Mystics use words strangely, associating them randomly or illogically. The many strong emotional associations that attach to words offer potential for them to be stripped of referential meaning and applied poetically for their emotional content alone. Non-sense sentence construction makes ordinary words mystical.

The works of seventeenth century poet George Herbert illustrate nonsensicalness in these terms. His poem *The Call* was set to music by English composer Ralph Vaughn Williams as one of five "mystical songs". The Call is frequently chosen as a wedding song and is sung at other church services. Parson Herbert's intention may have been to convey some coherent message through the words of his poetry, but it would be difficult to establish that as his object. The sentences that constitute The Call are clearly nonsense, written and sung to evoke their emotional associations.

THE CALL

Come, my Way, my Truth, my Life :

Such a Way, as gives us breath :

Such a Truth, as ends all strife :

And such a Life, as killeth death.

Come, my Light, my Feast, my Strength :

Such a Light, as shows a feast :

Such a Feast, as mends in length :

Such a Strength, as makes his guest.

Come, my Joy, my Love, my Heart :

Such a Joy, as none can move :

Such a Love, as none can part :

Such a Heart, as joyes in love

The reader is largely free to make what he/she chooses of this poetry. Though the words may communicate a sense of mystical musing, they describe nothing in strict sensory terms. They communicate feeling without conveying a rational message. Meaning is in their sentimental loading. The difference between most other poetry and that of George Herbert is the absence of any conventional literal meaning in the sentences formed by words. Standard poetry is written for literal meaning that is matched with the emotional tone of the words. Poets exploit the lyrical qualities of language. It is sentimental though not necessarily mystical.

Some standard religious words and usages are designed to be mystical in the sense of religiously sacred or holy. Terms like *Lord, God, heaven, thee, thou,* and *thine* are largely set aside for use in prayer and other mystical incantation. Many other words may be suspect for deep mystical nuance. Their ancient root meanings are searched out through reference to original language use. It is thought that later shifts in common usage may overlay older, deeper, mystical significance hidden under current usage.

The meaning of words does change over time. Some words shade into multiple variations of meaning, some change completely, some are abandoned. Mystical study can focus on old or ancient words, especially those that have lost or altered their original reference and emotional content. Very ancient texts are held in reverence for their potential to reveal hidden truths. Academics read them to better understand history, philosophy and literature. Theologians go deep into ancient religious writings for fuller access to the holy. Mystics look for echoes, hidden similes, curious contradictions as a source of mystical meaning.

Theology is of its nature mystical. Because its experience is fundamentally impenetrable, death is one of the greatest of mysteries. Love, forgiveness, atonement, unity all enjoy special status in mystical study. It is no surprise that each is fully loaded with intense emotional content. Meaning and feeling combine to create special inspiration as these words are read or spoken. They are the mystic's basic raw material. The deep insights derived from study of some words may trigger extraordinary feelings of connection with the infinite.

Mysticism begins with emotional loadings and ancient meaning of words, and progresses to dreams, imagination and belief systems. All of which can be permeated with presumed mystical qualities.

Prophetic dreams have long been thought to be mystical events and are reported in the Hebrew bible. The connection of mysticism and prophesy to dreams is probably impossible to demonstrate. Dream content is the most elusive of experiences. Those dreams that occur as one awakes can sometimes but not always be remembered. Psychological study of dream content requires that the dreamer be awakened and interrogated. Personal capture of dream content is very difficult. Unless quickly put into written or recorded words the content of dreams will likely be forgotten. The brain does not form dreams for storage in long term memory like it does sensory experience. That is the best evidence available that dreams must come either from within the brain's memory banks or from another unknown source. It is clear that the vast part of dreaming is beyond access by the speaking brain. Those intense dream events that abruptly awaken one may be quickly put into words, but most are sleeping visions and visceral sensations that are never articulated. Dreams are in a mental domain beyond that of words. Absent memory in words to call them up all those lost dreams are beyond grasp. Dreams as sleep events and as paths to changed states are all strange, somewhat otherworldly events that defy full explanation. There is, unarguably, a quality of the mystical about them.

Dreams in the sense of daydreaming may simulate the dreaming of sleep in the sense that they construct an unreal, alternative reality of imagination. Personal "dreams" that conceive a better state of personal being or the solution to a pressing issue can become the basis of real world action that enacts the dream state. If words can be used to model the process of translation from unreality to reality, the dream may come true. When put into language as foundation for pursuit, they become imagination.

Imagination is a powerful human faculty that is similar to dreaming. The capacity to visualize, plan and move toward realization of things and conditions not experienced makes man the most productive and audacious creature on the face of the earth. That which is not experienced can be modeled in words or pictures to be examined. Mentally created experience can be put into words that make it seem as real as any sensory experience. In strictly literal terms, though, it would be stretching to say that imagination is real before it has been brought to actuality. Successful actualization of that which has only been imagined is a special form of creation. When fantasy is transformed into reality the moment can be one of high drama.

Real imagination in original form is fantasy. It is clearly beyond immediate practical realization. Whether a current fantasy is one that can be made tangible or is forever beyond actualization is never entirely clear. Two hundred years ago, the industrial revolution was barely underway. At that moment it remained inconceivable that high-speed vehicular and aircraft travel, radio and television transmission, or travel beneath the sea could be more than story fantasies. The electromagnetic waves that produce long distance voice and image transmission existed no less then than now. They might have been fleetingly experienced as something strange that accidentally occurred with the crude electric apparatus then available, but they were still the stuff of mystery and magic. They are no less mysterious and magical in the current day because they are now fully actualized physical phenomena.

In the lifetime of many alive today, a rocket ship voyage to the moon was conceived, pursued and achieved. The televised event of setting foot on the surface of the moon was broadcast throughout the world for all to know that imagination can be actualized. That achievement required detailed engineering designs, colorful artists' renderings, selection of astronauts, flight simulations, test firing of rockets, orbital missions and much more to keep the imagined vision clear and on the path to realization. Extensive pre-test of, designs, equipment, skills all gave confidence that this was not just a fantasy. There was high confidence that it could be done. Yet, blast-off day was full of uncertainty. It had never been tried before and might not work. There is no knowing what fleeting and uncertain experiences imagined in the current age may be similarly brought into productive use at some future time.[1]

Not all imagination is creative innovation. Much is ordinary invention. One must discriminate between fantastic imagination and mere mental invention. Much that passes for creative imagination is little more than sensory experience alternatively conceived or rearranged. There is, for instance, very little new music based on a novel melody line. Almost any musical composition can be traced to tunes written or performed previously. The exact combination of notes may even be the same, with only small change in rhythm or tempo. This is not a matter of plagiarism so much as it is one of limited possibilities. Vast stores of musical literature exist that may be partly remembered or inadvertently repeated. Similarly most major narrative story plots have been used multiple times in the history of publishing. The real complexity of the characterizations, character interactions and story settings that are possible permits fresh combinations to be arranged. Sometimes, translation into contemporary language may be enough to justify nearly intact update of an old story. Fashions change just because they are fashions. Existing materials are used in different ways to achieve fresh application in clothing, furnishings, autos, anything. Imagination in fashion design, like music and literature, is likely to be only recombination of existing ideas materials or resources. Indeed, that is where much invention originates. Familiar existing ideas, materials, resources are rearranged and a something new is formed. The application of imagination may be entirely in polishing the details and they are certainly not imagination in any mystical sense.

Practical problem solving exists along a continuum of discovery from a simple notice that "it can be used for that" to "eureka, that's the answer everyone is looking for." Some reconfigurations are simple, others immensely complex. The defining quality of this kind of imagination is the search for something that generates significant social or technical change. As a driving force for change it looks for causal links that can be exploited. It seeks unexamined structure and untested utility. It is the indispensable cutting edge of growth and innovation. It is disciplined thinking that asks penetrating questions with potential to clarify sensory reality at its outer boundaries.

A prevalent and stubborn form of imagination is that which cannot be realized or demonstrated, but which is firmly believed. Religious mystery, extraterrestrials on earth, and nonprovable conspiracy notions all resist challenge. Evidence for these imagined realities is developed by like-minded believers who join together for confirmation through their testimony. Advocates firmly define beliefs as truth, as real. Such beliefs are comforting explanations for vexing issues. Abandoning them could bring despair.

Split brain phenomena supports the description of the human brain as a reason seeking, explanation generating instrument. Unverifiable belief might most generously be described as the best available hypothesis that explicates the inexplicable. Deeply troubling issues are thereby put to rest. The need to continue questioning and struggling is gone. They need only be defended from those who would question them as bulwarks against fear. Some unconfirmed beliefs may be necessary to maintain personal mental balance. Belief in the faithfulness of a spouse, in the safety of children out of sight, in the innocence of family or friend convicted of a crime can prevent one from being unhinged by fear or adversity. They are personal reality, fortified against an adverse, alternative reality. Doggedly held, they are truth. Tentatively held, they are hope. Hope always contains a tinge of the mystical.

Can We Define Natural And Unnatural Phenomena?

The problem with dealing with mystical events like dreams, imagination, and beliefs through words alone comes mostly from difficulty in defining natural and supernatural. Perhaps a better word would be *un*natural since the word supernatural evokes clumsy images of spirits and psychic visions. Because there is blurring between the words natural and supernatural it will be difficult or impossible to avoid confusion in their use. Natural versus unnatural is closer to a clean dichotomy.

Natural events and phenomena center on physical, experienced realities. Nature is testable. It can be manipulated.

By definition nature is real in time, space and substance. Natural things bump up against other natural things. Cause and effect sequences can be followed. Unnatural is beyond and outside natural. That which is unnatural may have power to enter consciousness, but it cannot act independently of the mind. There is no physical machinery involved, only words and images in the mind. Language is full of words for those images. Some may yet be opened to empirical demonstration.

The history of science and technology follows a course of discovery over which events that once seemed without cause were later understood. Thunder and lightning was once thought to be anger of the gods. Magnetism was once explained as spirit in stone. Magicians once kept their tricks and devices secret so they would be taken as magical power. Science has steadily progressed. Aristotle's four humors of earth, air, fire and water have morphed into the elements of the periodic table and moved on to particle physics. Given past experience with mysterious things and events that later turned out to be natural, it would be wise to classify all forces that have no observable physical effect on natural things as poorly understood natural phenomena. Eventually, it should be expected that an understanding of their workings can and will emerge. Experiences that cannot be accounted for other than by some strange inner workings of the mind may or may not be spiritual, which is to say, unnatural. We can at least entertain the possibility that the human mind might be capable of drawing on resources that are unnatural. The physical, time and space bound world operates within its own laws. The human mind may be partially outside those laws. It may at some future time be possible to use words to describe and explore that other world.

If the unnatural is restricted by definition solely to those events that occur in the experience of humans without any apparent basis in sensory experience, it becomes logical to accept the existence of spiritual input and throughput as a human capability. Dreams and other purely imaginary events are generated by the mind. Substitution of the word unnatural in place of the word *spiritual* might be acceptable in describing this capability. Mysticism might be redefined as exploration of human potential for encounter with the unnatural. That which is unnatural may at some point be better understood. Some in the present age already claim that understanding. Because it must be beyond material reality, though, it will always be difficult to demonstrate.

So where does this lead, where does this exercise in philosophic meandering take us? It has been argued that words are tools that allow sensory reality to be grasped and managed. It has also been proposed that words can become so firmly set as one's sense of reality that they are accepted as reality itself. Words are not just a reality map. To most they *are* reality. Does that leave room for the unnatural? It will be necessary to sort out the components of mental life to find an answer.

The one thing that is genuinely unexplainable about experience is consciousness -- the sense of being alive, aware, connected to the world. Explanations of consciousness tend to be philosophically and neurologically complex. On an abstract level, consciousness is called the soul by mystics, or, alternatively, it is described by some rigorous materialists as merely the firing of billions of neurons in the brain. Neither description goes much deeper than did earth, air, fire and water as natural science. Whatever the words used to map our sense of consciousness, none are yet fully satisfying. Consciousness cannot be measured or even shown to exist. The best evidence, perhaps, is that humans can communicate with words about what they see, hear, feel and know. We rely on experience of our own beingness as evidence of consciousness. I can experience mine but cannot confirm yours. Because you use words as I do, I can attribute consciousness to you. The independent consciousness of the mute, split-off right brain is verified only because it can communicate crudely with language. Without language it is just a piece of flesh. Without language any of us might as well be a potted plant.

Conscious experience need not necessarily be sensory experience. Conscious experience of the unnatural can be induced by direct stimulation of the brain. When locations on and in the brain are electrically or mechanically stimulated physical sensations are described and physical, muscular responses observed. It is clear from such brain research that perceptions can and do occur in the brain without input from the external sensors, the eyes, ears, skin, muscles. Lost legs and arms from injury or disease can continue to be experienced as if restored, so-called phantom limb phenomena. Brain injury and disease offer specific test of changes that happen when a part of the brain is damaged. A twentieth century explosion of population to over six billion humans means that extraordinarily rare types of brain injury that occur in only one in one-hundred million will yield sixty cases for study planet wide. The role of the damaged portion of the brain to conscious experience can be identified with considerable accuracy across confirming cases. The workings of the brain are better understood today than ever before.

We know that memory depends on the brain. Brain damage impairs or destroys memory. Storage of memory is distributed throughout the brain. Immediate, short term and long term memory reside in separate areas of the brain. Memory is created by consciousness and stored by the brain. Loss of long-term, autobiographical memory results in loss of sense of the social self. Consciousness as the sense of beingness and have-beenness is found in the string of memories we recall. Alzheimer's disease impairs memory creation and access so greatly that only immediate consciousness remains. It is a disease that can reduce a human being to pure consciousness without awareness of past or future. If life goes on without sense of self, what has happened to the self? Has it disappeared, or is it preserved in some mystical space?

Alternatively, we can ask what part of our selfness endures? The answer is not clear. With a disease like Alzheimer's the personality that was there appears to have left the house. Only memory and experience processed through a brain for preservation as written or recorded words remains testimony to the person's former existence. Put into recorded words, the self may endure beyond the grave. Otherwise, the self is gone. Words recorded may have the power to confer immortality, or something near it. As for eternal existence, the self from its wellspring of creative beingness can create new words that become part of the reality maps of future generations.

Words sing. Words seduce. Words reveal. Words destroy. Words hypnotize. Words create reality. The reality of words can endure. Words can be one's immortality. Words possess incredible power. Poetic words capture a wide range and depth of human feeling experience. Poets in every age have created images of heaven, hell, beauty, desolation. The emotional loading of words permits communication on a level of near pure feeling. It is intense feeling that many, perhaps most humans associate with spiritual power. Poetry is one of the more consistent realms of the mystical. It is the language of the mystic.

Words permit a living generation to benefit from the trial and error discoveries of an earlier one. Knowledge of food sources and cultivation, metal working, uses of fire, sources of water, applications of wood are all communicated in words. Life is a relay, each new generation of runners seizing the words of earlier ones to go forward. It is a process that itself should be celebrated as a mystical experience. Words in every form are the indispensable unifier of community. They have vast social power. Words are more than mere symbolic references to sensory phenomena. They are tools that give us power to create and understand the phenomenal world and ourselves. It is in such power that all words might be claimed to have mystical character.

The capacity of a human race on the planet Earth to examine the universe and its place within it is awesome. Somehow, the inner consciousness that we cannot prove to exist can use the words invented by an advanced brain to examine it all. There is certainly a mystical quality to the mind that can do that with mere words.

Notes and References

1. Language And The Mental Model Of Reality

1. Goodall, *My Life with the Chimps,* 1996.

2. Gardner, Gardner and VanCampford, 1989.

3. Reports of Feral Children have long generated public interest. Popular stories focus on children abandoned in the wild and raised by animals. The most frequently identified animal foster parents are wolves and dogs. Chimps, apes, monkeys, gazelles, ostriches, bears, jackals, leopards, sheep, cows and goats are all credited with having raised feral human children as their own. A web site, www. feralchildren.com lists more than one hundred such reports dating back to 250 CE.

4. Meshcheryakov, A., 1979. Also, the National Consortium on deaf-blindness, www.nationaldb.org.

5. Understanding of how specific impairments in the brain influence behavior has expanded greatly in the twentieth century. One of the most readable sources of information is Ramachandran's *Phantoms in the Brain.* College course texts like Beatty's *The Human Brain* or Gazzaniga's *Cognitive Neuroscience* are also authoritatively informative.

6. There is no question but that the brain can intuitively grasp language in all its complexity. Suggestions as to how that occurs are offered in Chapter 5.

7. Ganea, et al, 2007.

8. Richardson & Hayne, 2007. The question was taken further by these authors who studied memory in rats for a response conditioned to electric shock at an early stage of rats' neurological development. Physical response to shock matures progressively in rats, freezing first, with change in cardiovascular rate next, followed later by the startle response. Rats conditioned to shock paired with odor or sound at the freezing stage exhibited only the freezing response when the conditioning stimulus was introduced at a much later time after other response levels had matured. The earlier experience is apparently not updated by later maturation.

9. Psychologists study children's abstract use of language as an expression of *essentialism*. This is the notion that words which stand for abstract characteristics like race or gender are accepted as if based on hidden, non-obvious substantive qualities when, factually,

they are only arbitrary conventional categories. Psychologist Susan Gelman summarizes research and theory on psychological essentialism in her book, *The Essential Child.* Essentials are discussed in Chapter 19.

10. Exposure to Plato as an undergraduate student and by references encountered in a lifetime of reading are the beginning basis of these comments. To clarify thinking of them I have adopted a distinctly twenty-first century approach. Wikipedia, the free on line encyclopedia and the Encyclopedia Britannica Standard version were accessed to refresh and update memory. Wikipedia is written and revised on line by volunteer writers/scholars making it something of a competitively collaborative effort that yields a consensus of thinking among its authors. Britannica articles are commissioned to an expert author by the publisher. Comparing the two sources offers exposure to the best current thinking of the Platonic scholar community.

11. The notion of mapping in the brain, though not intended to be precisely literal as used here, has considerable support from the tendency of the brain to organize into topographic maps. These are arrangements of neurological activity that preserve the physical relations of their elements. For instance, a retinotopic map preserves the relations among retinal photoreceptors at the level of the cortex. Somatotopic maps preserve relations by location in the body. The special power of words as mapping devices derives from their status as symbols. Since they have no physical position in reality, the brain can arrange and rearrange them with near infinite plasticity. The concept of a mental, or cognitive, map was introduced by Edward Tollman in 1948 to account for the ability of rats to learn a route to food through a maze. Whether or not rats make maze maps in their brains is entirely speculative. That humans can do so is evident from their ability to draw from memory graphic representations of spatial arrangements. Not all humans are necessarily capable of thinking in topographical maps. Some such maps may be no more than a series of "landmarks" that guide one to a place or goal. The most efficient way to maintain landmark systems in memory would be to attach names to each point on the route. However, memory for some unique feature at each point would probably be sufficient. The simplest explanation for rat maze learning would be memory of smells or subtle visual cues along the maze path.

2. Linguistics And Culturally Unique Meaning

1. See www.wikipedia.org/wiki/list of language families.

2. The principal writings of Sapir and Whorf continue to be published under their names in edited collections and are available for purchase. The Sapir/Whorf hypothesis is well known to social science scholars and writers, but has only recently begun to exert major influence on linguistic theory through the writings of Anna Wierzbicka. The notion that language is a direct and inevitable reflection of its deep cultural base is difficult to grasp because of the generations, centuries, and even millennia over which invention has progressed into the present time. Arguing the evidence of that progression is the object of this chapter.

3. Sapir, 1966.

4. Whorf, 1956. The summary offered here is very close to Whorf's own words. He was quite clear and succinct and it's hard to do better.

5. Wierzbika, 1997, 2006.

6. Professor Wierzbika is part of an extended colleagueship of cultural and anthropological linguists who examine languages for differences and similarities. She has provided leadership in studying similarities with her *natural semantic metalanguage* (NSM). She has identified semantic primitives that can represent the foundation words of any language. These are described as (Wierzbika, 2006) "an irreducible core in terms of which the speakers can understand all complex thoughts and utterances". The test of this irreducible core is that words will be discovered that match the core across languages reflecting, again in her words, "the irreducible core of human thought". Semantic primitives are those "thoughts" that come naturally through the senses into human experience. The words that are invented to represent these core thoughts are offered as the foundation of every culture's language. Professor Wierzbika's Table of Semantic Primitives is reproduced here for reference.

Table of Semantic primes: English Version

Substantives......................I, YOU, SOMEBODY/PERSON,
Quantifiers ....ONE, TWO, SOME, ALL, MUCH/MANY
Evaluators...........................GOOD, BAD
Descriptors ....BIG, SMALL
Mental/experiential
  predicates.........................THINK, KNOW, WANT, FEEL, SEE, HEAR

Speech	SAY, WORDS, TRUE
Actions, events, movement	DO, HAPPEN, MOVE
Existence & possession	THERE, IS/EXIST, HAVE
Life and death	LIVE, DIE
Time	WHEN, TIME, NOW, BEFORE, AFTER A LONG TIME, FOR SOME TIME, MOMENT
Space	WHERE/PLACE, BE (SOMEWHERE), HERE, ABOVE, BELOW, FAR, NEAR, SIDE, INSIDE, TOUCHING
Logical concepts	NOT, MAYBE, CAN, BECAUSE, IF
Augmenter, intensifier	VERY, MORE
Similarity	LIKE, (AS, HOW)

7. Etymology is the historical compilation of word usage. In any time and era, some words are always in the process of evolutionary change. Change across centuries illustrates how the cultural environment has shaped common sense thinking into the present. The etymological reference source used here is a very convenient, on line compilation of several published sources augmented by on line user input, www.etymonline.com. On line resources offer the advantage of many minds reviewing, evaluating and adding to common knowledge. There is also the very great convenience of having reference information available at the touch of the keyboard.

8. Reading Anna Wierzbika's *ENGLISH; Meaning and Culture* was a journey into the depths of word meaning through examination of usage. My explication of the foregoing sub-cultural differences of meaning in *fear, freedom* and *pride* follow her example.

9. The game of baseball even has its own instructions for fans. Try Zack Hample's *Watching Baseball Smarter; A Professional Fan's Guide for Beginners, Semi-Experts and Deeply Serious Geeks*, 2007, Vintage Books.

3. Culture And The Language Imperative

1. Translation: Hunting Parties become corporations, large kill is a nice profit, attacks from animals are law suits and other tribes are competitors.

2. Wojtan, 1993.

3. Wierzbicka, 1997.

4. Samuels, D., 2007.

5. Schonberger, 1982; Ohno, 1988.

6. Janis, I., 1972.

7. Patai, R., 1983.

4. Intellect And The Written Word

1. Wickapedia: "Lescaux"

2. Wickapedia: "Johannes Gutenberg"

3. Direct sales of this iconic book and other material continues to the present time. The direct Bible sales culture was captured in the 1969 film docudrama, *Salesman*, directed by the Maysles brothers and preserved by the Library of Congress in the National Film Registry.

5. The Neuroplastic Associative Brain And How It Acquires Language

1. Watson, J. B., (1930). *Behaviorism* (Revised edition). Chicago: University of Chicago Press.

2. Wikipedia: "Feral Child"

3. Elizabeth Hess, 2008. *Nim Chimsky: The Chimp Who Would be Human.* Fouts, Roger, 1998. *Next of Kin: My Conversations with Champanzees,* Living Planet

4. Normal Doidge, 2007. *The Brain that Changes Itself,* Penguin.

5. Jean Aitchison, 2008. *The Articulate Mammal,* Routledge

6. Laura Wagner & Laura Lakusta, 2009. *"Using Language to Navigate the Infant Mind." Perspectives on Psychological Science,* 4:177

7. Wikipedia: "Nicaraguan Sign Language"

6. Psychology And Language; Is The Speaking Brain Your Mind?

1. Once one is made aware of Pavlovian conditioning it is apparent everywhere. Experimental Psychologists routinely demonstrate the phenomenon with animal (usually rat) experiments that pair a noxious stimulus like mild electric shock with a specific noise or odor to train behavior.

2. Watson and Skinner doggedly insisted that free will is a myth. They credited the totality of human behavior to a lifetime of accumulated Pavlovian conditioned responses.

3. Chomsky, N., 1973.

4. Wikapedia: "positron emission tomography" or "magnetic resonance imaging"

5. See www.rogersperry.org where Sperry's comprehensive biography is offered on line.

6. Gazziniga, Michael, 1985, 1992. Gazziniga was a doctoral student under Roger Sperry in the early 1960s and subsequently promoted split brain method and theory as a practitioner in the expanding field of cognitive neurology.

7. Gazziniga, M., 1985, 1982.

8. Beatty, J., 2001. Milner, B., 1973.

9. Gazziniga, M. & Sperry, R., 1967.

10. Ramachandran, V.S. & Blakeslee, S., 1998.

7. How The Brain Restores Order When Chaos Prevails

1. Wells, T. & Leo, R.A., 2008.

2. See www.innocenseproject.org. Names of mistakenly convicted offenders and a summary of the investigations before and after vindication are provided on the website.

3. Myers, D., 2008. Professor Myers devotes an entire chapter of his textbook to the subject of Social Psychology in Court.

4. See www.fmsfonline.org is a website maintained by the False Memory Syndrome Foundation.

5. Kassin, S.M. & Kiechel, K.L., 1996. This research is posted on Professor Kassin's faculty web site at Williams College, Williamstown, MA.

8. Social Responsiveness; Authority, Conformity And Suggestibility

1. Ganea, Shutts, Spelke & DeLoache, 2007.

2. Schumaker, J.F., 1991. Suggestibility is most dramatically demonstrated by hypnotic phenomena. Suggestibility, though, is in play in just about every form or theater of human interaction.

3. Groth-Marnat, G., 1991.

4. Milgram, 2004. This republication of Milgram's research report nearly fifty years after the event demonstrates how significant this work was. His conclusions are still an open wound in the community of social psychology.

5. Zimbardo, P., 2007. Abu Garib stimulated republication of Zimbardo's work.

6. Asch, S.E., 1973. The research report reproduced in this "Classic Contributions" compilation of readings was published in 1952 as a chapter in Asch's text *Social Psychology.*

7. Bond & Smith, 1996.

8. Wikipedia: "Stockholm Syndrome"

9. Wikipedia: "brainwashing"

10. Wikipedia: "neurolinguistic programming"

9. Words And The Inner Experience

1. Kelley, H.H., & Nisbett, R.E., 1972. Fosterling, 2001.

2. For a useful thumbnail of his life and work search Sigmund Freud in Wikipedia.org.

3. Use Wikipedia.org to bring up Carl Jung if you want to go a little deeper.

4. Costa & McRae, 1988.

5. The "Big 5" personality factors are closely related to many other personality tests and temperament inventories. This is not the only approach to creating personality tests, though. Jungian and other personality typologies continue to be popular. A variety of internet sites offer free personality testing. One of the most open and least restrictive is www.similarminds.com. IQ tests can also be found and sampled at this web site.

6. Ashton, Lee & May, 2007.

7. Smith, D.B., 2007.

8. Lucidly explored by V.S. Ramachandran in *Phantoms in the Brain.*

9. Quoted from V.S. Ramachandran in *Phantoms in the Brain.*

10. Words Of Passion

1. Beatty, J., 2001, Ramachandran, V., 1998.

2. The Harvard Business School MBA program had trained George W. Bush to "make decisions." That program had evidently not made specific that there are two classes of decisions, those made with full information and those made in partial ignorance. The former decisions are no-brainers that have been made for

you. The latter *must not* be made until all options to resolve uncertainties are exhausted and/or cost will be high if it is not made. Decisions made in partial ignorance are always dangerous and must wait until circumstances clearly force them. Iraq appears to have been an HBS MBA "OK, let's do it!" decision made in an artificial environment of rational confidence and under substantial ignorance.

3. Chang, L. & Kornbluh, P., 1962; Kennedy, R.F. & Schlesinger, A., 1999.

4. Moon & Mackle, 2007.

5. Kensinger, E.A., 2007.

11. Loaded Words: Hot And Cool Language

1. Eric Berne, 1996.

12. Inventions Of The Mind

1. This account is drawn from Gerald Posner's book, *Case Closed.*

2. Enron was so monumental an example of corporate misbehavior that it had to be extensively documented in the courts and the press. Swartz' and Watkins' *Power Failure,* McLean's and Elkind's literary account of *The Smartest Guys in the Room* and the motion picture documentary with the same title all tell a tale of intellectual arrogance and bad business judgment arising out of overly inventive word play.

13. Propaganda; The Language Of Manipulation

1. Wikipedia: "propaganda fide"

2. Wikipedia: "radio free europe" and "Voice of America"

3. Wikipedia: "nazi propaganda"

4. Wells. R.A., 2002. See also Wikipedia: "Committee on Public Information"

5. Wikipedia: "Four Minute Men"

6. See www.fax.libs.uga.edu/wwwpost/ The University of Georgia library website offers viewing of over 400 WWI and WWII propaganda posters. Posters are also found at

    Wikipedia: "Propaganda"

7. Asch. S., 1972.

8. Noam Chomsky in partnership with Edward Herman unleashed a classic polemic on World War I propaganda using Creel's own words in its title, "Manufacturing Consent: The Political Economy of the Mass Media." (1988, Pantheon Books).

9. King. E.G., 1989.

10. Bernays, E., 1928.

14. Words That Create Markets And Social Movements

1. Word etymology is sourced from www.etymonline.com

2. Brandweek Magazine, June 26, 2007. or www.brandweek.com.

3. See www.adcouncil.org.

4. Sivulka, 2001.

5. This is a sampling of ads from the glossy pages of the New York Times Sunday Magazine's pages for June 7, 2007.

6. Wikipedia: "Advertising Slogan" for more of the same.

15. Rhetorical language: The Words of Politics and Public Policy

1. Luntz, F., 2007. Political rhetoric tends to evolve much like language itself. It is invented by politicians to meet the demands of the moment. Dr. Luntz has made a career of systematically constructing political rhetoric. The pride he takes in his craft and product is given expression in his book. By telling his story in print he offers a convenient and perhaps unique example of political spin in use.

2. See www.faireconomy.org/estatetax/

3. See www.brookings.edu/opinions/2004/1101saving_aaron.aspx for arguments against privatization of social security and www.socialsecurity.org/dailys/12-09-99.html for arguments in favor.

4. For contrasting arguments see www.schoolchoices.org/roo/vouchers.htm for a favorable argument and www.nea.org/vouchers/ for the rebuttal.

5. Wikipedia: "Environmentalism"

6. Wikipedia: "John Muir"

7. Carlson, R., 1962.

8. United Nations, 2001.

9. Wikipedia: "Intergovernmental Panel on Climate Change"

10. See www.globalwarming.org/primer for the arguments made by those who reject global warming.

11. Luntz, 2007.

16. Economica: The Words Of Wealth, Welfare And Public Policy

1. See www.econlib.org/library/Smith/smWN.html. Other useful economic reference sources are found here also.

2. Wikipedia: "Adam Smith"

3. Wikipedia.org/wiki/socialism also, www.wikipedia.org/wiki/capitalism.

4. Wikipedia: "strike action"

5. Wikipedia: "labor unions in the United States"

6. Wikipedia: "National Labor Relations Act"

7. See www.annualreportservice.com and look under "financial disclosure" in any corporation's annual report. This quote is taken from the disclosure section of United Technology Corporation's 2004 annual report. It is nearly identical to hundreds of others published each year.

17. Abstracting The Size Of The World; Words For Numeration

1. Russell, B., 1971.

2. Wikipedia: "calculus"

3. Wikipedia: "probability"

4. Taleb. N.N., Nassim Taleb has eloquently pointed out in *The Black Swan* that extreme or unusual events otherwise disregarded as improbable can change the course of history. Probability theory that dismisses them as merely unlikely can mislead catastrophically.

5. NEJM permits all issues over six months old to be directly accessed and read or down loaded on line free of charge. This is an enlightened scientific policy that should be made standard by all serious academic journals.

6. Wikipedia "eugenics". In political and ethical ways the field of eugenics remains alive and controversial.

7. Gross, M.L., 1962.

8. The very best talent of the IBM corporation was applied to this problem. Though the computer may have "won," the cost of approximating human talent was tens of thousands of hours of programming manpower and reliance on RAM memories of ninety computers. To remain current, the entire data base must periodically by revised and updated. At best the program could be described as no more than a device for calculating the probabilities of word associations for this one contest. Even so, though response was lightning fast, it was not perfect.

18. Science; Sensory Phenomena in the Abstract

1. Wikipedia: "Periodic Table of the Elements"
2. Asimov, I., 1962.
3. Darwin, C. & Jones, S., 2001. See also Wikipedia "Charles Darwin"
4. Wikipedia: "Opinion Poll"
5. See www.publicagenda.org Search environmental issues for red flags on this site.
6. Taubes, G., 2007. Gary Taubes' *Good Calories, Bad Calories* is a well researched look at both the epidemiological "bad science" and the biochemically based "good science" pertaining to heart disease, diabetes, and obesity. Medical and pharmaceutical communities settled into an early, quasi-scientific consensus on cholesterol and dietary fat as the culprits. Cholesterol as the widely presumed cause of these scourges now represents too big and profitable a commitment to back away from. Other critiques of the cholesterol hypothesis include *The Cholesterol Hoax* by Sheldon Serdon, *The Cholesterol Myths* by Uffe Ravnskov, and *The Great Cholesterol Con* by Dr. Malcolm Kendrick.
7. The prefix "co-" has the meaning "together" or "jointly". Things that are correlated occur together. Lots of things occur together randomly or only under certain circumstances. The proper scientific response to correlation of variables is "Hello! What's really going on here?"
8. Taubes, 2011 See also www.mayoclinic.com/health/statins/ CL00010. and Business Week Magazine, 1/17/08.
9. Wikipedia: "Vitamins" also "Nutrition"
10. Pollan, M. 2007, M., 2007.

19. Philosophers at Work: Language Under Construction

1. Philosophers are what they are because they push the boundaries of language. They struggle with the meaning of words, revise old meaning and invent new words. They are notable for the influence they have on language use and evolution. Because they are at the edges of language usage for their time, it is often necessary to connect with them first through the changes in word use they have produced. Evolution in language use and prevailing dialects must be taken into account. Philosophy in a language other than one's own suffers the further impediment of requiring translation of philosophical usage that can differ from conventional usage of the time and tongue. Philosophical scholars strive to enter the mind of their philosopher subject. A certain amount of imagination is needed to do that.

2. To begin penetrating their intent and meaning, students of philosophy must focus on those philosophers that interest them and learn the language of the philosopher and word usages of his era. Philosophers of an earlier age are studied by communities of scholars who struggle for consensus in their interpretation of a philosopher's body of work. The rest of us, including this author, must depend on the working agreements that interpret each philosophy. To access philosophical consensus as fully and simply as possible for purposes of this writing, those summaries extant written, revised and critiqued by an open scholarly community were referenced. Wikipedia, the on line free encyclopedia, was compared to a summary offered by a designated (and paid) Encyclopedia Britannica scholar author. Summaries offered here reflect the most consistent scholarly agreement available from those sources. Choice of Philosophies and Philosophers was a function of the author's acquaintance with their names and ideas over a lifetime of reading and study.

3. Wikipedia: "Plato", and Hamilton E., & Cairns, H., 1973.

4. Wikipedia: "Issac Newson"

5. Wikipedia: "John Locke"

6. Wikipedia: "Emmanuel Kant"

7. Wikipedia: "Jeremy Bentham"

8. Wikipedia: "Karl Marx"

9. Wikipedia: "Charles Peirce"

10. Wikipedia: "Particle Physics"

20. Non-sense Language: Abstractions and Essences

1.   From Plato's *Republic*.

2.   On-line etymology at www.etymonline.com.

3.   Isaiah 40:4, "Prepare in the wilderness a road for the Lord. Fill every valley; level every mountain. The hills will become a plain and the rough country will be made smooth." *The Good News Bible; English Version*. Modern road builders obviously are followers of the Bible.

4.   Wikipedia: "Social Contract"

5.   Wikipedia: "Justice"

6.   Wikipedia: "Boolean algebra"

7.   Gelman, S.A., 2003, 2005.

21. Is it Redundant to say that Words are Mystical?

1.   Ramachandran, V.S., 1998.

Bibliographic List

Asch, S.D., "Group Forces in the Modification and Distortion of Judgments". In Hollander E. P., & Hunt, R.G., 1972, Classic Contributions to Social Psychology.

Ashton, M.C. & Lee, K., May 2007. "Empirical, Theoretical and Practical Advantages of the HEXACO Model of Personality Structure" in Personality and Social Psychology Review, 11,2, pp 150-166.

Asimov I., 1962. The Search For The Elements. Basic Books.

Bandura, A., 1997. Self Efficacy; The Exercise of Control. Worth Publishers.

Beatty, J., 2001. The Human Brain, Sage Publications.

Berlow, Alan, 2007. "What Happened in Norfolk?" New York Times Sunday Magazine, August 19.

Bernays, E., 1928. Propaganda. Liveright, New York.

Berne, E., 1973. Games People Play. Ballantine.

Bond, R. & Smith, P.B., 1996. "Culture and Conformity: A Meta-Analysis of Studies Using Asch's Line Judgment Task" in Psychological Bulletin, V. 119, No. 1, 111-137.

Business Week Magazine, January 17, 2008. Do Cholesterol Drugs Do Any Good?

Carlson, R.. 1962. The Silent Spring. Crest.

Carver, C.M., 1991. A History of English in Its Own Words. Harper Collins.

Chang, L. & Kornbluh, P., 1962. Cuban Missile Crisis; A National Archives Reader. New Press.

Chomsky, N. "On Skinner's 'Verbal Behavior". In Hollander E. P., & Hunt, R.G., 1972. Classic Contributions to Social Psychology.

Chrystal, D., 2007. The Fight for English. Oxford University Press.

Costa, P.T., JR. & McCrae, R.R., 1988. From Catalog to Classification: Murray's Needs and the five-factor model. Journal of Personality and Social Psychology, 55, 258-265.

Darwin, C. & Jones, S., 2001. Voyage of the Beagle. Modern Library.

Dawkins, R., 1976, The Selfish Gene. Oxford University Press.

Fouts, R. & Mills, S.T., 1998. Next of Kin: My Conversations with Chimpanzees. Harper Paperbacks.

Fosterling, F., 2001. Attribution: An Introduction to Theories, Research and Applications. The Psychology Press.

Ganea, P.A., Shutts J., Spelke, E.S., & DeLoache, J.S., 2007 "Thinking of Things Unseen", Psychological Science, V18,#8, August, 2007.

Gardner, R.A., Gardner, B.T. & VanCantford, T.E., 1989. Teaching Sign Language to Chimpanzees. Albany, SUNY Press.

Gazzaniga, M., 1985. The Social Brain, Basic Books.

Gazzaniga, M.S., 1992. Nature's Mind. Basic Books.

Gazziniga, M.S., Ivry, R. B. & Mangun, G.R., 1998. Cognitive Neuroscience: The Biology of the Mind. Norton.

Gazziniga, M.S. & Sperry, R.W., 1967. "Language After Section of the Cerebral Commissures", in Brain, Volume 90, pp. 131-148.

Gelman, S.A., 2003. The Essential Child. Oxford.

Gelman, S.A., 2005. "Essentialism in Everyday Thought". APA On-Line Psychological Science Agenda. V19, No.5, May. www.apa.org/science/psa.

Goodall, J., 1996. My Life with the Chimps. Aladdin Books.

Grandin, Temple, 1995. Thinking In Pictures. Doubleday.

Gross, M.L., 1962. The Brain Watchers. Random House.

Groth-Marnat, G. "Hypnotizability, Suggestibility and Psychopathology", in Schumaker, J.F. (ed.), 1991. Human Suggestibility. Routledge.

Hamilton, E, & Cairns, H., 1973. Plato: The Collected Dialogs. Bollingen Series LXXI, Princeton University Press.

Hogg, M.A. & Cooper, J., 2007, The Sage Handbook of Social Psychology, Sage Publications.

Huntington, S.P., 1996. The Clash of Civilizations and the Remaking of World Order. Touchstone Books.

Janis, I., 1972. Victims of Groupthink. Houghton, Mifflin.

Jaynes, J., 1976. The Origin of Consciousness in the Breakdown of the Bicameral Mind. Houghton Mifflin.

Kassin, S.M. & Kiechel, K.L., 1996. "The Social Psychology of False Confessions: Compliance, Internalization and Confabulation". Psychological Science. V7, #3., May.

Kelley, H.H., & Nisbett, R.E., 1972 Attribution: Perceiving the Causes of Behavior. General Learning Press.

Kennedy, R.F. & Schlesinger, A., 1999. Thirteen Days; A Memoir of the Cuban Missile Crisis. W.W. Norton & Co.

Kensinger, E.A. ,"Negative Emotion Enhances Memory Accuracy" Current Directions in Psychological Science, V16, #1, August, 2007.

King, E.G., 1989. "Exposing the 'Age of Lies: The Propaganda Menace as Portrayed in American Magazines in the Aftermath of World War I". Journal of American Culture, 12:1:35-40.

Lee, C.D. & Smagorinsky, P., 2005. Vygotskian Perspectives on Literacy Research. Cambridge.

Locke, E. and Latham, G., 1990. A Theory of Goal Setting and Task Performance. Prentice Hall College Division.

Luntz, F., 2007. <u>Words That Work: It's Not What You Say It's What People Hear</u>. Hyperion.

Meshcheryakov, A., 1979. <u>Awakening to Life: Forming Behavior and the Mind in Blind-Deaf Children</u>. Progress.

Myers, D., 2008. <u>Social Psychology</u>, ninth edition. McGraw-Hill.

McLean B. & Elkind, P., 2003. <u>The Smartest Guys in the Room</u>, Portfolio.

Milgram, S., 2004. <u>Obedience to Authority: An Experimental View</u>. Harper Perennial Modern Classics.

Milner, B., 1973 "<u>Hemispheric Specialization: Scope and Limits</u>." In Schmitt, F.O. and Worden, F.G. (Eds.) <u>The Neurosciences: Third Study Program</u>. M.I.T. Press.

Moon, W., & Mackle, D.M., May, 2007, "Thinking Straight While Seeing Red: The Influence of Anger on Information Processing", <u>Personality and Social Psychology Bulletin</u>, Vol 33, #5.

Ohno, D., 1988. <u>Workplace Management</u>. Productivity Press.

Panksepp, J., 2007, "Neurologizing the Psychology of Affects", <u>Perspectives in Psychological Science</u>, V2, #3, September.

Patai, R., 1983. <u>The Arab Mind</u>. Scribners.

Pollan, M., 2007. "Unhappy Meals: The Age of Nutritionism" in <u>The New York Times Sunday Magazine</u>, January 28, 2007.

Posner, G., 1993. <u>Case Closed</u>, Random House, New York.

Prentice, D.A., & Miller, D.T., 2007. "Psychological Essentialism of Human Categories" <u>Current Directions in Psychological Science</u>, V16, #4 August.

Ramachandran, V.S. & Blakeslee, S., 1998, <u>Phantoms in the Brain</u>. Morrow.

Richardson, R., & Hayne, H., 2007. "You Can't Take It With You". <u>Current Directions in Psychological Science</u>, V16,#2, August, 2007.

Rieber, R.W.,(ed.), 1983. Dialogues on the Psychology of Language and Thought. Plenum Press.

Ruhlen, Merritt, (1987). A guide to the world's languages. Stanford: Stanford University Press.

Russell, B., 1971. Introduction to Mathematical Philosophy. Simon & Schuster.

Samuels, D., May, 2007. "Let's Die Together", Atlantic Magazine.

Sapir, Edward, 1966. Culture, Language and Personality. University of California Press.

Schonberger, D.J., 1982. Japanese Manufacturing Techniques. The Free Press.

Schumaker, J.F. (ed.), 1991. Human Suggestibility. Routledge

Sivulka, J., 1998. Soap, Sex and Cigarettes. Wadsworth.

Sivulka, J., 2001. Stronger than Dirt: A Cultural History of Advertising Personal Hygiene in America, 1875 to 1940. Humanity Books.

Smith, Adam., 2000. The Wealth of Nations. Modern Library Classics.

Smith, D.B., 2007. Can You Live With the Voices in Your Head? New York Sunday Times Magazine, March 25, 2007.

Taleb, N.N., 2007. The Black Swan, Random House.

Taubes, G., 2007. Good Calories, Bad Calories: Challenging the Conventional Wisdom on Diet, Weight Control and Disease. Anchor Press.

Taubes, G., 2011. Is Sugar Toxic? New York Times Sunday Magazine, April 17, 2011.

Trowbridge, B.C., 2003. "Suggestibility and Confessions". American Journal of Forensic Psychology. Vol21, #1. Available on-line at www.trowbridgefoundation.org/docs/suggestibility.htm.

United Nations, 2001. Report of the International Panel on Climate Change (IPCC). UN Publication.

Wells, T. & Leo, R.A., 2008. The Wrong Guys: Murder, False Confessions and the Norfolk Four. New Press.

Wells, G.L., Memon, A., & Penrod, S.D., 2006, "Eyewitness Evidence: Improving its Probative Value", Psychological Science in the Public Interest, V7, #2, November 2006.

Wells, R.A., 2002. "Mobilizing Public Support for War: An Analysis of American Propaganda During World War I". Proceedings of the International Studies Association, 2002.

Whitehead, A.N. and Russell, B., 1997. Principia Mathematica. Cambridge University Press.

Whorf, B.L., 1956. Language, Thought and Reality. The MIT Press.

Wierzbicka, A., 1997. Understanding Cultures Through their Key Words. Oxford University Press.

Wierzbicka, A., 2006. English: Meaning and Culture. Oxford.

Wojtan, Linda S., Nov., 1993. "Rice: It's More than Food in Japan". Stanford University Program on International and Cross-Cultural Education. Reference on line: www://spice.stanford.edu/docs/145#edu.

Zimbardo, P., 2007. The Lucifer Effect: Understanding How Good People Turn Evil. Random House.